WORLD
PICTURE
ATLAS

TEXT WRITTEN BY

ANNE WEBB

PREPARED IN CONSULTATION WITH

BRIAN P. PRICE

B.Sc. (Lond.), F.R.G.S.

FIRST PUBLISHED IN GREAT BRITAIN 1970
YOUNG WORLD PRODUCTIONS LTD.
© VALLARDI INDUSTRIE GRAFICHE

Photographs have been supplied by: Allan Cash p. 7b, 30a, 80. - Brake-Magnum p. 17a, 106b, 107. - Burri-Magnum p. 50. - Canali p. 29a. - Cirani p. 61b, 64. - Comet-Magnum p. 18, 62, 83, 87, 91, 93, 109. - E.N.I. archivio p. 58. - E.P.S. p. 7, 46, 77, 79, 95. - Foto B p. 17b, 55, 60, 69, 81. - Glinn-Magnum p. 33. - Mariani p. 44a. - Nimatallah p. 32a. - Perorelli-Magnum p. 67. - Prato Previde p. 49, 103. - Quilici-Moana p. 35. - S.E.F. p. 19, 26, 27, 28, 29b, 30b, 31, 32b, 42, 43, 44b, 45, 47, 48, 59, 61a, 63, 66, 75, 76, 89, 90, 92, 94, 101, 104, 105, 106a. (a = above, b = below)

contents

WORLD PICTURE ATLAS

YOUNG WORLD PRODUCTIONS

LIMITED

LONDON

THE WORLD

The many wonders to be found in this world have fascinated men for thousands of years. Explorers and scientists have often toiled and risked their lives tempting the Earth to yield more and more of its secrets. Even now man is still exploring the land to discover new crops and natural resources which will help to further his achievements in the realms of science, medicine, industry and agriculture.

In 1492 Christopher Columbus discovered an unknown land. Today that New World of America has become one of the most advanced and powerful countries in the world. In 1953 Hillary and Tenzing stood on the summit of Mount Everest—the roof of the world—and they were the first men ever to do so.

But it is not only those few who find new lands or conquer great mountains who go down in history. Equally important contributions come from those who succeed in harnessing and exploiting the natural resources of the Earth or discover new ways of feeding her ever-increasing population.

Imagine, if you can, how uncomfortable and inconvenient life would be today without the gas and electrical appliances found in our homes. We owe a very large debt of gratitude to those men who discovered and harnessed the power of water, gas and electricity to provide mankind with heat, light and the power to drive machines.

And even now that our world is becoming a springboard to the Moon, Mars and other planets, our scientists and explorers are still at work here—under the oceans, beneath the ice caps and boring into the centre of the Earth—to discover more and more secrets which may enrich our lives.

In this atlas the reader will be taken on a tour, in words and pictures, through the various continents and countries, looking at some of the natural features of each area and being introduced to the many peoples of the world—their customs, ways of life, forms of government, industry and agriculture. But before starting out, first consider how our wonderful world came into being . . .

No-one can be certain about how our world was formed. One of the most popular theories is that many millions of years ago there was a terrific explosion which created our galaxy. After the explosion, some of the gases set free were drawn together by the force of gravity, and condensed into what we today call stars.

Other matter from the explosion was then attracted to these stars, again by gravity, and began to whirl around them. One of these stars is our sun, and one of the fragments spinning round it is our own earth.

At first, the Earth might have been compared with a huge ball of molten material. Later, some of this material flew off into space, began rotating round the Earth and became our Moon. Some people believe that our Moon was torn from the bed of the Pacific Ocean and that this accounts for the imbalance of land areas in the world. If you look at a globe, you will see that the Pacific Ocean does occupy nearly half of its surface, broken only by groups of tiny islands; the continents are all concentrated in the other half of the globe.

On the other hand, you may have noticed that the shapes of our continents are such that they could be pieced together like a jig-saw puzzle. This fact has prompted some people to suggest that the continents were once a single land mass, and that they have broken away from each other over a long period of time.

Another theory is that the sun condensed from a cloud of dust particles which was rotating very quickly. An unconsolidated mass rotating at speed tends to become flattened at top and bottom and as it condensed and contracted it achieved its present size and became circled by a disc of gas from which the planets formed. Within this gas the heavier elements tended to condense first, forming the denser planets including Earth. As these heavier elements condensed out of it, the cloud disc moved outwards and the larger, lighter planets, Saturn

THE INTERIOR OF THE EARTH

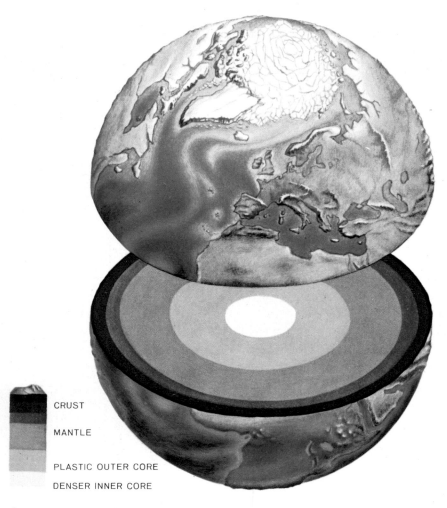

CRUST

MANTLE

PLASTIC OUTER CORE

DENSER INNER CORE

Continued on page 17

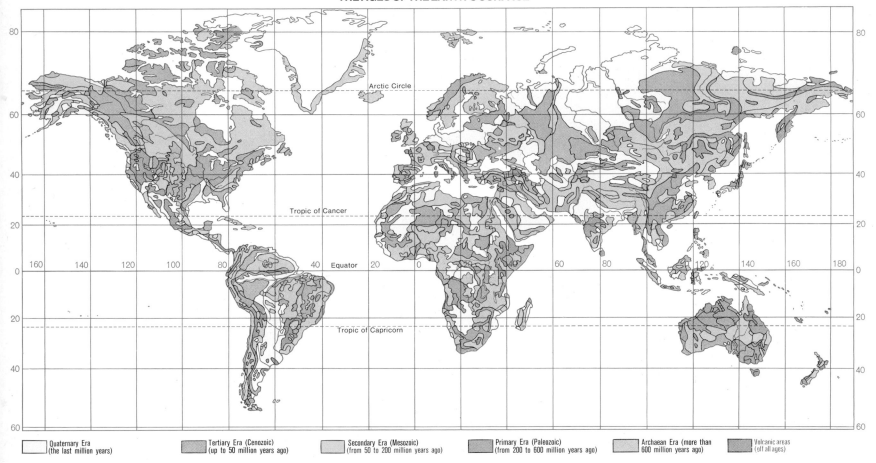

Quaternary Era (the last million years)	Tertiary Era (Cenozoic) (up to 50 million years ago)	Secondary Era (Mesozoic) (from 50 to 200 million years ago)	Primary Era (Paleozoic) (from 200 to 600 million years ago)	Archaean Era (more than 600 million years ago)	Volcanic areas (of all ages)

The distribution of various ages of rocks on the earth's surface is very complex. However, large areas of the oldest rocks can be seen in Scandinavia and much of Canada, the secondary and tertiary rocks are often found in areas of recently formed mountains, such as the Alps, whilst the youngest rocks are found in lowlands and river valleys.

OUR WONDERFUL WORLD

Estimated age
4,500 million years, at least

Population
Over 3,250 million

Superficial area
509,610,000 sq. km. (196,836,000 sq. miles)

Equatorial circumference
40,000 km. (24,902 miles)

Highest point
Mt. Everest, 8,880 metres (29,028ft.)

Lowest exposed point
Shores of Dead Sea, Palestine (393 metres (1,286ft.) below sea level)

Lowest known land level
Beneath the Antarctic Ice Cap (approx. 2,500 metres (8,200ft.) below sea level)

Greatest recorded ocean depth
Marianas Trench (off Philippines) 10,860 metres (36,198ft.) below sea level

Longest river
Nile (Africa) 6,660 km. (4,145 miles)

Largest lake
Caspian Sea (U.S.S.R.-Iran) (salt) approx. 440,000 sq. km. (170,000 sq. miles)

Largest ocean
Pacific 178,000,000 sq. km. (69,000,000 sq. miles)

Number of active volcanoes
485 on Earth's surface; possibly 80 below sea level

Tallest building
Empire State Building, New York, U.S.A. 382 metres (1,250ft.) to the 102nd floor; 449 metres (1,472ft.) to the top of the TV tower

Number of languages
2,800 approx.

Highest recorded temperature
58°C (136.4°F) at El Azizia (Libya) in September 1922 and also at San Luis de Potosi (Mexico) in August 1933

Lowest recorded temperature
—88.3°C (—125.3°F) Vostok (Antarctica) in August 1958

Greatest rainfall in a single day
1,162mm. (45.99in.) at Baguio, Philippines in July 1911

Longest drought on record
Over 300 years in the Atacama Desert

Greatest snowfall in a day
1,925mm. (76in.) at Silver Lake, Colorado in April 1921

Largest hailstones ever seen
Approx. 2 kilogrammes (4.4lb.) in weight in Kazakhstan in September 1959

TEMPERATURE (January)

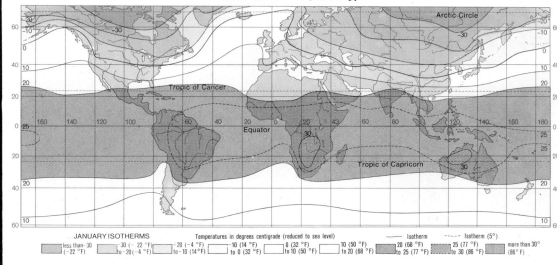

JANUARY ISOTHERMS — Temperatures in degrees centigrade (reduced to sea level) — Isotherm ---- Isotherm (5°)

| less than -30 (-22 °F) | -30 (-22 °F) to -20 (-4 °F) | -20 (-4 °F) to -10 (14 °F) | -10 (14 °F) to 0 (32 °F) | 0 (32 °F) to 10 (50 °F) | 10 (50 °F) to 20 (68 °F) | 20 (68 °F) to 25 (77 °F) | 25 (77 °F) to 30 (86 °F) | more than 30° (86° F) |

TEMPERATURE (July)

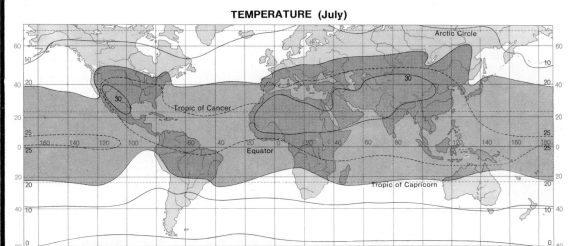

JULY ISOTHERMS — Temperatures in degrees centigrade (reduced to sea level) — Isotherm ---- Isotherm (5°)

| -10 (14 °F) to 0 (32 °F) | 0 (32 °F) to 10 (50 °F) | 10 (50 °F) to 20 (68 °F) | 20 (68 °F) to 25 (77 °F) | 25 (77 °F) to 30 (86 °F) | more than 30 (86 °F) |

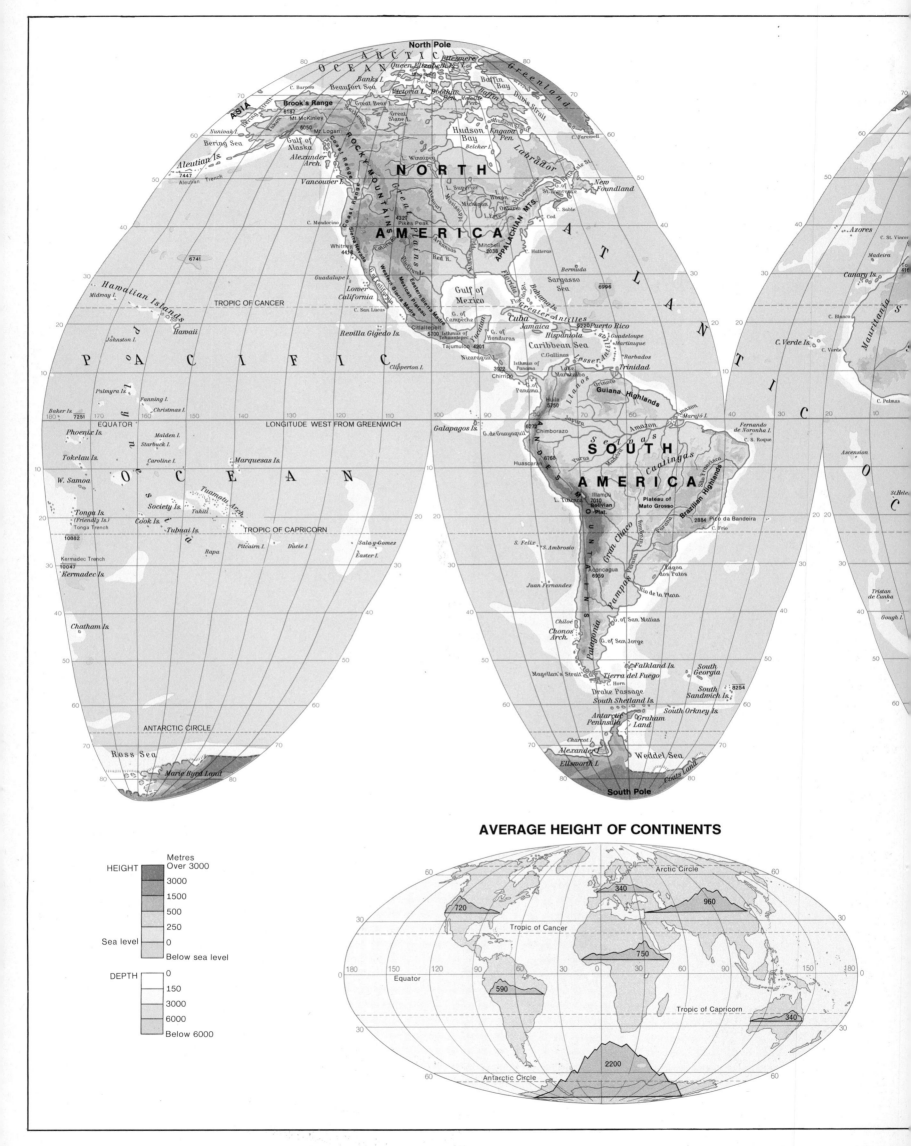

North Pole

ARCTIC OCEAN

Ellesmere

80

Queen Elizabeth Is.

Magnetic Pole

Banks I. Beaufort Sea

Victoria L. Boothia Pen.

Baffin Bay

Greenland

80

C. Barrow

70

Brook's Range

Melville Pen.

Baffin I.

Davis Strait

70

ASIA

Great Bear L.

Mackenzie

Hudson Strait

C. Farewell

6187 Mt. McKinley

Ungava Pen.

6050 Mt. Logan

Great Slave L.

Hudson Bay

Nunivak I.

Bering Sea

Gulf of Alaska

Belcher I.

Labrador

60

60

Aleutian Is.

Alexander Arch.

L. Winnipeg

ROCKY MOUNTAINS

N O R T H

7447

Vancouver I.

L. Superior

L. Huron

New Foundland

50

Aleutian Trench

Coast Ranges

Great Plains

Missouri

Michigan

Ontario

St. Lawrence

50

C. Mendocino

Sierra Nevada

4327 Pikes Peak

A M E R I C A

Mississippi

L. Erie

APPALACHIAN MTS.

C. Sable

40

Whitney 4418

Colorado

M o u n t a i n s

Arkansas

Mitchell 2038

Hatteras

40

6741

Guadalupe

Great Basin

Eastern Sierra Madre

Red R.

Bermuda

30

Lower California

Mexican Plateau

Gulf of Mexico

Florida

6996

30

TROPIC OF CANCER

C. San Lucas

Western Sierra Madre

Bahamas

Sargasso Sea

Hawaiian Islands

Midway I.

G. of Campeche

Yucatan

Cuba

Greater Antilles

20

Hawaii

Citlaltepetl 5700

Isthmus of Tehuantepec

G. of Honduras

Jamaica

Hispaniola

9220 Puerto Rico

Guadeloupe

Martinique

20

Johnston I.

Revilla Gigedo Is.

Tajumulco 4201

C. Gallinas

Caribbean Sea

Lesser Antilles

Barbados

10

Palmyra Is.

Clipperton I.

Nicaragua

3922 Chirripo

Isthmus of Panama

Lake Maracaibo

Trinidad

10

Fanning I.

Christmas I.

G. of Panama

Orinoco

Guiana Highlands

180 Baker Is. 7251

170

160

150

140

130

120

110

100

90

Galapagos Is.

Huila 5750

Llanos

EQUATOR

Phoenix Is.

G. de Guayaquil

6272

Chimborazo

Japura

Amazon

Marajó I.

Fernando de Noronha I.

Tokelau Is.

Malden I.

Starbuck I.

Caroline I.

Marquesas Is.

Andes

S O U T H

Selvas

Purus

Madeira

C. S. Roque

10

W. Samoa

6768 Huascarán

A M E R I C A

Caatingas

10

Tonga Is. (Friendly Is.)

Society Is.

Tahiti

Tuamotu Arch.

L. Titicaca

Illampu 7010 Bolivian Plat.

Plateau of Mato Grosso

Brazilian Highlands

São Francisco

20

Cook Is.

Tubuai Is.

TROPIC OF CAPRICORN

2884 Pico da Bandeira

20

10882 Tonga Trench

Rapa

Pitcairn I.

Ducie I.

Sala-y-Gomez

Easter I.

Gran Chaco

Parana

C. Frio

Kermadec Trench

Paraguay

30

10047 Kermadec Is.

S. Felix

S. Ambrosio

Pampas

Uruguay

30

Aconcagua 6959

Rio de la Plata

Chatham Is.

Juan Fernandez

Lagoa dos Patos

40

Chiloé

Andes Mountains

G. of San Matias

40

Chonos Arch.

Patagonia

G. of San Jorge

50

Magellan's Strait

Falkland Is.

South Georgia

50

Tierra del Fuego

C. Horn

Drake Passage

8254

60

South Shetland Is.

South Orkney Is.

South Sandwich Is.

60

Antarctic Peninsula

Graham Land

70

Ross Sea

Charcot I.

Alexander I.

Weddel Sea

70

Ellsworth I.

Coats Land

80

Marie Byrd Land

80

ANTARCTIC CIRCLE

South Pole

70

80

Azores

C. St. Vincent

Madeira

4168 Canary Is.

Mauritania

C. Blanco

C. Verde Is.

C. Verde

C. Palmas

Ascension

St. Helena

Tristan de Cunha

Gough I.

AVERAGE HEIGHT OF CONTINENTS

Arctic Circle

HEIGHT	Metres
	Over 3000
	3000
	1500
	500
	250
Sea level	0
	Below sea level
DEPTH	0
	150
	3000
	6000
	Below 6000

340

960

720

Tropic of Cancer

750

Equator

590

Tropic of Capricorn

340

Antarctic Circle

2200

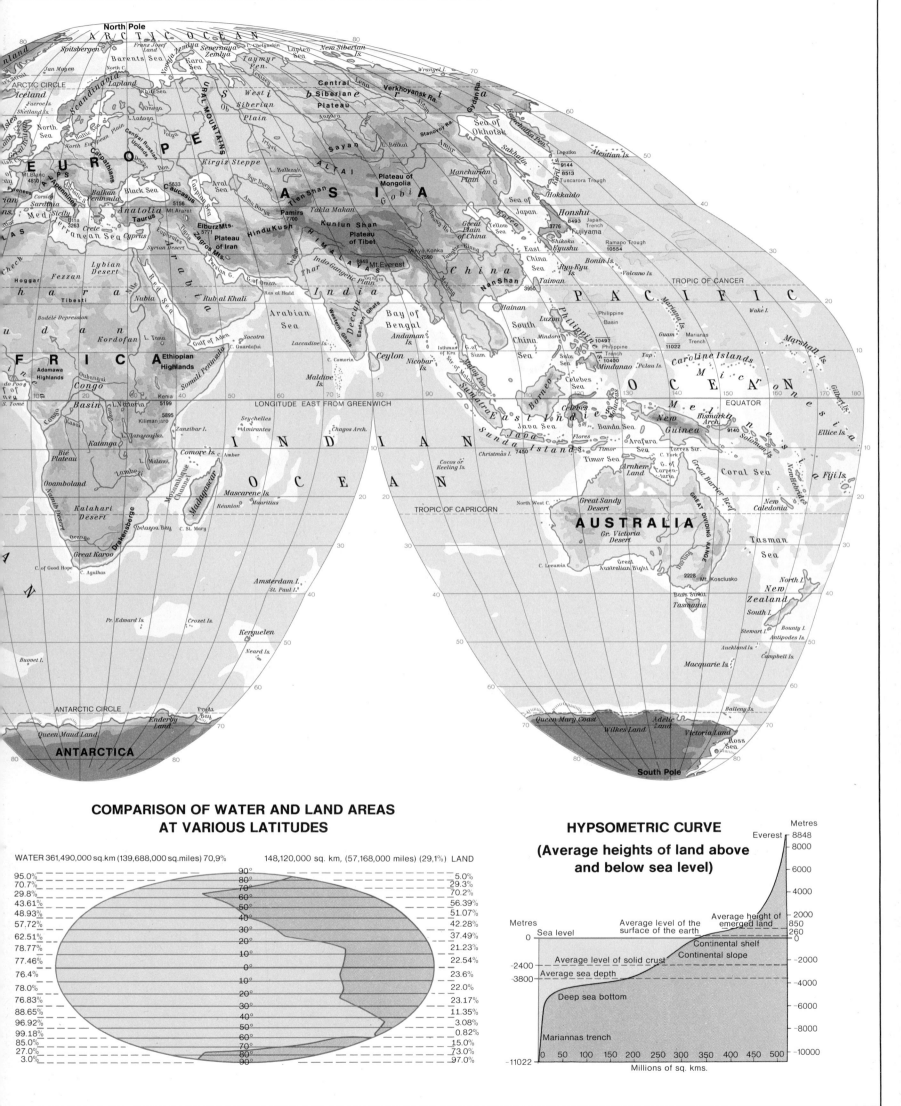

COMPARISON OF WATER AND LAND AREAS AT VARIOUS LATITUDES

WATER 361,490,000 sq.km (139,688,000 sq.miles) 70,9%   148,120,000 sq.km, (57,168,000 miles) (29,1%) LAND

WATER	Latitude	LAND
95.0%	90°	5.0%
70.7%	80°	29.3%
29.8%	70°	70.2%
43.61%	60°	56.39%
48.93%	50°	51.07%
57.72%	40°	42.28%
62.51%	30°	37.49%
78.77%	20°	21.23%
77.46%	10°	22.54%
76.4%	0°	23.6%
78.0%	10°	22.0%
76.83%	20°	23.17%
88.65%	30°	11.35%
96.92%	40°	3.08%
99.18%	50°	0.82%
85.0%	60°	15.0%
27.0%	70°	73.0%
3.0%	80°	97.0%
	90°	

HYPSOMETRIC CURVE
(Average heights of land above and below sea level)

Metres
Everest 8848
8000
6000
4000
2000
850
260
Average height of emerged land
Average level of the surface of the earth
Continental shelf
Continental slope
Metres
Sea level 0
Average level of solid crust
−2400
Average sea depth
−3800
Deep sea bottom
Mariannas trench
−11022

0 50 100 150 200 250 300 350 400 450 500
Millions of sq. kms.

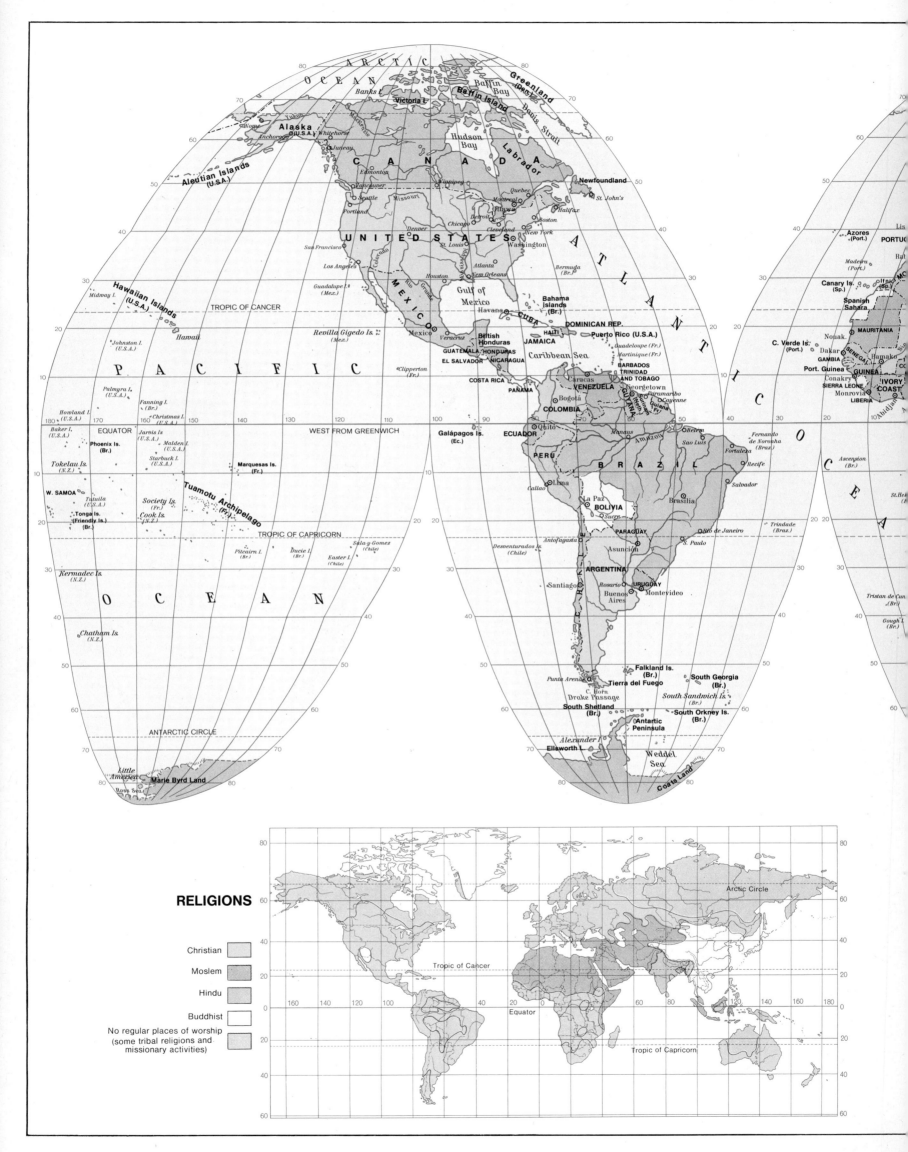

ARCTIC OCEAN

Greenland (Den.)

Baffin Bay

Banks I.

Victoria I.

Baffin Island

Davis Strait

70

80

Nome

Alaska (U.S.A.)

Anchorage

Whitehorse

Yukon

Juneau

Aleutian Islands (U.S.A.)

Mackenzie

CANADA

Hudson Bay

LABRADOR

Edmonton

Vancouver

Seattle

Portland

Winnipeg

Missouri

Quebec

Montreal

Ottawa

Detroit

Cleveland

Boston

New York

Newfoundland

St. John's

Halifax

UNITED STATES

San Francisco

Denver

Colorado

St. Louis

Chicago

Atlanta

Washington

New Orleans

Bermuda (Br.)

Los Angeles

Houston

Rio Grande

MEXICO

Gulf of Mexico

Havana

CUBA

Bahama Islands

TROPIC OF CANCER

Hawaiian Islands (U.S.A.)

Midway I.

Hawaii

Johnston I. (U.S.A.)

Revilla Gigedo Is. (Mex.)

Mexico

Veracruz

British Honduras

GUATEMALA

EL SALVADOR

HONDURAS

NICARAGUA

Guadalupe (Mex.)

DOMINICAN REP.

HAITI

JAMAICA

Puerto Rico (U.S.A.)

Guadeloupe (Fr.)

Martinique (Fr.)

Caribbean Sea

BARBADOS

TRINIDAD AND TOBAGO

COSTA RICA

PANAMA

Caracas

VENEZUELA

Bogotá

COLOMBIA

Georgetown

GUYANA

Paramaribo

Cayenne

Guiana (Neth.)

Guiana

PACIFIC

Palmyra I. (U.S.A.)

Fanning I. (Br.)

Christmas I. (U.S.A.)

Clipperton (Fr.)

Homland I. (U.S.A.)

Baker I. (U.S.A.)

EQUATOR

Jarvis Is. (U.S.A.)

Malden I. (U.S.A.)

Starbuck I. (U.S.A.)

Phoenix Is. (Br.)

Marquesas Is. (Fr.)

Galápagos Is. (Ec.)

ECUADOR

Quito

PERU

Manaus

Amazon

Belém

São Luís

Fortaleza

Fernando de Noronha (Braz.)

Recife

Ascension (Br.)

Tokelau Is. (N.Z.)

Callao

Lima

BRAZIL

Salvador

W. SAMOA

Tutuila (U.S.A.)

Society Is. (Fr.)

Tuamotu Archipelago (Fr.)

La Paz

BOLIVIA

Sucre

Brasília

Trindade (Braz.)

Tonga Is. (Friendly Is.) (Br.)

Cook Is. (N.Z.)

TROPIC OF CAPRICORN

PARAGUAY

Asunción

Rio de Janeiro

S. Paulo

Pitcairn I. (Br.)

Ducie I. (Br.)

Easter I. (Chile)

Sala-y-Gomez (Chile)

Desventuradas Is. (Chile)

Antofagasta

Kermadec Is. (N.Z.)

ARGENTINA

URUGUAY

Tristan de Cunha (Br.)

Santiago

Rosario

Buenos Aires

Montevideo

Gough I. (Br.)

Chatham Is. (N.Z.)

OCEAN

Falkland Is. (Br.)

South Georgia (Br.)

Punta Arenas

Tierra del Fuego

C. Horn

Drake Passage

South Shetland (Br.)

South Sandwich Is. (Br.)

South Orkney Is. (Br.)

ANTARCTIC CIRCLE

Alexander I.

Ellsworth L.

Antarctic Peninsula

Weddell Sea

Little America

Marie Byrd Land

Ross Sea

Coats Land

ATLANTIC OCEAN

Azores (Port.)

PORTUGAL

Madeira (Port.)

Canary Is. (Sp.)

Ifni (Sp.)

Spanish Sahara

C. Verde Is. (Port.)

Nouak.

Dakar

MAURITANIA

SENEGAL

Bamako

GAMBIA

Port. Guinea

GUINEA

Conakry

SIERRA LEONE

Monrovia

IVORY COAST

LIBERIA

Abidjan

RELIGIONS

Christian

Moslem

Hindu

Buddhist

No regular places of worship (some tribal religions and missionary activities)

Arctic Circle

Tropic of Cancer

Equator

Tropic of Capricorn

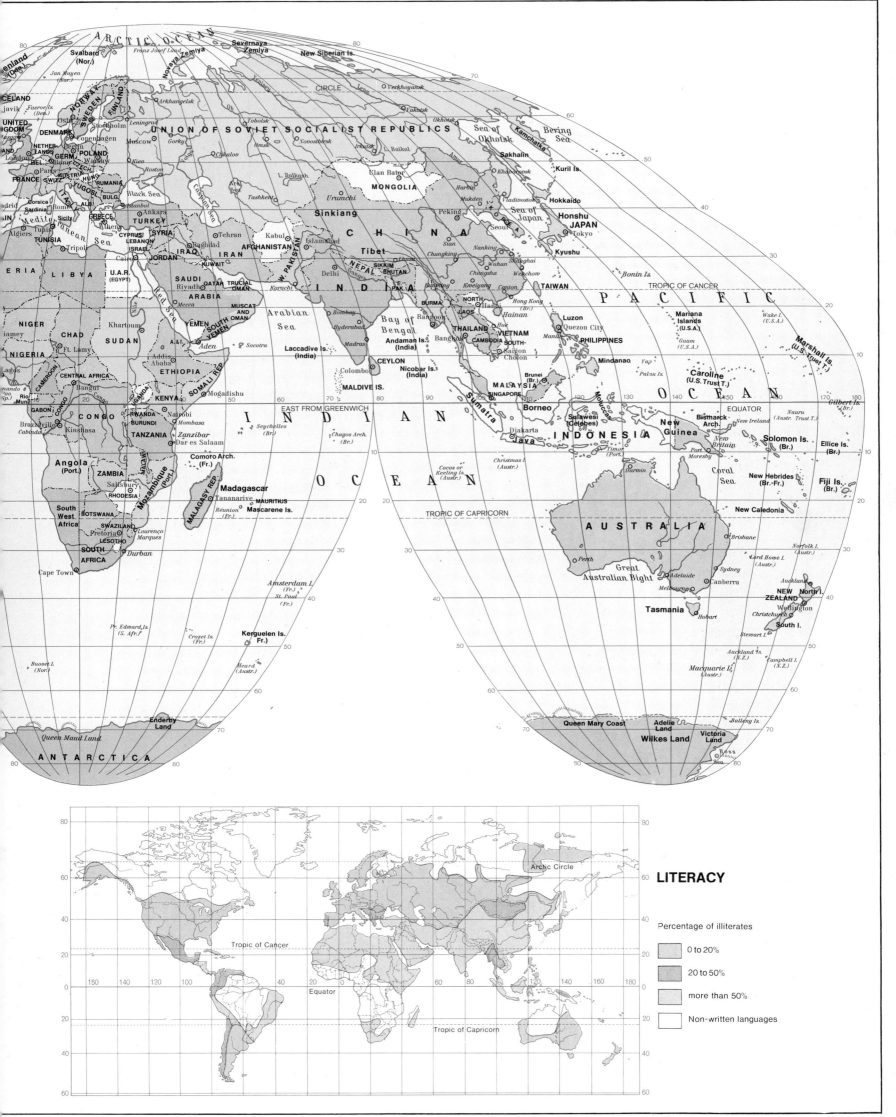

LITERACY

Percentage of illiterates

0 to 20%

20 to 50%

more than 50%

Non-written languages

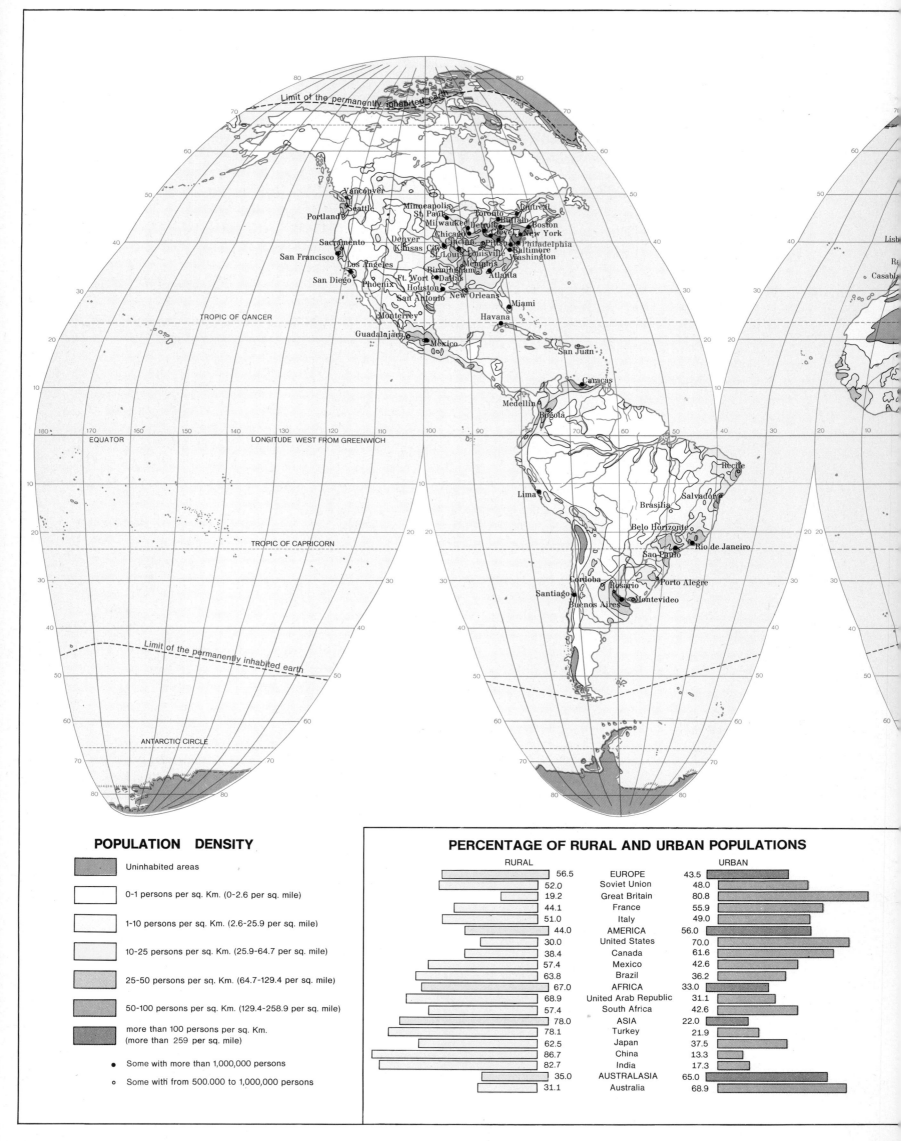

POPULATION DENSITY

Uninhabited areas

0-1 persons per sq. Km. (0-2.6 per sq. mile)

1-10 persons per sq. Km. (2.6-25.9 per sq. mile)

10-25 persons per sq. Km. (25.9-64.7 per sq. mile)

25-50 persons per sq. Km. (64.7-129.4 per sq. mile)

50-100 persons per sq. Km. (129.4-258.9 per sq. mile)

more than 100 persons per sq. Km.
(more than 259 per sq. mile)

● Some with more than 1,000,000 persons

○ Some with from 500,000 to 1,000,000 persons

PERCENTAGE OF RURAL AND URBAN POPULATIONS

RURAL		URBAN
56.5	EUROPE	43.5
52.0	Soviet Union	48.0
19.2	Great Britain	80.8
44.1	France	55.9
51.0	Italy	49.0
44.0	AMERICA	56.0
30.0	United States	70.0
38.4	Canada	61.6
57.4	Mexico	42.6
63.8	Brazil	36.2
67.0	AFRICA	33.0
68.9	United Arab Republic	31.1
57.4	South Africa	42.6
78.0	ASIA	22.0
78.1	Turkey	21.9
62.5	Japan	37.5
86.7	China	13.3
82.7	India	17.3
35.0	AUSTRALASIA	65.0
31.1	Australia	68.9

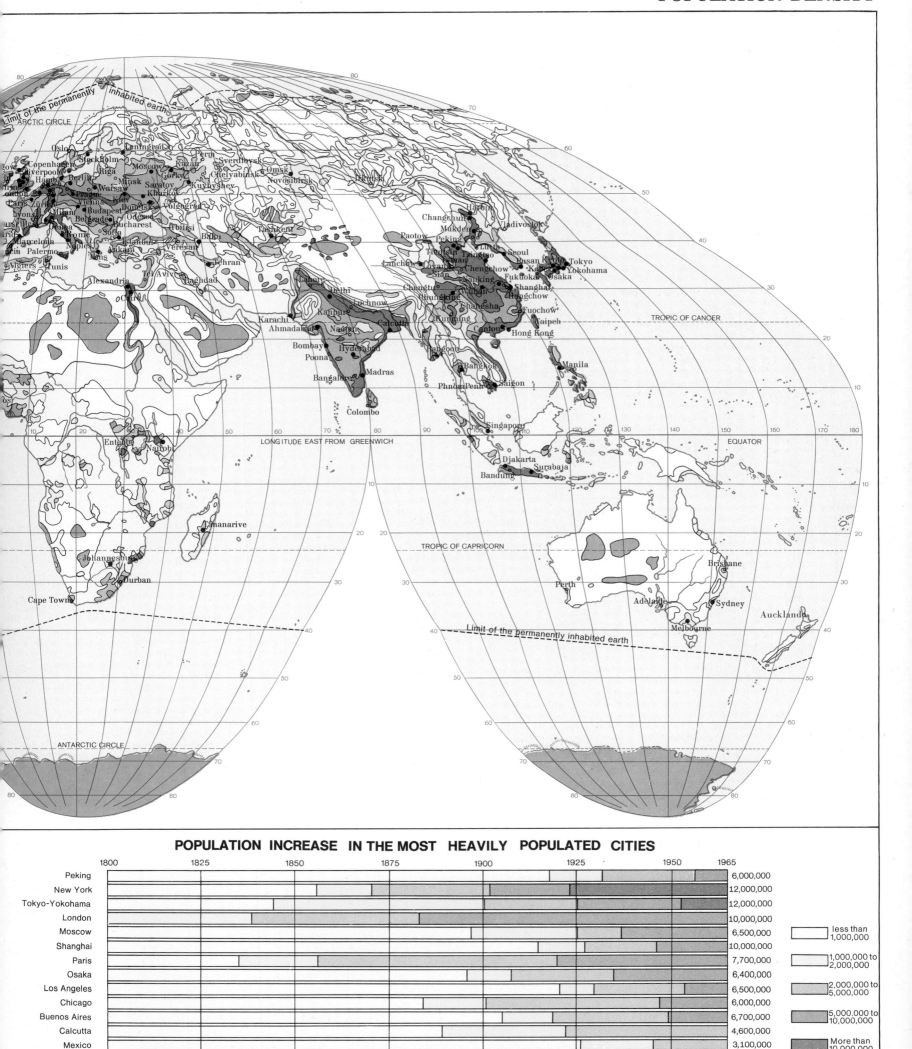

ARCTIC CIRCLE

Limit of the permanently inhabited earth

Oslo
Copenhagen Stockholm Leningrad
Liverpool Riga Moscow Kazan Perm Sverdlovsk
Hamburg Berlin Minsk Gorky Chelyabinsk Omsk Novosibirsk Irkutsk
Paris Zürich Warsaw Saratov Kharkov Kuybyshev
Prague Vienna Kiev Donets Volgograd
Milan Budapest Bucharest Odessa
Belgrade Sofia Tbilisi
Rome Istanbul Yerevan Baku Tashkent
Barcelona Naples Ankara
Palermo Tehran
Algiers Tunis

Harbin
Changchun Vladivostok
Mukden
Paotow Peking

Alexandria Baghdad
Cairo Tel Aviv
Lanchow Tientsin Tsingtao Seoul Pusan Kyoto Tokyo
Sian Chengchow Loyang Fukuoka Kobe Osaka Yokohama
Chengtu Nanking Shanghai
Lahore Chungking Wuhan Hangchow
Delhi Changsha
Lucknow Fuochow
Kanpur Kunming Taipeh
Karachi Calcutta Canton
Ahmadabad Nagpur Hong Kong
Bombay Hyderabad
Poona Rangoon
Bangkok
Bangalore Madras Manila
Colombo PhnomPenh Saigon

TROPIC OF CANCER

LONGITUDE EAST FROM GREENWICH

Singapore

Entebbe Nairobi

Djakarta
Bandung Surabaja

Tamanarive

Brisbane

TROPIC OF CAPRICORN

Perth

Johannesburg

Durban
Adelaide Sydney
Cape Town
Auckland

Melbourne
Limit of the permanently inhabited earth

ANTARCTIC CIRCLE

POPULATION INCREASE IN THE MOST HEAVILY POPULATED CITIES

	1800	1825	1850	1875	1900	1925	1950	1965	
Peking									6,000,000
New York									12,000,000
Tokyo-Yokohama									12,000,000
London									10,000,000
Moscow									6,500,000
Shanghai									10,000,000
Paris									7,700,000
Osaka									6,400,000
Los Angeles									6,500,000
Chicago									6,000,000
Buenos Aires									6,700,000
Calcutta									4,600,000
Mexico									3,100,000
Sao Paulo									5,250,000
Berlin									3,600,000
Leningrad									3,600,000

less than 1,000,000

1,000,000 to 2,000,000

2,000,000 to 5,000,000

5,000,000 to 10,000,000

More than 10,000,000

Copyright Vallardi Ind. graf.

NATURAL VEGETATION

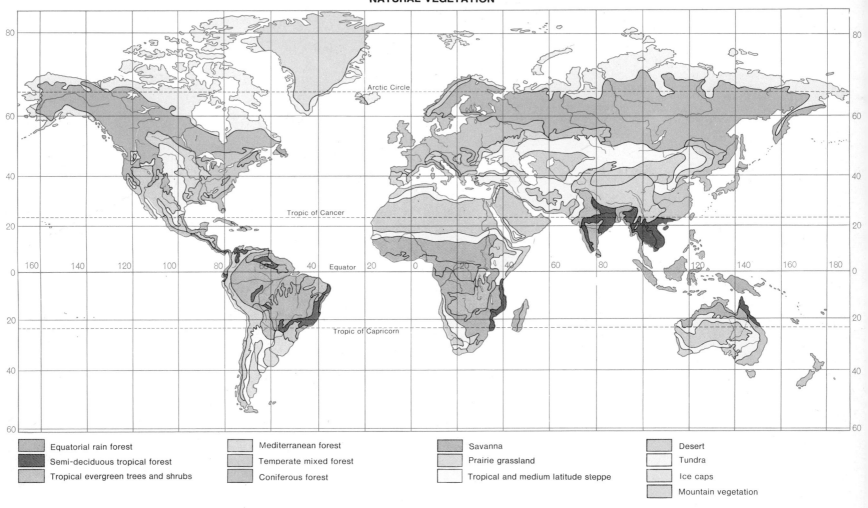

Equatorial rain forest	Mediterranean forest	Savanna	Desert
Semi-deciduous tropical forest	Temperate mixed forest	Prairie grassland	Tundra
Tropical evergreen trees and shrubs	Coniferous forest	Tropical and medium latitude steppe	Ice caps
			Mountain vegetation

There are two main zones of forests on the earth's surface; the equatorial and tropical zone, and to both north and south, a temperate zone. Besides the forests, areas of grassland and others of desert are found in some tropical areas and the interiors of the continents.

Maximum rainfall occurs in the equatorial zone and in the monsoon areas, minimum rainfall in the desert and sub-polar zones.

ANNUAL PRECIPITATION

Millimetres of rainfall per year

0 to 250 (0 to 9.85 in)	250 to 500 (9.85 to 19.7 in)	500 to 1000 (19.7 to 39.4 in)	1000 to 1500 (39.4 to 59.1 in)	1500 to 2000 (59.1 to 78.8 in)	more than 2000 (78.8 in)

and Jupiter, were formed.

Whichever of these, or any other theories, you accept about how the Earth was formed, it is known that it was at first very hot. Over a period of millions of years, it began to cool down and a thin crust formed. This crust is never more than 48 km. (30 miles) thick; beneath it is the mantle, the thickest of the Earth's layers, the plastic outer core and the denser inner core.

Not only did the molten material cool down to form rocks on the Earth's surface, water formed the seas and oceans. Since water always finds the lowest level, this has collected in the basins of the world, leaving the higher parts of the crust standing up as the land masses.

Nature is rarely static and the face of our Earth is constantly changing. Convection currents beneath the crust lead to a build-up of tension at the surface; such tension can only be released in an earthquake. Over a longer period of time, such movements result in the creation of new mountain ranges. In the early Tertiary Era, many thousands of feet of rock were compressed to form the Alps and Himalayas.

Sometimes hot, viscous material from the Earth's interior erupts on the surface, or the sea floor. In the 1940's, a Mexican farmer observed that one of his fields was smoking; today, Mount Paracutin stands in that area. In the early 1960's, the Atlantic Ocean just south of Iceland began to froth and boil; today, the volcanic island of Surtsey rises from the water at that spot. These island volcanoes often cause a great deal of damage with the tidal waves they create. Such a wave killed 36,000 people when Krakatoa erupted in Indonesia in 1883.

Over a period of some 300 years, another dramatic change can be shown. When Hendrik Hudson sailed into Hudson Bay, he stopped at the entrance and made a mark on the cliff at sea level. Today that same mark is 20 metres (60ft.) above sea level, proving that the land in that part of North America has risen 20 metres (60ft.) in 300 years.

The forces of erosion and deposition are constantly at work, gradually reshaping the landscape. The wind, rivers and moving ice erode rocks and soils from many parts of the Earth's surface. This is later deposited at lower levels, sometimes on the sea floor, sometimes in valleys and plains.

Man has only appeared on the Earth in comparatively recent times. If we imagine that life on Earth has existed for only 24 hours, man's stay here would amount to only a few seconds. But during this comparatively brief period, he has proved his superiority over the rest of the animal kingdom, increased astonishingly in numbers and organised himself into groups or nations. And although there has always been a tendency towards rivalry and wars between nations, this is gradually being replaced by a spirit of commercial competition and even, at times, co-operation, as mankind strives to make this wonderful world into a happy place in which to live.

Some waves have gradually built up this sandy beach at Cape Reinga in New Zealand; others are slowly destroying the headland beyond it.

A typical sandy desert in Death Valley, California. The almost complete absence of rain leads to very little plant life. Because of this lack of vegetation, the sand on the surface is loose and is blown by the wind to form large dunes and smaller wave-like formations.

EUROPE

Europe has a total area of nearly 12,000,000 sq. km. (more than 4 million square miles) and this makes it the second smallest of the seven great land masses which we call continents. However, during the last twenty centuries it has become the home of the most progressive civilisations, and has had a dominating influence on all the other six continents.

Europe has only one land boundary—the one on the east which divides it from Asia. This boundary, which runs through the U.S.S.R., is made up of the Ural Mountains, the Ural River and the Caucasus Mountains. Although part of the U.S.S.R. is in Europe and part in Asia, it is dealt with at the end of the European section of this atlas, being treated separately (and out of alphabetical order) from the truly European countries. The U.S.S.R. can be said to form a bridge between Europe and Asia.

Europe's other boundaries are the Atlantic Ocean to the west, the Arctic Ocean to the north, and the Mediter-ranean to the south. These maritime boundaries are rich in peninsulas, bays, inlets and islands (such as the British Isles) giving Europe a surprisingly long coastline for its size.

Europe's rivers can roughly be divided into three groups: those that drain west and north to the Atlantic Ocean and the Baltic Sea such as the Tagus, Garonne, Seine, Loire, Meuse, Rhine, Moselle, Weser, Elbe, Oder and Vistula; those that drain south to the Mediterranean such as the Ebro, Rhone, Tiber and Po; and, finally, those draining to the Black Sea, the greatest of which is the Danube; others crossing the plains of European Russia include the Dniester, Dnieper and Don. The great Volga system ultimately reaches the land-locked Caspian Sea.

These large rivers are important because their basins are major areas of agriculture. Some of them serve as inland waterways, ports are situated at their mouths and some crossing places have formed the sites of large towns and cities, e.g. Paris, Rome, Budapest, Vienna.

Europe's vegetation reflects the various climatic conditions. In the cold north (Iceland, northern Scandinavia and northern Russia) tundra prevails. Southwards, this passes into coniferous forests and then to the mixed forests of conifers and broad-leaved trees in much of central Europe. In regions of Mediterranean climates, small evergreen trees and shrubs prevail.

Europe's population is about 14% of the world total. Historical developments, and the advent of industrialisation, have caused this population to become somewhat irregular in distribution, and alongside areas of dense population such as central Belgium and the Po Basin in Italy can be found others with few inhabitants—the Ardennes and the Alps. Countries with severe climates such as Iceland and Finland also have comparatively few people living in them. The most heavily populated areas form a broad belt from central England, across north east France, Belgium and the southern Netherlands to Rhineland-Westphalia, Saxony and Silesia. That these areas are heavily industralised stems originally from the presence of large deposits of coal.

Continued on page 24

Despite the fact that it is well on the way to industrialisation, Rumania still retains many of its traditional characteristics, such as these horse-drawn carts.

The Kaiser-Wilhelm memorial church in West Berlin. Damaged during the Second World War, it was left in this state as a memorial. It provides a striking contrast with the modern buildings of the Reit-scheidplatz which surround it. Notice that in West Berlin, as in many European cities, tram-cars are still an important method of public transport.

21

Copyright, Vallardi Ind.Graf.

N   O   35   P   40   Q   45   R   S   T   U   V   70   Z   75   80

North C.
Vadsö
Pechenga
Kolguyev I.
Kanin Pen.
Murmansk
Kola Pen.
Naryan-Mar
Vorkuta
Salekhard
2
Ob
Berezovo
Khanty-Mansiysk
3
55
Rovaniemi
Kandalaksha
White Sea
Mezen
Pechora
Kozhva
Ukhta
Tara
Tobolsk
OMSK
Tornio
L. Onega
Arkhángelsk
N. Dvina
Ishim
Irtysh
Luleä
Onega
Kotlas
Syktyvkar
Vel Ustyug
PERM
SVERDLOVSK
Tyumen
Kurgan
Petropavlovsk
50
Oulu
Petrozavodsk
Konosha
Kirov
Izhevsk
Sarapul
CHELYABINSK
Kustanai
Krasnoe
Tselinograd
Tampere
L. Ladoga
Vologda
KAZAN
UFA
Magnitogorsk
L. Tengiz
HELSINKI
Vyborg
Cherepovets
L. Rybinsk
Sterlitamak
Baikonur
G. of Finland
LENINGRAD
Novgorod
YAROSLAVL
Ivanovo
GORKI
Abdulino
Orenburg
Orsk
Turgay
Tallin
ESTONIA
Chudskoye L.
Bologoye
Volga
Ulyanovsk
KUYBYSHEV
6
Tartu
Kalinin
MOSCOW
Oka
Arzamas
Saransk
Penza
Uralsk
Aktyubinsk
Aralsk
RIGA
Pskov
Velikie Luki
Vyazma
Volga
Ryazan
Chelkar
Novo Kazalinsk
LATVIA
Daugavpils
Vitebsk
Smolensk
Tula
Tambov
Volga
SARATOV
Uralsk
45
Klaipeda
LITHUANIA
Kaunas
WHITE
Bryansk
Orel
Yelets
Aral Sea
Vilnius
MINSK
RUSSIA
Gomel
Kursk
VORONEZH
VOLGOGRAD
Guryev
KAZAKHSTAN
Bialystok
Baranovichi
Pripet
Belgorod
Millerovo
Astrakhan
UZBEKISTAN
WARSAW
Brest
Konotop
KHARKOV
Volga
7
Radom
Rovno
KIEV
Poltava
Dnieper
DNEPROPETROVSK
DONETSK
Shakhty
ROSTOV
Stepnoy
FortShevchenko
Kungrad
Amu Nukus
Lublin
Zhitomir
UKRAINE
Krivoy Rog
ZAPOROZHYE
Taganrog
Volga
Tashauz
LVOV
Chernovtsy
Dniester
Nikolayev
Zhdanov
Yeysk
Manych
Stavropol
Kuma
Urgench
40
Kishinev
Kherson
Sea
Krasnodar
Pyatigorsk
CASPIAN
Kara Bogaz Gol
Daroaza
Botoşani
Prut
MOLDAVIA
of Azov
Kerch
Kuban
Maykop
Grozhyy
Dagestan
Makhachkala
Debrecen
Cluj
Iaşi
ODESSA
Perekop
Crimea
Krasnodar
Armavir
Ordzhonikidze
Krasnovodsk
TURKMENISTAN
Arad
Sibiu
Braşov
Galaţi
Simferopol
Yalta
Tuapse
Sukhumi
Kutaisi
Nukha
Kizyl Arvat
8
Timişoara
ROMANIA
Sevastopol
Balaklava
Batumi
GEORGIA
TBILISI
Kirovabad
BAKU
Ashkhabad
Turnu Severin
Ploeşti
BUCHAREST
Constanţa
BLACK SEA
ARMENIA
AZERBAIJAN
SEA
Bojnürd
Craiova
Danube
Ruse
Varna
Sinop
Trabzon
Leninakan
YEREVAN
Nakhichevan
Lenkoran
Bandar e Shāh
BELGRADE
Pleven
BULGARIA
Burgas
Samsun
Erzurum
Tabriz
Rasht
Shāhrūd
35
SOFIA
Plovdiv
Edirne
Zonguldak
Sivas
Tigris
L. Van
Van
Urmia
Skopje
Kapalla
Bosporus
ISTANBUL
Üsküdar
Diyarbakir
Rizaiyeh (Urmia)
TEHRAN
GREECE
Geliboiu
Saf Marmara
ANKARA
ANATOLIA
T U R K E Y
Erbil
Kāshān
Thessaloniki
Bandirma
Bursa
Eskişehir
Malatya
Mosul
IRAN
Ioánnina
Larisa
Manisa
Afyon
Kayseri
Gaziantep
Kirkuk
Kermānshāh
Esfahan
Khalkís
Khios
Izmir
Konya
Adana
Iskenderun
Dayr az Zawr
BAGHDAD
Yazd
Patras
ATHENS
Piraeus
Aydin
Isparta
HALAB (ALEPPO)
IRAQ
Dezful
Kalamai
Antalya
G. of Antalya
Hama
SYRIA
Euphrates
Ahvaz
Bandar e Shahpur
C. Matapan
Rhodes
Nicosia
Homs
Tigris
Al Hadithah
An Najaf
Al Basrah
Abadan
Shiraz
Iraklion
Kharpatos
CYPRUS
BEIRUT
LEBANON
DAMASCUS
Persian Gulf
Crete
SEA
Haifa
ISR.

23

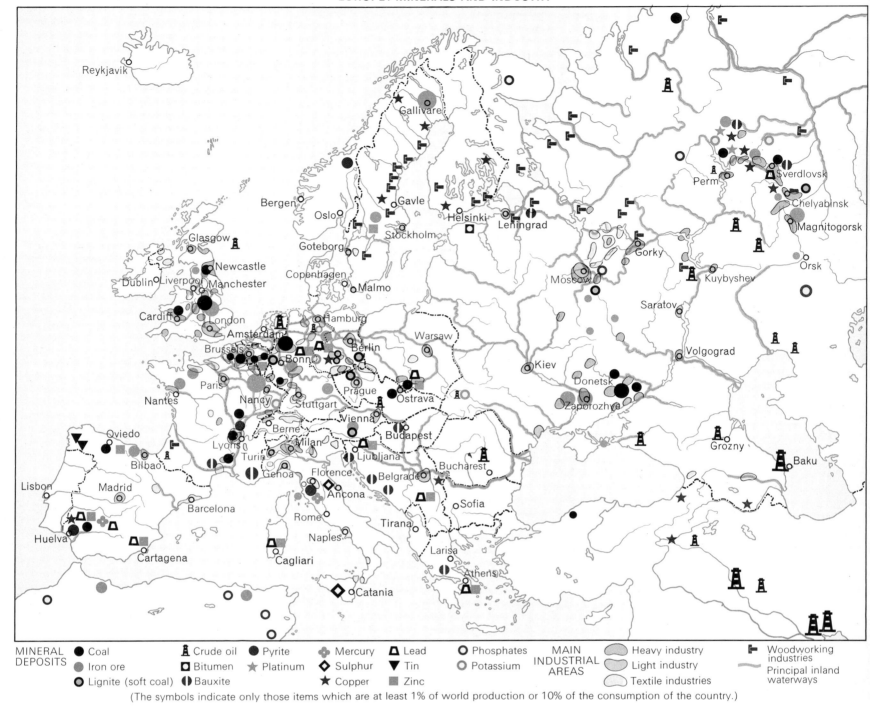

MINERAL DEPOSITS

● Coal
● Iron ore
◉ Lignite (soft coal)

⚱ Crude oil
▣ Bitumen
◑ Bauxite

● Pyrite
★ Platinum
★ Copper

✛ Mercury
◇ Sulphur
▼ Tin

⬒ Lead
▼ Tin
▪ Zinc

○ Phosphates
○ Potassium

MAIN INDUSTRIAL AREAS

Heavy industry
Light industry
Textile industries

⚑ Woodworking industries
Principal inland waterways

(The symbols indicate only those items which are at least 1% of world production or 10% of the consumption of the country.)

Europe is an important continent agriculturally, although about half of its land is unproductive because of the relief, climate, soil or because it has been built over by man. Cultivation is usually intensive and scientific, using rotation of crops and heavy fertilising, resulting in good yields. The world's highest yields of wheat are in the U.S.S.R., Denmark and the Netherlands. Even excluding the U.S.S.R., Europe produces one third of the world's wheat, two thirds of the potatoes, more than half of the dairy produce, a quarter of the sugar and three quarters of the wine.

Denmark and the Netherlands are major exporters of livestock products. About two fifths of Europe's sheep are in Britain and Spain while two fifths of her cattle are in France, West Germany and Britain.

The most highly industrialised countries in Europe, measured by the total number of people employed in manufacturing, are the United Kingdom, West Germany, Italy, France, the Netherlands and Belgium. Switzerland and Sweden also have a high proportion of their small populations so employed. Since the Revolution, the U.S.S.R. has become a leading industrial country, and

now occupies second place in the world, after the U.S.A.

All branches of manufacturing have been developed in Europe, but most notably iron and steel and other metals, engineering, textiles and food processing. The two World Wars hindered both industrial and agricultural development, and in comparatively recent years associations between European countries have been formed with the aim of encouraging both economic and political co-operation.

The European Coal and Steel Community was established in 1952 between France, Italy, West Germany and the Benelux countries, removing tariff and quota restrictions on coal and steel. In 1957 the European Economic Community (the Common Market) came into being when the same six countries signed the Treaty of Rome whose provisions encouraged trade between them. In 1960 Sweden, Norway, Denmark, Austria, Switzerland, Portugal and the U.K. formed a customs union and trading bloc, called the European Free Trade Association. The EFTA agreement provides for progressive reductions of tariffs and quota restrictions between members. Bulgaria, Czechoslovakia, East Germany, Hungary, Poland,

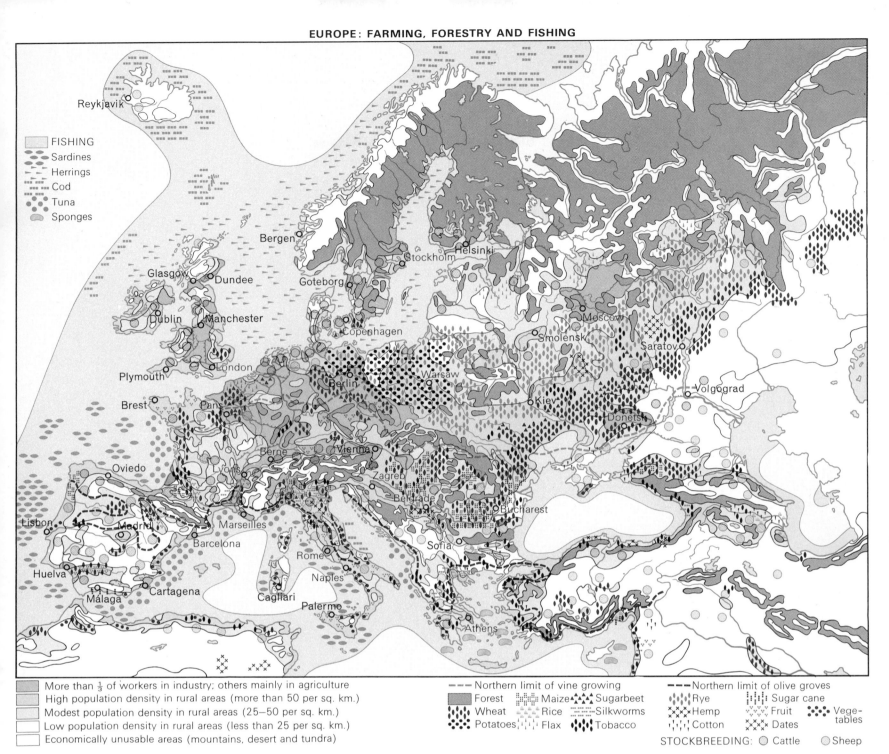

FISHING
- Sardines
- Herrings
- Cod
- Tuna
- Sponges

More than ⅓ of workers in industry; others mainly in agriculture
High population density in rural areas (more than 50 per sq. km.)
Modest population density in rural areas (25–50 per sq. km.)
Low population density in rural areas (less than 25 per sq. km.)
Economically unusable areas (mountains, desert and tundra)

--- Northern limit of vine growing   --- Northern limit of olive groves

Forest	Maize	Sugarbeet	Rye	Sugar cane
Wheat	Rice	Silkworms	Hemp	Fruit	Vegetables
Potatoes	Flax	Tobacco	Cotton	Dates	

STOCKBREEDING: ○ Cattle   ○ Sheep

EUROPE: BASES OF INDUSTRIAL PRODUCTION

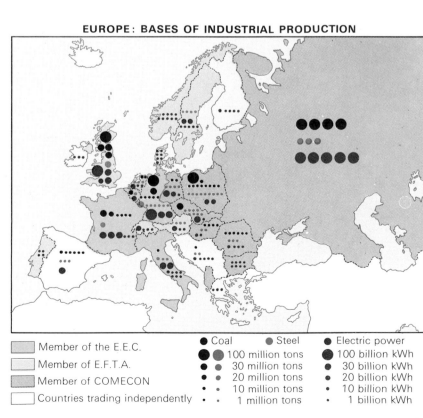

Rumania and the U.S.S.R. are all members of an economic union known as the Comecon.

Europe is divided into numerous countries and states and has many cultural and religious groupings of people. More than 70 languages are spoken within Europe and one reason for this is thought to be the complex movements of populations by invasions and migrations. Other reasons are probably the great geographic variations with mountain areas isolating lowland basins, and the many islands along the coastlines.

Apart from Soviet Russia, France and Spain are the largest states with over 551,000 sq. km. (nearly 213,000 sq. miles) and over 503,000 sq. km. (nearly 190,000 sq. miles) respectively. Next comes Sweden with 460,000 sq. km. approx. (175,000 sq. miles). Norway, Poland and Finland are all larger than the United Kingdom which, with approximately a quarter of a million sq. km. (94,215 sq. miles) is a little smaller than the German Federal Republic. Europe also has some very tiny states—Andorra, San Marino, Malta, Gibraltar, Monaco, Liechtenstein and the Vatican City—each with less than 518 sq. km. (200 sq. miles).

Member of the E.E.C.
Member of E.F.T.A.
Member of COMECON
Countries trading independently

● Coal   ● Steel   ● Electric power
● 100 million tons   ● 100 billion kWh
● 30 million tons   ● 30 billion kWh
● 20 million tons   ● 20 billion kWh
● 10 million tons   ● 10 billion kWh
· 1 million tons   · 1 billion kWh

ALBANIA

Albania is a mountainous state between Yugoslavia and Greece, ruled by the Communist Party. The Koritsa Basin and the coastal plain are the main areas of farming. Some parts have been reclaimed and irrigated. Maize, wheat, tobacco, fruit and vegetables are the most important crops; there are more than one million sheep and goats. Oil, copper, chrome, iron ore and lignite are mined, largely for export, and various small-scale industries are carried on. The largely Moslem population speaks a language related to ancient Illyrian and unlike any other modern language. Albania became a People's Democracy in 1945 after being invaded and controlled by Italy in 1939 and later Germany during the Second World War. *Capital: Tirana. Population: 1.7 million. Highest point: Mount Korab, 2,754 metres (9,028ft.). Land area: 28,748 sq. km. (11,097 sq. miles).*

ANDORRA

Andorra is a mountainous "pocket" principality in the eastern Pyrenees. It has a curious semi-independent status for, whilst it pays dues to France and to the bishop of a neighbouring Spanish diocese (Urgel), it is left very much to its own devices. It is a country of valleys and ridges enclosed by high mountain ranges, the lowest entry pass from the north rising to nearly 2,500 metres (8,000ft.) although access is much easier from Spain. The Catalan-speaking population rear sheep and goats and grow some wheat, maize and tobacco. There is also a little industry. Tourists have been encouraged to visit Andorra in recent years by new roads and hotels which have been constructed. Government is by a council of twenty-four members, elected by heads of families. *Capital: Andorra la Vella. Population: 14,000. Land area: 465 sq. km. (180 sq. miles).*

AUSTRIA

Austria is a mountainous federal republic in central Europe with an elected President and National Assembly. Dairying, arable farming and iron and steel production are all important activities. Natural resources include iron ore, lead and zinc and a major world deposit of graphite. The Danube is important for transport. Tourists to Vienna and various Alpine resorts provide a major source of income. The German-speaking population is unevenly distributed, one quarter living in Vienna. Religion is predominantly Roman Catholic. Austria was annexed to Germany in 1938 during Hitler's regime, was divided into four allied zones after the war but regained her independence in 1955. *Capital: Vienna. Population: 7.4 million. Highest point: Gross Glockner, 3,802 metres (12,465ft.). Principal river: Danube. Land area: 83,849 sq. km. (32,366 sq. miles).*

BELGIUM

Belgium is a north-west European kingdom. It is the most densely populated country in Europe and is highly industrialised—textiles, iron and steel, food processing and engineering being most important. Dairy farming, beet and potatoes and cereal production are the main agricultural activities. More than half the population speaks Flemish, a language akin to Dutch, while the Walloons, mainly in the south, speak French. Both languages are official and legally equal. Belgium has a constitutional monarchy with a chamber of deputies and a Senate. In 1948 she entered into a customs agreement, the Benelux Union, with the Netherlands and Luxembourg. This is now part of the Common Market. Belgium established an important overseas Empire (part of the Congo, in Africa) to which independence was granted in 1959 as a result of African impatience. *Capital: Brussels. Population: 9.6 million. Principal river: Meuse. Land area: 30,513 sq. km. (11,778 sq. miles).*

BULGARIA

Bulgaria is a mountainous country, bordered on the north by the lower Danube and opening eastward onto the Black Sea. It is essentially agricultural with tobacco, grapes, maize, wheat and attar of roses (rose oil) of most importance. Industrial output is increasing, especially coal, lead, zinc, copper, cement, steel and electricity. The population are mainly Orthodox Christians although there is a small Turkish Moslem minority. The language, Bulgarian, is the oldest and simplest of the Slavonic languages. The country has been independent since 1908 and adopted a Socialist form of government after the Second World War. Since 1947 private enterprise in major industry has been replaced by state ownership, and most agriculture is collectivised. *Capital: Sofia. Population: 8.3 million. Highest point: Pic Stalin, 2,926 metres (9,593ft.). Land area: 110,912 sq. km. (42,812 sq. miles).*

Austria. **A typical alpine view. This is the village of Werfen in the Valley of the Salzach.**

Bulgaria. **The Bay of Nessebar on the Black Sea.**

Belgium. **Ghent, the old building of the city next to the Grand Palace.**

CZECHOSLOVAKIA

Czechoslovakia is a central European Republic. It was originally created in 1918 out of parts of Austria-Hungary, later becoming a People's Democracy within the Soviet bloc. Its highly efficient agricultural economy produces sugar beet, grain, hops and malt. Coal and iron resources in the Erz Gebirge provide the basis for a steel industry; copper, lead, silver, graphite and uranium are also mined. Machinery and other manufactured goods—glass, porcelain, pencils and beer—are exported. Industry and trade are nationalised. Czechs are for the most part Roman Catholic; churches are subject to state control, clergymen being paid by the state to which they take an oath of allegiance. Two languages are spoken—Czech in Bohemia and Moravia, and Slovak in Slovakia. *Capital: Prague. Population: 14.3 million. Highest point: Stalinov Stit, 2,665 metres (8,737ft.). Principal river: Vltava. Land area: 127,870 sq. km. (49,357 sq. miles).*

DENMARK

Denmark is a small, low-lying Scandinavian kingdom including a number of islands, notably Zealand and Funen, many of which are linked by bridges and ferries. It is mainly an agricultural country with a co-operative marketing system; much of the dairy produce is exported. Denmark has a large merchant marine and fishing fleet, and important shipyards. Industrial progress in engineering, textiles, chemicals and furniture production has been rapid. The Danes have a very high standard of living and excellent educational and social security schemes. Their religion is predominantly Lutheran. Denmark is an independent constitutional monarchy and the parliament (Folketing) consists of one chamber with members elected by proportional representation for a term of four years. *Capital: Copenhagen. Population: 4.8 million. Land area: 43,069 sq. km. (16,625 sq. miles).*

FINLAND

Finland is an independent republic in north-east Scandinavia with more than 70% of its total area covered with forests and lakes. Paper, pulp and timber are the major exports, but metal, manufactured goods and dairy produce are also sent abroad. Most houses are made of timber and vast quantities of wood are burned in domestic stoves during the long winters. Europe's largest copper reserve is at Outokumpu. Finland has one of the lowest population densities in Europe and more than half live along the south coast. Swedish is spoken by about 9% of the population; the remainder speak Finnish (Suomi). Religion is 93% Lutheran. The President, elected for six years, appoints a Cabinet responsible to the House of Representatives, a single chamber of 200 members. *Capital: Helsinki. Population: 4.7 million. Principal river: Kemijoki. Land area: 305,475 sq. km. (117,913 sq. miles).*

FRANCE

France is the largest country in Europe, with the exception of Russia. It has long Atlantic, Mediterranean and Channel coastlines. About one fifth of the population works on the land. Wheat, potatoes and sugar beet are major crops; many cattle, sheep and pigs are reared. In the south, rice, citrus fruits and silk worms are important. France produces about 30% of the world's wine. Heavy industry is found in Lorraine and the north; the valley of the River Rhône, and the estuary towns of western France, are centres of other industries. Religion is predominantly Roman Catholic. Government is by a President, elected for seven years by a special body of electors, and Parliament comprising the Senate and National Assembly, the latter elected by the nation's vote. *Capital: Paris. Population: 46.9 million. Principal river: Seine. Land area: 551,601 sq. km. (212,918 sq. miles).*

GERMANY (Eastern)

East Germany has a Socialist form of government and is known as the German Democratic Republic. It is an importer of raw materials and an exporter of manufactured goods, mainly machinery. Optical goods are also manufactured. The chief industrial cities are Leipzig, Dresden and East Berlin. Mineral resources include the largest world output of lignite—which is the basis of the chemical industry and used for generating electric power— and potash, a fertiliser. Agriculture is broadly based and very important. In 1961 the East German government erected a wall across Berlin sealing off the flow of East Germans to the west. The question of German reunification is a major issue in world affairs at the present time. *Capital: East Berlin. Population: 17.3 million. Principal river: Elbe. Land area: 108,174 sq. km. (41,755 sq. miles), excluding East Berlin.*

Denmark. **Copenhagen, the impressive town hall, built in the typical Scandinavian style.**

France. **Paris, an aerial view of the Palais de Chaillot.**

Czechoslovakia. **Prague, the Charles IV bridge on the Vltava river.**

GERMANY (Western)

West Germany is a Western-type democracy, officially known as the German Federal Republic. After financial reform in 1948, West Germany rapidly returned to prosperity and has become a leading industrial country in Western Europe. Industry is largely concentrated in the Ruhr region. Principal products are coal, iron and steel. Exports of manufactured goods include machinery, ships, cars, electrical goods and chemicals. The principal seaport is Hamburg. Agricultural production is important, especially on the plains in the north. A feature of West Germany's post-war policy has been its close co-operation with other European powers through the North Atlantic Treaty Organisation, the European Economic Community and the West European Union. West Berlin is part of the Federal Republic. *Capital: Bonn. Population: 60.5 million. Principal river: Rhine. Land area: 248,546 sq. km. (95,939 sq. miles), including West Berlin.*

West Germany. **The Rhine at Oberwesel and the Castle of Schonburg.**

GIBRALTAR

Gibraltar is a rocky peninsula, joined to the Spanish mainland by a narrow causeway. In history it was part of the "Pillars of Hercules", was settled by Romans, Arabs and Berbers and became part of Spain in 1462. Sir George Rooke captured it for Britain in 1704 since when it has been a Crown Colony and British naval base, guarding the entrance to the Mediterranean Sea. In recent years there has been trouble with Spain over the future of the Rock. Spain would like Britain to hand it back to her. The Rock—a limestone cliff riddled with caves and tunnels—rises sheerly above the artificial harbour of Gibraltar. Most of the population are engaged in dockyard work and supply services. Barbary apes, the only monkeys at large in Europe, are found on the Rock. They live under the protection of the Governor. *Population: 26,000. Land area: 6.5 sq. km. (2½ sq. miles).*

Gibraltar. **A view of the Rock of Gibraltar, taken from Europa Point.**

GREECE

Greece is a kingdom in the southernmost part of the Balkan Peninsula with a number of islands in the Aegean and Ionian Seas, the most important being Rhodes, Crete and Patmos. The country is mountainous and not very fertile. Only about 30% of the land is cultivated but cotton, tobacco, vines, olives and citrus fruits thrive in the Mediterranean climate and are exported. Currants take their name from the Greek city of Corinth where they were first grown. Industry suffers from lack of minerals but bauxite, iron ore, magnesite and chromite are exported. Tourist traffic to the architectural remains of the ancient Greek civilisation is heavy. Religion is mainly Eastern Orthodox. *Capital: Athens. Population: 8.5 million. Highest point: Mount Olympus, 2,920 metres (9,573ft.). Land area (including the islands): 131,944 sq. km. (50,930 sq. miles).*

HUNGARY

Hungary is a central European republic which has adopted a Socialist form of government since the Second World War. It is rich agriculturally with 75% of its farming on a co-operative basis and 14% state run. Major crops are wheat, maize, vegetables, sugar beet and tobacco. There are substantial deposits of coal, bauxite and lignite. Industries producing foodstuffs, metals, vehicles and textiles are concentrated around Budapest. The population is two-thirds Roman Catholic; one-third Calvinist. Their language, Magyar, has no obvious link with any other European language but is probably related to Finnish. Under the 1949 Constitution, a 'Republic of Workers and Working Peasants' with a National Assembly elects a Council of Ministers and a Presidential Council. *Capital: Budapest. Population: 10.2 million. Principal river: Danube. Land area: 93,030 sq. km. (35,909 sq. miles).*

ICELAND

Iceland is an independent island republic in the North Atlantic Ocean, just south of the Arctic Circle. The country is mountainous with volcanoes and geysers and three quarters is uninhabitable. Fishing, fish-processing and sheep raising are the main occupations. Over 90% of the exports are of fish produce. Heat from the geysers is used for domestic heating, in industry and for heating glass-houses. The volcanic phenomena are a tourist attraction. The majority of the population speaks Icelandic which is the most archaic of the northern Germanic languages. Religion is Lutheran. The Althing (parliament) elects one third of its members to serve as an Upper House. Iceland was ruled by Denmark from 1380 to 1918 when it became independent but still recognised the King of Denmark as its sovereign. The union with Denmark was dissolved in 1944 and a republic was proclaimed. *Capital: Reykjavik. Population: 197,000. Land area: 103,000 sq. km. (39,750 sq. miles) (approx.).*

Hungary. **Budapest, a beautiful view of the city and the River Danube. On the far bank is the domed Parliament building.**

IRELAND

The Republic of Ireland (Eire) is an independent state comprising 26 counties and occupying the southern part of Ireland. The other six counties in the north east are within the United Kingdom. Agricultural and industrial outputs are nearly equal each year. Farming is predominantly pastoral; brewing and food processing are the most valuable industries. The language is mostly English although Gaelic is spoken among the country people. Government is by a parliamentary democracy: Dail Eireann and a President are elected by the nation's vote. Religion is 96% Roman Catholic. *Capital: Dublin. Population: 2.8 million. Principal river: Shannon. Land area: 68,893 sq. km. (26,593 sq. miles).*

ITALY

The republic of Italy is a mountainous boot-shaped peninsula projecting into the Mediterranean Sea. In the river basins and on some lower mountain slopes cereals, vegetables, fruit, olives and vines are produced. Cattle and sheep are equally numerous. In the north are areas of industrial activity—motor car, shipping, engineering and textile manufacture. Southern Italy is less well developed. Principal exports are fruit, vegetables and consumer goods. Tourists flock to Venice, Rome and Florence. Religion is Roman Catholic. Since the Second World War, governments have been coalitions dominated by Christian Democrats. *Capital: Rome. Population: 53.6 million. Principal river: Po. Highest point: Monte Bianco, 4,810 metres (15,782ft.). Land area: 301,224 sq. km. (116,272 sq. miles).*

Italy. **Rome, buildings and monuments of different periods blend harmoniously in Navona Square.**

LIECHTENSTEIN

Liechtenstein is a small independent principality in central Europe, situated on the upper Rhine, just south of Lake Constance, between Austria and Switzerland. The population is mainly engaged in light industry, including precision instrument making, food canning, textiles and ceramics. The frequent issue of attractive postage stamps is another source of income. The country is linked economically with Switzerland. The language is German. The ruling prince lives in a 16th century castle at Vaduz. Liechtenstein was founded in 1719, although its history goes back to 1342, and it became independent in 1866. It remained neutral during both world wars. The National Anthem has the same tune as "God Save the Queen". *Capital: Vaduz. Population: 19,000. Land area: 160 sq. km. (62 sq. miles).*

LUXEMBOURG

The Grand Duchy of Luxembourg is an independent state situated between Belgium, France and Germany. It has extensive iron ore deposits and is an important producer of steel. Luxembourg City is the headquarters of the European Coal and Steel Community. In 1948 it entered the Benelux Union. The languages spoken are German, French and a distinctive German dialect called Letzeburgesch. Luxembourg was occupied by Germany in both world wars, despite the fact that it had been declared a neutral territory in 1867. In 1948 it abandoned its neutrality and joined NATO. It has been a Grand Duchy since 1918 and the sovereign is a member of the House of Nassau. Religion is Roman Catholic. Government is by a Chamber of Deputies elected by the nation's vote and an upper Chamber appointed by the sovereign. *Capital: Luxembourg City. Population: 335,000. Principal river: Sûre. Land area: 2,586 sq. km. (998 sq. miles).*

Italy. **Valle d'Aosta. A cable car leaving Courmayeur. In the background is Mont Blanc.**

MALTA

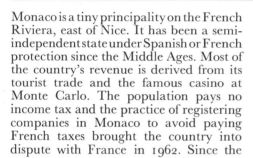

Malta is a small Mediterranean island in the straits between Sicily and North Africa. The docks are the major centre of employment, though a number of new industries have been established in the last decade. Wheat, barley and potatoes are the leading crops. Malta was ceded to Britain in 1814, became self-governing in 1921 and served as a British naval base during the Second World War. In 1942 she was awarded the George Cross in recognition of the bravery of her people under continual heavy bombing. She became an independent nation within the British Commonwealth in 1964. The language, Maltese, is a dialect of the Semitic languages. Italian and English are also used. Religion is Roman Catholic. Malta has a thriving tourist trade. The islands of Gozo and Comino are part of Malta. *Capital: Valetta. Population: 330,000. Land area: 316 sq. km. (122 sq. miles).*

MONACO

Monaco is a tiny principality on the French Riviera, east of Nice. It has been a semi-independent state under Spanish or French protection since the Middle Ages. Most of the country's revenue is derived from its tourist trade and the famous casino at Monte Carlo. The population pays no income tax and the practice of registering companies in Monaco to avoid paying French taxes brought the country into dispute with France in 1962. Since the 13th century, Monaco has been ruled by a member of the Grimaldi family. Should there be no male heir, however, Monaco would become a French protectorate. The old town of Monaco is built on a rocky headland projecting into the Mediterranean. It has a 16th century castle and an important oceanographic institute. The Condamine, a luxury trading centre, adjoins the harbour. *Population: 21,700. Land area: 149 hectares (368 acres).*

NETHERLANDS

The flat, low-lying kingdom of the Netherlands is distinguished for its dune coast and sea walls. Behind these, many thousands of hectares (1 acre = 0.405 hectares) of land have been reclaimed; many of these are below sea-level. An intricate system of dams, ditches, dykes and pumping stations protects this land. Dairy and market-garden produce and manufactured goods (electronic products, bicycles, ships and textiles) are exported. The Netherlands is a member of the Benelux Union. Government is by a Premier, responsible to the States-General, consisting of a Senate elected by the Diets of the provincial states and a second chamber elected by the nation's vote for a period of four years. The voting age is 23 and voting compulsory. Religion is Protestant with a substantial Roman Catholic minority. *Capitals: Amsterdam and The Hague. Population: 12.5 million. Principal river: Rhine. Land area: 33,397 sq. km. (12,891 sq. miles).*

NORWAY

Norway is an independent Scandinavian state with a constitutional hereditary monarchy. Because of the rugged terrain, about 74% of the land is unproductive and 23% is forested. Forestry and fishing are the main activities. Cheap hydro-electric power is the base for many industries, including pulp and paper production and aluminium refining. Norway's merchant marine is the third largest in the world. Exports include base metals, fishery products, timber, paper and pulp. Tourists come for winter sports and to travel in the fjords of the south-west and into the land of the Midnight Sun. Religion is mainly Lutheran. Legislative power is vested in the Storting (Parliament) comprising 150 representatives elected every four years, and executive functions are carried out by the Prime Minister and Cabinet. *Capital: Oslo. Population: 3.7 million. Highest point: Mt. Galdhopiggen, 2,469 metres (8,095ft.). Land area: 323,884 sq. km. (125,019 sq. miles).*

POLAND

Poland is an Eastern European country, lying between the U.S.S.R. and East Germany. Potatoes are the most valuable crop but rye, barley, sugar beet and wheat are also important. Industrial activity is great in the south western area of Silesia where Europe's second largest coalfield is situated. Steel and zinc production are particularly important in this area. Main industries are nationalised but 86% of the land is farmed on a co-operative basis. Chief exports include coal, ships, railway rolling stock and cement. Poland adopted a Socialist form of government in 1945. Under the 1952 Constitution, supreme power is vested in the Sejm (parliament) elected by the nation's vote. Religion is mainly Roman Catholic. *Capital: Warsaw. Population: 32.4 million. Highest point: Rysy, 2,499 metres (8,202ft.). Principal river: Vistula. Land area: 312,520 sq. km. (120,633 sq. miles).*

Netherlands. **Intensive horticultural activity is economically very important in the Low Countries and much of the produce is exported.**

Poland. **Warsaw, the impressive Building of Culture.**

PORTUGAL

Portugal is a small country in the west of the Iberian peninsula. Just less than half of the land is cultivated, whilst waste land and forest each occupy about one quarter. Over half of the world's cork comes from the cork oak trees of Portugal. Port wine, timber, sardines and scarce minerals such as wolfram also go abroad. Textiles, pottery, glass, paper and fertilisers are manufactured. The standard of living is low and about half the population is illiterate.

Government is by an elected President, a single chamber with limited powers and a Corporative Chamber of representatives of industry and local authorities. Portugal's overseas provinces include Madeira, the Azores, Cape Verde Islands, Macao, Portuguese Guinea, Angola and Mozambique. Religion is mainly Roman Catholic. *Capital: Lisbon. Population: 9.3 million. Principal river: Tagus. Land area: 91,561 sq. km. (35,343 sq. miles).*

RUMANIA

Rumania is a Socialist People's Republic on the Black Sea, situated at the mouth of the Danube, between Bulgaria and the U.S.S.R. Principal crops are wheat and maize, grown in the fertile lowlands of Moldavia, Walachia and Dobregea. Wine is produced in the foothill areas. Rumania's oilfields are in the foothills of the Carpathian Mountains. She is the leading East European producer of oil, outside the U.S.S.R. The main refining centre is

Ploesti and a pipeline carries the oil to the Black Sea port of Constanta. In addition to oil products and grain, Rumania also exports manganese, timber and machinery. The Danube is used by ocean-going ships as far as Braila. Religion is Eastern Orthodox. *Capital: Bucharest. Highest point: Moldoveanul, 2,543 metres (8,346ft.). Principal river: Danube. Population: 19.1 million. Land area: 237,428 sq. km. (91,647 sq. miles).*

SAN MARINO

San Marino is a tiny republic on the eastern slopes of the Apennines; it is completely engulfed by Italy. Principal products are ceramics, skins, wine and barley, many of which are sent to the nearby city of Rimini. The sale of attractive postage stamps to collectors is one of the main sources of revenue. San Marino is reputedly the oldest republic in the world,

having been founded by a stonecutter in the 4th century. It has resisted the claims of the Papacy and Italy respects its sovereignty. It is governed by two Captains-Regent and a ten-man State Congress with a legislative council elected for five years by the nation's vote. *Capital: San Marino. Population: 17,000. Land area: 61 sq. km. (23 sq. miles).*

SPAIN

Spain is an independent state, sharing the Iberian peninsula in the south-west of Europe with Portugal. Spain is primarily an agricultural country, growing wheat, potatoes, barley and maize for domestic consumption. Grapes and olives are leading crops and the vineyards are famed for sherry and Malaga wines. Other exports include cork, almonds, oranges, figs and melons. There are also important mineral resources, notably iron. Since petroleum is lacking, industry depends on coal and

hydro-electric power. There is a thriving tourist industry. Religion is Roman Catholic. Spain remained neutral during the Second World War. She was declared a monarchy in 1947 and Franco was confirmed as head of state, charged with naming his successor. Spain was admitted to the U.N. in 1955. Spanish possessions include the Balearic and Canary Islands. *Capital: Madrid. Population: 31.3 million. Principal river: Ebro. Land area: 503,545 sq. km. (194,368 sq. miles).*

SWEDEN

Sweden is a kingdom in the Scandinavian peninsula and is one of the most prosperous countries in Europe. About 55% of the country is forested and lumbering, paper and pulp-milling are important. Modern farming methods obtain high yields of sugar beet, flax, potatoes and grain from the small amount (about 10%) of cultivated land. High-grade iron ore is exported and also supplies the steel industry in the towns of the north and the central

lowlands. Metal and timber products form a major part of Sweden's exports. Sweden's standard of living is thought to be the highest in the world. Religion is Lutheran. Government is by a Council of Ministers responsible to a Parliament (Riksdag) of two chambers. Sweden was admitted to the United Nations in 1946. *Capital: Stockholm. Population: 7.9 million. Land area: 411,406 sq. km. (158,803 sq. miles).*

Spain. **Grenada, a corner of the Generalife, a beautiful example of Moorish art.**

Switzerland. **The Melide bridge on Lake Lugano. This remarkable feat of engineering divides the lake into two parts.**

SWITZERLAND

Switzerland is a mountainous country of central Europe. Less than one sixth of the population is employed in agriculture, yet the land is well farmed and Swiss dairy produce is famous. Switzerland exports milk products (cheese, chocolate, condensed milk etc.), watches and precision instruments, textiles, toys and pharmaceutical products. The Alpine landscape attracts many tourists in all seasons of the year. Another major source of revenue is international banking. Since the 16th century, Switzerland has pursued a policy of neutrality; it is for this reason that Geneva has been chosen in recent times as the headquarters of the Red Cross, the League of Nations, the International Labour Organisation and various other international bodies. Yet, Switzerland is not a full member of the United Nations. The country was originally made up of three cantons (states) but there are now 22, each with its own parliament and government. Swiss women have just gained the vote. The official languages are German, French and Italian with Romansch as a local minority language. About 53% of the Swiss are Protestants, 46% Roman Catholics. *Capital: Berne. Population: 5.8 million. Highest point: Monte Rosa, 4,634 metres (15,203ft.). Land area: 41,288 sq. km. (15,937 sq. miles).*

United Kingdom. **Tower Bridge and the Pool of London, on the Thames. London is one of Europe's most active cities and was at one time the centre of the political and economic life of a third of the world.**

UNITED KINGDOM

The United Kingdom is a group of islands in western Europe, which is separated from the mainland by the North Sea and the English Channel. The constituent members of the Union are England, Scotland, Wales and Northern Ireland. Agriculture is well-developed and high yields are obtained. Nevertheless the United Kingdom only produces about one half of its food requirements. She has few mineral resources apart from coal and iron ore but she is able to obtain others from members of The Commonwealth, her European neighbours and other countries. To pay for these imports, the United Kingdom is essentially an industrial country and exports huge quantities of manufactured goods. London, the capital, is an important commercial and financial centre and a busy port. The United Kingdom is the parent state of The Commonwealth but since 1945 many former colonies have been granted independence (e.g. Nigeria; India; Ghana, which was previously known as The Gold Coast). She is a member of the North Atlantic and South East Asia Treaty Organisations and one of the five permanent members of the Security Council of the United Nations Organisation. She is also a member of the European Free Trade Association. The United Kingdom still has military commitments in the Near and Far East and maintains an army in Germany. The Church of England is the established church but there are free church communities and a Roman Catholic minority. The United Kingdom is a monarchy, governed by a parliament elected by the nation's vote. *Capital: London. Population 53.4 million. Highest point: Ben Nevis, 1,344 metres (4,406ft.). Principal river: Thames. Land area: 240,914 sq. km. (93,053 sq. miles).*

VATICAN CITY

The Vatican City is a sovereign state within the city limits of Rome, ruled over by the Pope. It is situated on the right bank of the River Tiber. It contains the Lateran Palace (the city residence of the Pope), the administrative offices of the Roman Catholic Church, the cathedral church of St. Peter, the Vatican Library and Museum, and Castle Gandolfo (the Pope's country residence). It has its own citizenship, postage stamps, coinage, diplomatic corps and radio station. Civil government is by a Governor and Council appointed by the Pope whose chief advisers are the College of Cardinals and the administrative Curia Romana. Many pilgrims and tourists visit the Vatican. The General Council of Roman Catholic leaders, called to the Vatican in 1962 by the late Pope John, was only the second in history to be held there. *Population: 940. Land area: 44 hectares (109 acres).*

YUGOSLAVIA

Yugoslavia is a mountainous Balkan country, formed in 1918 as a result of the union of the south Slavic peoples—the Croats, Serbs, Slovenes and Macedonians. About 5% of the population work on the land. Grapes, fruit, olives and tobacco are grown in the sunny areas of Macedonia and Dalmatia. Maize and wheat are grown in the fertile plains of the Sava and Danube. Industry has developed considerably during recent years. Mineral resources include copper, bauxite, lead, zinc and chrome. Heavy industries were nationalised in 1945 but most enterprises are run by local workers' councils. Principal exports are cement, bauxite, mercury, fruit (especially prunes), eggs, tobacco and timber. Yugoslavia has adopted a socialist form of government. The official language is Serbo-Croat. Religion is 41% Eastern Orthodox, 32% Roman Catholic and 12% Moslem. *Capital: Belgrade. Population: 19 million. Principal river: Danube. Land area: 255,804 sq. km. (98,740 sq. miles).*

Yugoslavia. **Belgrade, the parliament building in the centre of the city.**

U.S.S.R.

The U.S.S.R. (Union of Soviet Socialist Republics) is the largest nation in the world, forming one eighth of the entire land surface. The country's population is concentrated in a triangular area around Moscow, with the cities of Leningrad, Odessa and Sverdlovsk on its margins. This area contains forest land, most of the large cities and the greater part of the fertile farmland. In the rest of the country the climate is less attractive to settlement. Principal crops are wheat, sugar beet and cotton. The U.S.S.R. has considerable mineral resources and has become a leading industrial power, second in the world to the United States. Particularly important is the chemical industry and this is being developed because of the boost it could give to agriculture. Since the Second World War, large sums have been invested in nuclear physics and space research and the U.S.S.R. accomplished the first manned space flight in 1961. Although half of its borders are maritime, these coastlines are either frozen or closed seas. Railways, roads and canals are used for internal transport, but even these are hampered by the harshness of the Soviet winter. After the Revolution of 1917 when power was seized from the Czar (ruler), the Soviet State which emerged adopted a policy of collectivisation of agriculture and state control of industry. The local and national government councils are directly elected: the legislative organ is the Supreme Soviet, elected for four years. Everyone is able to vote but the only legal political party is the Communist party which approves candidates for office. The Constitution permits freedom of religious worship and anti-religious propaganda. The Eastern Orthodox Church is disestablished and congregations must maintain their churches and clergy. Some 120 languages are spoken within the U.S.S.R. but Russian is the official language. *Capital: Moscow. Population: 237 million. Principal river: Volga. Land area: 22.4 million sq. km. (8.65 million sq. miles).*

U.S.S.R. **Moscow, a large political demonstration in Red Square. In the background is St. Basil's Cathedral.**

U.S.S.R.: AGRICULTURAL AND INDUSTRIAL REGIONS

Spring sown wheat, sugar beet and cattle farming

Winter sown wheat, maize and other cash crops

Flax, fodder and stock rearing

Cereals and stock rearing

Mainly forest, with some farming in river valleys

Fruit and vineyards

Arid and semi-arid grazing lands

Winter sown cereals, sugar beet and other cash crops

Intensive fruit and vegetable farming with cattle

Tea and citrus fruits

Upland pastures (for sheep) with mixed farming in valleys

Cattle rearing with some grain farming

Sheep in Central Asia with cotton, fruit and cereals

Reindeer herding in the Tundra region

Cattle and horse breeding

Industrial regions

ASIA

Asia is the largest of all the continents with a total area of approximately 44,000,000 sq. km. (nearly 17 million square miles). This is almost one third of the total land surface of the world. The continent is, in fact, so large that when the sun is setting on its Pacific margins in the east, it is rising on its western boundaries; this in March and September when the sun is overhead at the Equator. During the northern winter, continual night reigns at its most northerly point; in March and September, on the Equator, day and night are equal in length.

Asia is divided from Europe by a 3,200 km. (2,000 mile) land boundary, marked in part by the long chain of the Ural Mountains. Asia is also joined to another continent—Africa—by the narrow isthmus of Suez which forms a bridge between the Mediterranean and Red Seas.

Northern Asia faces the ice-bound Arctic Ocean through which no reliable seaway exists, even in summer. In the east, the U.S.S.R., China and the smaller countries of S.E. Asia all border onto the Pacific Ocean.

Most of Asia's great rivers rise in the central highland zone. Some of them, such as the Ob, Yenisey and Lena, drain to the Arctic and are frozen for a number of months in the winter. Others drain to the Pacific—the Amus (which is also frozen in winter), the Yellow River, the Yangtze and the Mekong. And a third group drain to the Indian Ocean—the Salween and Irrawaddy in the east, the Ganges, the Brahmaputra and the Indus further

west and the Tigris and Euphrates draining to the Persian Gulf.

Along the Arctic coast and for up to 400 km. (250 miles) inland, is the tundra area where the land is frozen and covered by snow for almost two thirds of the year. During the summer, moss and lichen cover the surface for a short time but, about a foot below the surface, the earth remains frozen.

Southwards from the pole, the climate tends to vary according to the distance of the area from the oceans which warm or cool the land according to the season.

South of the tundra belt lies a huge forest region. Practically the whole of Siberia lies in this forest area where spruce and pine trees predominate in the west and larch in the east. The climate of Siberia is extreme. In fact, the coldest part of the northern hemisphere lies in the mountain basins of north-east Siberia and not at the north pole as might be expected. Both Oimyakon and Verkoyansk have recorded a temperature of −68°C (−90.4°F); Verkoyansk has an average temperature of −50°C (−58°F) in January. Throughout the forest region a thin covering of snow lies from October to March but precipitation is low—less than 510 mm. (20in.) per year. Yet, despite the bitterly cold winters, summer temperatures are high, sometimes reaching 32°C (90°F). Difficult conditions occur during the summer as the surface snows and ice melt; since most of the roads are unpaved, travel is very difficult. For the same reason, the foundations of buildings have to be prepared with special care.

Towards the centre of the continent stretches a strip of valuable grasslands or steppe. South again, huge deserts and semi-deserts stretch from Arabia to Mongolia. The low rainfall totals reduce vegetation to grasses and scattered bushes and the land is really suitable only for occupation by nomads rearing cattle. Mountain slopes provide forest and fairly good pasture land but cultivation of the soil is possible only where the oases are found or where irrigation has been introduced.

In the heart of the Asian deserts, like the Arabian and Gobi, crop cultivation and animal rearing are quite impossible.

South of the mountain ranges which conveniently divide Asia into north and south, the climate is totally different, being dominated by the monsoons. During the summer the land warms up more than the sea, and thus creates a large area of low pressure over the continent; in winter, the land becomes colder than

Continued on page 40

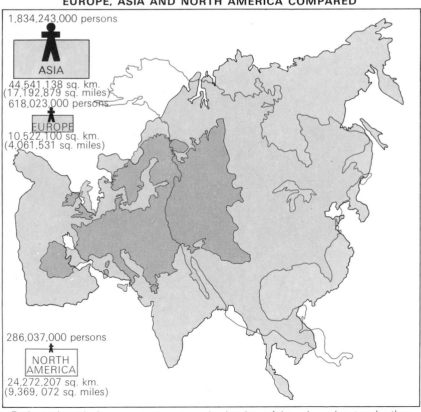

EUROPE, ASIA AND NORTH AMERICA COMPARED

1,834,243,000 persons

ASIA
44,541,138 sq. km.
(17,192,879 sq. miles)

618,023,000 persons

EUROPE
10,522,100 sq. km.
(4,061,531 sq. miles)

286,037,000 persons

NORTH AMERICA
24,272,207 sq. km.
(9,369,072 sq. miles)

Each continent is drawn on a common scale; the sizes of the coloured rectangles then represent the land areas whilst the sizes of the human figures show the respective populations.

Singapore is one of south-east Asia's great commercial centres. It is a typical example of an entrepot port, handling all types of cargoes destined for other parts of the world. Its population includes representatives of most Asian races.

Main Map (left)

Alaska Nome C.Pr.of Wales
Bering Str.
70 C.Dezhneva St.Lawrence I. 60 4 50 5 40
(East C.)
C.Dezhnev
Wrangel I.
Chukchi Pen.
Chukot Ra. Gulf of Anadyr St.Matthew I.
2320 C.Navarin Bering
Chersky Ra. Koryak Ra. Atka I. Sea
Bear I. 2115 Andreanof Is.
Gydan Ra. (Kolyma) C.Navarin Aleutian Is.
3147 567 Rat Is.
Kolyma 2222 Near Is. 7679
Plain 4775 5513
Omolon Kamchatka Pen. Komandorskiye Is.
yansk Range 2959 Klyuchevsk Vol.
Stanovoy Ra. C.Lopatka
2520 Okhotsk Sea
Dzhugdzhur Ra. of
Shantar Is. Okhotsk Paramushir I. 2339
Uchur Sakhalin Simushir I. 3658 9144
1609 Iturup I. 8513
Amur Kuril Is.
2078 La Perouse Str.
Little Khingan Mts. Hokkaidō 2290
Great Khingan Mts. Sikhote Alin Ra. Hakodate
Manchurian Plain Vladivostok Sado
Khanka Sea of Japan Fuji Yama 2542
Sungari Changpai Shan 2744 Tokyo 3775
Res. Honshu Osaka
Yalu 1708 Korea Str. Shikoku
Peking Kwen G.of Chihli Seoul Kyūshū Tanega I.
Shantung Yellow Nagasaki 5996
2996 Pen. Sea Cheju Do 10554
Wutai Shan Grand Canal Amami Is.
Nanking Shanghai East Okinawa Bonin Is.
Poyang China Daitō Is.
3052 Wuhan Sea Ryukyu Is. Volcano Is.
Tapa Shan 7505
Wu Yi Shan Ishigaki I.
Nan Shan Taiwan 3950
Canton (Formosa)
Si-Kiang Hong Kong Batan Is.
G.of Babuyan Is. Yap Is.
Tonking Luzon 8527
Hainan Pulog Philippines Caroline Islands
1879 2928 9138
Manila 2428 Palau Is.
2596 Samar 10497
Mindoro Panay Leyte
Ataouat Palawan Negros Mindanao
2598 5576 2958
Mui Varella Sulu Sea Talaud Is.
Cambodia Balabac Str. 6218
Saigon Kinabalu Celebes Sangi Is. Halmahera
Cholon Sulu Arch. Sea Bacan Is. Waigeo Biak
Ca Mau Pt. 4100 Moluccas
Mekong Borneo Molucca Sea New
2999 Guinea
South China Sea G.of Tomini Ceram Aru Is.
Bunguran Is. Iran Ra. Buru Kai Is.
Singapore Kapuas Schwaner Ra. 5800 Ceram Sea Tanimbar Is.
Riouw Arch. Celebes Banda Sea
Lingga Arch. Rahtemario Buling Makassar Wetar Arafura Sea
Bangka 3440 2871 Flores Sea
Belitung 2392 Flores Timor
Barisan Mts. Str.of Makassar Sumba Sumbawa
Greater Sunda Is. Bali Lesser Sunda Is. Roti
Djakarta Semeru Java
Java Sea 3019 3676

ALTITUDES
Metres / Feet
5000 / 16404
4000 / 13123
3000 / 9843
2000 / 6562
1000 / 3281
500 / 1640
200 / 656
Sea level / 0
Depression

DEPTHS
0
200 / 656
2000 / 6562
4000 / 13123
Over

PACIFIC OCEAN
Japan OCEAN

North Pacific / Arctic Inset

140 a 150 b 160 c 170 d 180 e 170 f 160 g 150 h 140
NORTH PACIFIC OCEAN
0 300 600 Kms.
Arctic Ocean
Bear Is. Wrangel I. Pt.Barrow
Kolima Aion I. Barrow Brooks Ra.
Plain De Long Str. C.Dezhnev (East C.)
Sredne Kolymsk Yukon
Siberia Kolyma Chukot Ra. Fairbanks 11
Chersky Ra. Nizhne 2320 Mt.McKinley
Stolbonoye Kolymsk 6187 Alaska Ra.
Magadan Gydan Ra.(Kolyma) Chukchi Seward Anchorage
2222 Anadyr Pen. Pen. Nome 3063
60 Shelekhan Penzhina G. Gulf St.Pr.of Wales 60
Sea of Bay of Anadyr Kodiak I.
Okhotsk Koryak Range St.Lawrence I.
Karaginsk I. C.Navarin Pribilof Brist.B. Alaska Pen.
3335 C.Otyotorski Is. Kodiak
Kamchatka Pen. Unimak I. 12
4658 St.Matthew I. Bering Unalaska I.
Klyuchevsk Vol. Nunivak I. Sea Umnak I.
Petropavlovsk Komandorskiye Is.
Kamchatsky Aleutian Islands
C.Lopatka Near Is. Atka I.
Rat Is. Andreanof Is. 50

Java Inset

l m
Seputih Java Sea Karamian 5
Sumatra Karimundjawa Is. Selembu Is.
Teluk C.Krawang Bawean
Betung Sunda Strait Djakarta C.Indramaju
Krakatau I. Bogor C.Bugel Surabaja Str.
Panaitan I. 2211 Tjirebon 1602 Madura I.
3019 3078 Tjareme Semarang Murjo 13
Djungkul Bandung Slamet Merbabu Surabaja Madura Str.
Pen. Pangrango 2621 3428 3371 Surakarta 3265 3348 3676 3088 Raung
Penandjung B. Tjikuraj Sumbing 3142 Lawu Arjuno Semero 3332 Bali
C.Genteng Djogjakarta Bali Str.
Java Blambangan Pen.
3900 Barung
INDIAN OCEAN
1200
10 JAVA
Christmas I. 0 100 200 Kms.
n 110 East from Greenwich o

Central Himalaya Inset

p q
CENTRAL HIMALAYA
0 10 Km.
8189 7897 Khartachangri
Cho Oyu Gyachung Kang Khartaphu
West Rongbu Gl. 7205
Nup La Changtse Karma Changri
Lingtren 7547 Karpo La 16
Pumori Lho La Rapiu La Pethang
7145 6060 Kangshung Glacier Ringmo
Changri 8848 Everest (Chomolungma)
Lhotse Pethangtse
Labuche Nuptse 8501
Dzonglu 7589 Chomo Lonzo
Cholatse Duglha Pk.38 7790
Nang Pheriche Oto Polu Makalu II
Taweche Shanti 8481 Makalu 17
Khumbila Kangtega Khumbu Ama Dablam Baruntse
5881 Yaral Peak 4 Peak 3
Thangnoche Thyangboche
Tesinga 7317
Thammu Namche Bazar Kangtega
Thamserku Chatharbu
Copyright.Vallardi Ind.Graf.

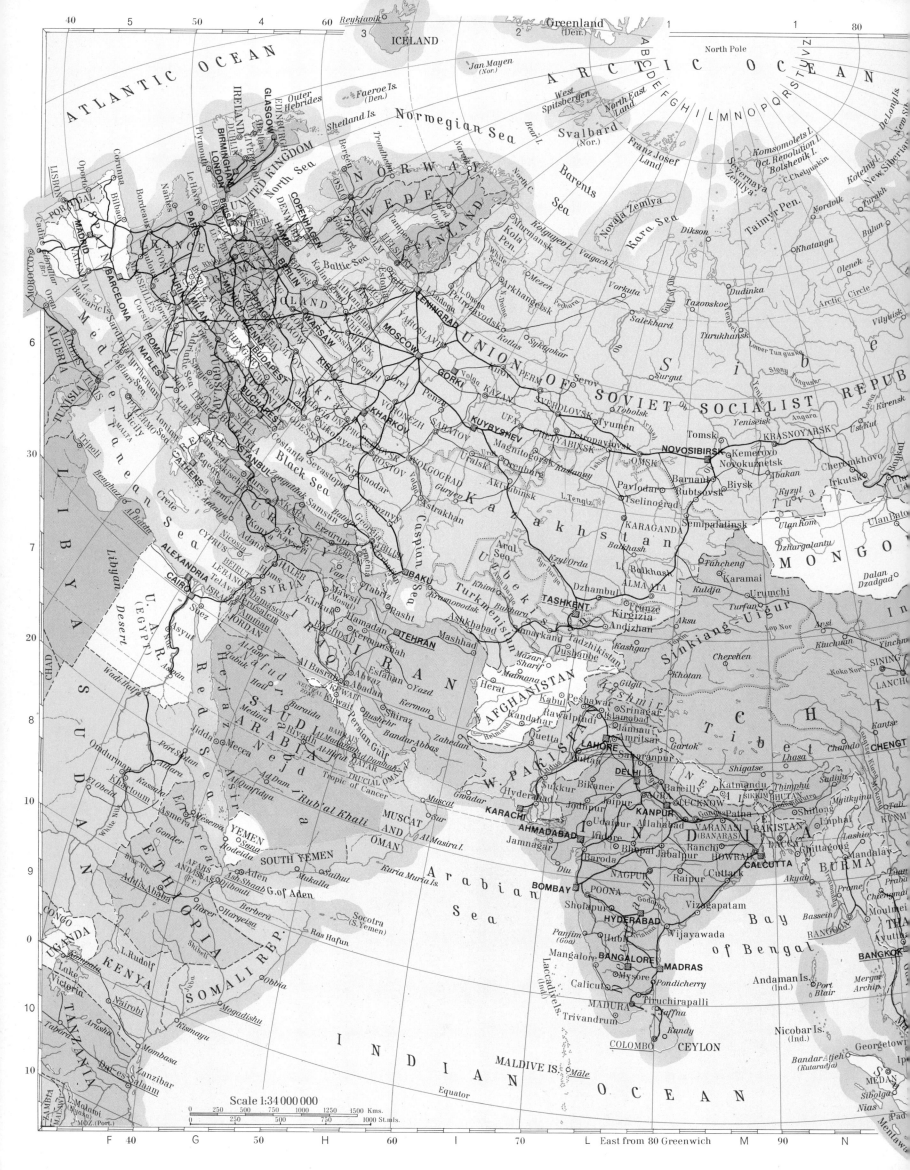

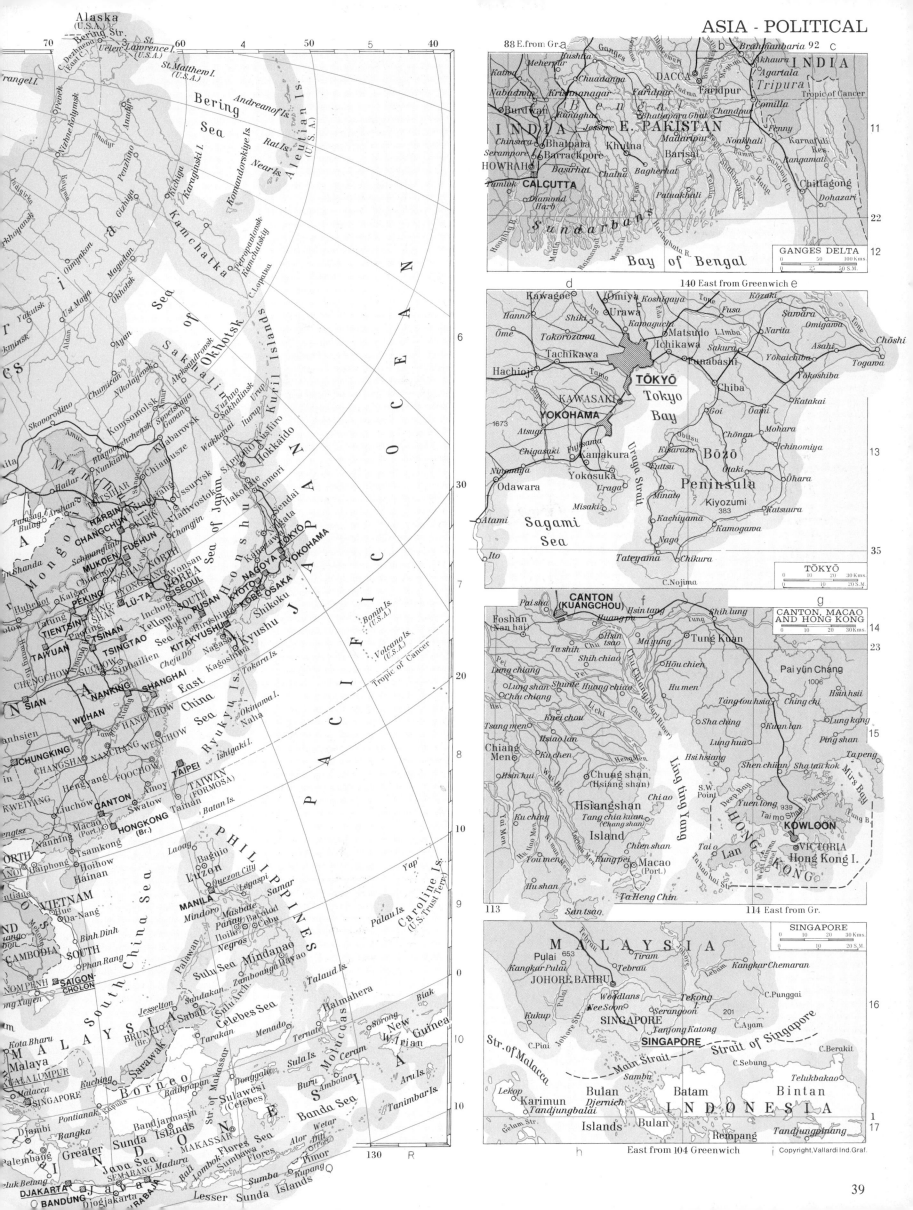

Main map labels (clockwise/regional):

Alaska (U.S.A.)
Bering Str.
St. Lawrence I. (U.S.A.)
Uelen C. (East C.) (U.S.A.)
Bering Sea
Andreanof Is.
Aleutian Is. (U.S.A.)
Rat Is.
Near Is.
Komandorskije Is.

Sea of Okhotsk
Kamchatka
Sakhalin
Kuril Is.
Hokkaido
Sea of Japan
Honshu
HONSHU
JAPAN
TŌKYŌ
YOKOHAMA
NAGOYA
KYOTO
KOBE OSAKA
Shikoku
Kyushu
KITAKYUSHU
Ryukyu Is.
Okinawa I.
Naha

PACIFIC OCEAN

MONGOLIA
HARBIN
CHANGCHUN
FUSHUN
MUKDEN
NORTH KOREA
PYONGYANG
SEOUL
SOUTH KOREA
PUSAN
PEKING
TIENTSIN
TSINAN
TSINGTAO
TAIYUAN
SIAN
WUHAN
NANKING
SHANGHAI
HANGCHOW
SUCHOW
CHENGCHOW
CHUNGKING
CHANGSHA
NANCHANG
WENCHOW
FOOCHOW
TAIPEI
TAIWAN (FORMOSA)
Tainan
CANTON
Swatow
Amoy
Macao (Port.)
HONGKONG (Br.)
KWEIYANG
Liuchow
Nanning
Hainan
Hoihow

Yellow Sea
East China Sea
South China Sea

PHILIPPINES
Luzon
Baguio
Quezon City
MANILA
Mindoro
Masbate
Samar
Panay
Cebu
Negros
Palawan
Mindanao
Davao
Zamboanga
Sulu Sea
Celebes Sea

VIETNAM
Hue
Da-Nang
Binh Dinh
SOUTH VIETNAM
Phan Rang
SAIGON-CHOLON
CAMBODIA
PNOMPENH

Bonin Is. (U.S.A.)
Volcano Is. (U.S.A.)
Tropic of Cancer
Yap
Palau Is.
Caroline Is. (U.S. Trust Terr.)
New Guinea
W. Irian

MALAYSIA
Malaya
KUALA LUMPUR
SINGAPORE
BRUNEI (Br.)
Sarawak
Sabah
Borneo
Kuching
Jesselton
Sandakan
Sulu Arch.

INDONESIA
Sumatra
Greater Sunda Islands
Java
DJAKARTA
BANDUNG
SEMARANG
SURABAYA
Madura
Bali
Lombok
Sumbawa
Flores
Timor
Lesser Sunda Islands
Sula Is.
Moluccas
Ceram
Banda Sea
Celebes Sea
Sulawesi (Celebes)
Makassar
Str. of Makassar
Banjarmasin
Balikpapan

GANGES DELTA inset

INDIA
E. PAKISTAN
DACCA
Faridpur
Tripura
Agartala
Comilla
Chittagong
Dohazari
Chandpur
Noakhali
Barisal
Khulna
Jessore
HOWRAH
CALCUTTA
Tamluk
Diamond Harb.
Sundarbans
Bay of Bengal
Tropic of Cancer
Burdwan
Barrackpore
Serampore
Bhatpara
Chinsura
Krishnanagar
Chuadanga
Nabadwip
Meherpur
Kushtia
Ganges
Brahmanbaria
Akhaura

88 E. from Gr.
92

Scale: 0 50 100 Kms. / 25 50 S.M.

TŌKYŌ inset

140 East from Greenwich
Kawagoe
Ōmiya
Koshigaya
Kōzaki
Hanno
Urawa
Sawara
Omigawa
Tone
Ōme
Tokorozawa
Matsudo
Narita
Asahi
Chōshi
Tachikawa
Ichikawa
Sakura
Yōkaichiba
Togawa
Hachioji
Funabashi
Yokoshiba
TŌKYŌ
Tokyo Bay
Chiba
KAWASAKI
Goi
Ōami
Katakai
YOKOHAMA
Atsugi
Chōnan
Mohara
Ichinomiya
Chigasaki
Kamakura
Kisarazu
Bōzō Peninsula
Nirayama
Yokosuka
Uraga
Otaki
Ōhara
Odawara
Minato
Kiyozumi
Katsuura
Atami
Misaki
Kachiyama
Kamogawa
Sagami Sea
Nago
Tateyama
Chikura
Ito
C. Nojima

Scale: 0 10 20 30 Kms. / 0 10 20 S.M.

CANTON, MACAO AND HONG KONG inset

CANTON (KUANGCHOU)
Pai sha
Hsin tang
Shih lung
Foshan (Nan hai)
Huangpu
Tung Kuan
Pai yün Chang
Chu Chiang (Pearl River)
Hu men
Täng tou hsia
Ching chi
Hsin hsii
Lung kang
Ping shan
Ta peng
Mirs Bay
Shen chüan
Sha tau kok
HONG KONG
KOWLOON
VICTORIA
Hong Kong I.
Lan tao
Ling ting Yang
Macao (Port.)
Chung shan (Hsiang shan)
Hsiangshan Island
Ta heng Chin
San tsao

113
114 East from Gr.

Scale: 0 10 20 30 Kms.

SINGAPORE inset

MALAYSIA
Pulai
Tiram
Kangkar Pulai
Tebrau
Kangkar Chemaran
JOHORE BAHRU
Woodlands
Tekong I.
C. Punggai
Nee Soon
Serangoon
Kukup
SINGAPORE
Tanjong Katong
C. Ayam
SINGAPORE
Strait of Singapore
Str. of Malacca
Main Strait
C. Piai
Johore Str.
C. Sebung
C. Berakit
Bulan
Batam
Bintan
Telukbakao
Karimun
Djernich
Sambu
Tandjungbalai
INDONESIA
Bulan Islands
Rempang
Tandjungpinang

East from 104 Greenwich
Copyright, Vallardi Ind. Graf.

39

the sea, and so creates an area of high pressure. Winds always blow away from areas of higher pressure and towards areas of lower pressure. Thus, from May to September winds blow off the Indian Ocean and onto the S.E. Asian lands from the south and south-west, whilst in October the winds reverse and start to blow off the land from a northerly or north-easterly quarter.

In most parts of South East Asia, except for coasts which face the north and north-east, May to September is by far the wettest season. For example, Calcutta receives 1,362mm. (53.6in.) of rain between May and September, whilst October until April brings only 250mm. (10.7in.). In the foothills of the Himalayas, some of the earth's highest rainfall totals are recorded; at Cherrapunji in the Khasi Hills, the average annual total is 11,615mm. (457in.); June and July totals both exceed 2,540mm. (100in.).

Nine tenths of Asia's population live in these monsoon regions. Their principal occupation is agriculture. In the fertile river valleys, large quantities of rice (the staple diet) are grown. Wheat, sugar cane and millet are also important crops; tea is grown in China for domestic consumption and in Northern India and Ceylon for export.

Further south still, there is an equatorial region with consistently heavy rainfall and dense jungles and forests. In this area economic development is largely based on the coconut palm and its products and on the tree (which is not native to Asia) which produces latex from which rubber is made.

Asia produces about 90% of the world's rice but few areas produce enough to be able to export any. More important in world trade is tea, of which Asia produces over 95% of the world crop. Asia also produces about 90% of the world's jute and natural rubber. Of minerals, one is outstanding—tin—and in South East Asia production accounts for more than half of the world's total. South-west Asia now produces about one fifth of the world's oil.

Compared with European and North American standards, Asian industrial development is very limited. However, there are immense resources of iron ore, coal and water power but as yet they are not fully exploited. Industrial expansion in central Asia and China has been rapid since the Second World War whilst Japan has largely transformed itself into a highly competitive industrial country and has become the world's leading shipbuilder.

The Trans-Siberian from Moscow to Vladivostok is the only west-east trans-continental railway in Asia. India and some of the island countries have well developed railway systems, but amongst the islands and peninsulas sea travel is more important. There is no through railway and no trunk road from north to south.

It is sometimes claimed that every major world religion started in Asia. In the west, Judaism and Christianity were born, and on the confines of the Arabian desert, Mohammedanism sprang up. Mohammedanism prevails over most of the south and west of Asia, except in the Deccan and Tibet. It is also the religion of the majority in the Malay Peninsula and many of the south eastern islands. In India, Brahminism and its offshoot Buddhism arose. Buddhism is also practised in China, along with Confucianism and Taoism.

About half of the world's population lives in southern and eastern Asia and in large parts of the monsoon areas the average density of population is over 600 persons to the square mile. In the more productive rural areas, as many as 10,000 people may live in a square mile; in urban districts the figure often exceeds 100,000. Such figures constitute gross over-population; the living standards of these peoples is far below that of most Europeans. However, India and China, following Japan's example, are trying to counter the problems of over-population and food shortage; to do this, schemes to introduce power and industry, schemes to utilise the land more efficiently, revised schemes of land-holding, and educational schemes leading to a reduction in the birth rate are being introduced. It is thus hoped that the total population will not rise so quickly, that the natural resources of the lands may be put to better use and that the average annual earnings of the population will be increased.

Other small Asian countries, and countries in other continents, are watching India and China as they attempt to counter the problems of over-population and food shortage.

THE MONSOONS IN SOUTH EAST ASIA

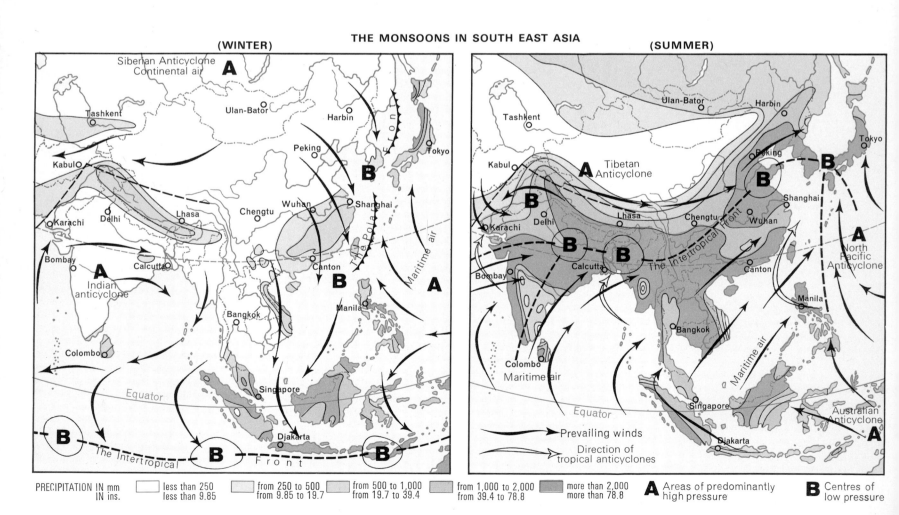

PRECIPITATION IN mm / IN ins. — less than 250 / less than 9.85 — from 250 to 500 / from 9.85 to 19.7 — from 500 to 1,000 / from 19.7 to 39.4 — from 1,000 to 2,000 / from 39.4 to 78.8 — more than 2,000 / more than 78.8 — **A** Areas of predominantly high pressure — **B** Centres of low pressure

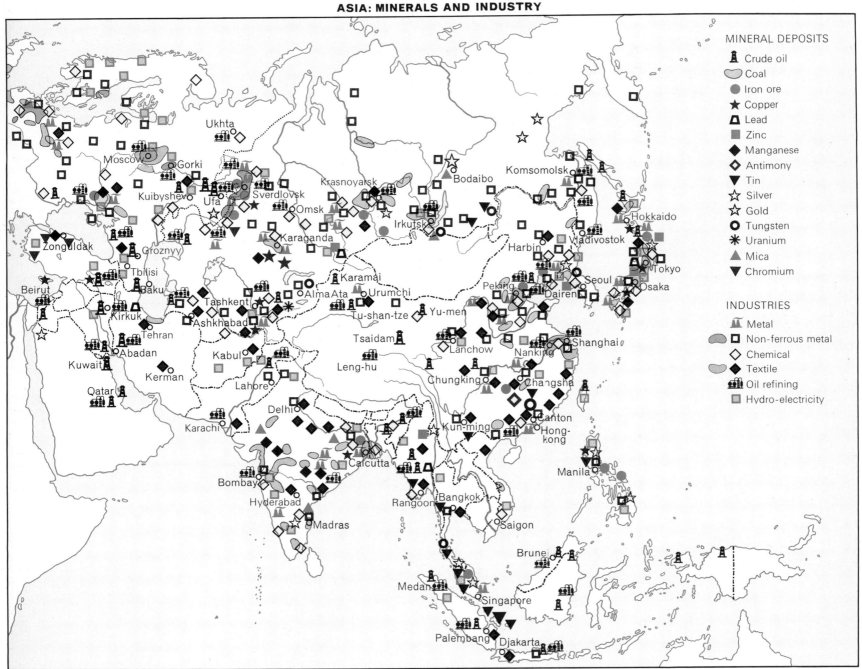

MINERAL DEPOSITS

- Crude oil
- Coal
- Iron ore
- Copper
- Lead
- Zinc
- Manganese
- Antimony
- Tin
- Silver
- Gold
- Tungsten
- Uranium
- Mica
- Chromium

INDUSTRIES

- Metal
- Non-ferrous metal
- Chemical
- Textile
- Oil refining
- Hydro-electricity

AFGHANISTAN

Afghanistan is a kingdom between Pakistan, Iran and the U.S.S.R. Only about 5% of the land is cultivated, the remainder being the mountainous Hindu Kush and the surrounding desert plateaux. Wheat is the most important food crop. Cotton and sugar beet are also grown and fresh and dried fruit is exported. Livestock raising is important, particularly among the large nomadic population, and large quantities of Persian lamb skins are exported. Camel and mule caravans are important for transport—there are no railways and few good roads. Religion is mainly Moslem. *Capital: Kabul. Population: 13.8 million. Highest point: Noshaq, 7,492 metres (24,581ft.). Land area: 657,500 sq. km. (253,800 sq. miles).*

BHUTAN

Bhutan is a small Indian state in the Himalayas. In 1949 she signed a treaty with India under which her independence was guaranteed but she agreed to accept guidance in foreign affairs. Population density is low because of the mountainous nature of the land. Most people work on the land and much trade is conducted by barter. The most important crops are rice, maize and millet. Yaks, elephants and ponies are raised. Forestry and forest crafts are important. The standard of living is good and most houses resemble Swiss chalets. The majority of the population are Buddhists. *Capital: Thimphu. Population: 750,000. Highest point: Chomo Lhari, 7,299 metres (23,930ft.). Land area: 46,600 sq. km. (17,988 sq. miles).*

BAHRAIN

The Bahrain islands are at the entrance to the Persian Gulf, between the peninsula of Qatar and the Hasa coast of Saudi Arabia. They form an independent sheikdom under British protection as regards defence and foreign affairs. Since 1934, Bahrein has been an important source of oil. Crude oil is also piped from the nearby Saudi Arabian oilfields to Bahrain's refineries. Recently, a new harbour has been developed at Mina Sulman; this includes a free transit and growing industrial area. There are also important archaeological remains. Most of the population are Arab and Moslem. The Sheik has executive and legislative powers. *Capital: Manama. Population: 182,200. Land area: 598 sq. km. (231 sq. miles).*

BRUNEI

Brunei is a self-governing sultanate on the north coast of Borneo, under British protection. The country is surrounded by the former British colony of Sarawak. 75% of the land is under forest but at present it is largely untouched; a little timber is exported to Hong Kong. Rice is the staple diet and is grown for home consumption. Boat-building, weaving and craft metal work are important native industries. About 80% of the cleared land is planted with rubber trees which provide one valuable product for export. The chief wealth lies in the oil-field at Seria, though the field is now declining in its annual output. *Capital: Brunei. Population: 127,200. Land area: 5,800 sq. km. (2,239 sq. miles).*

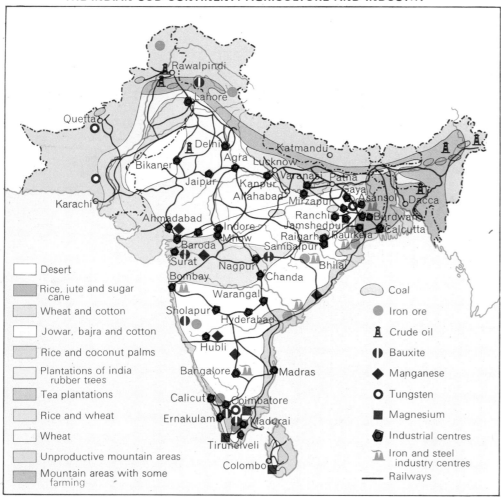

Map labels: Rawalpindi, Lahore, Quetta, Delhi, Katmandu, Bikaner, Agra, Lucknow, Jaipur, Kanpur, Varanasi, Patna, Gaya, Karachi, Allahabad, Mirzapur, Asansol, Dacca, Ahmadabad, Ranchi, Burdwan, Indore, Jamshedpur, Calcutta, Mhow, Raigarh, Raurkela, Baroda, Sambalpur, Surat, Nagpur, Bhilai, Bombay, Chanda, Warangal, Sholapur, Hyderabad, Hubli, Bangalore, Madras, Calicut, Coimbatore, Ernakulam, Madurai, Tirunelveli, Colombo

Legend:
- Desert
- Rice, jute and sugar cane
- Wheat and cotton
- Jowar, bajra and cotton
- Rice and coconut palms
- Plantations of india rubber trees
- Tea plantations
- Rice and wheat
- Wheat
- Unproductive mountain areas
- Mountain areas with some farming

- Coal
- Iron ore
- Crude oil
- Bauxite
- Manganese
- Tungsten
- Magnesium
- Industrial centres
- Iron and steel industry centres
- Railways

BURMA

Burma is a federal republic between East Pakistan, India, China, Laos and Thailand. It is cut off from its neighbours by high mountains. Rice, which accounts for 75% of Burma's exports, is grown in the valleys and coastal plains. Other exports include cotton, rubber, teak, petroleum, lead and zinc ores, some silver and precious stones. Religion is mainly Buddhist. *Capital: Rangoon. Population: 25,800,000. Highest point: Hkakabo Razi, 5,885 metres (19,296ft.). Principal river: Irrawaddy. Land area: 678,000 sq. km. (261,708 sq. miles).*

CAMBODIA

Cambodia is a south-east Asian kingdom on the Gulf of Siam, bordered by Thailand, South Vietnam and Laos. Rice, which is the main food crop, occupies about 80% of the cultivated land; some rice is exported, mainly to France. Rubber, maize and pepper are also grown for export. Small amounts of phosphate, iron ore and precious stones are mined. Industry and tourism are expanding. Cambodians, comprising 90% of the population, are Buddhists. The rest are Chinese, Europeans and Vietnamese. Cambodia was under French protection until 1954 when it became independent after the Indo-Chinese War. *Capital: Phnom-Penh. Population: 6,260,000. Principal river: Mekong. Land area: 181,000 sq. km. (69,866 sq. miles).*

CEYLON

Ceylon is an island off the south-east of India. Rice is the principal food crop. Rubber, tea and coconuts are major export items. Graphite is the most important mineral; some gem stones are also mined. The population consists of 70% Sinhalese, 20% Tamils and 6% Moors and Burghers. Britain gained control of Ceylon in 1796, governing it as a crown colony from 1798 until 1948 when she became a self-governing dominion within the British Commonwealth. Since independence, Ceylon has pursued a neutral policy in world affairs. Religion is mainly Buddhist. *Capital: Colombo. Population: 11.5 million. Principal river: Mahaveliganga. Highest point: Pidurutalagala, 2,529 metres (8,291ft.). Land area: 65,610 sq. km. (25,325 sq. miles).*

CHINA

China is the second largest country in Asia. There are three large river basins, the Si Kiang, the Yangtse and the Hwang in the east. The south-west and the west are dominated by high mountains and plateaux. Much of the north is dry steppe land or cold desert.

The country has a rich history dating back into the pre-Christian eras. A succession of dynasties, culminating in the Mongul (1279-1368), the Ming (1368-1644) and the Manchu (1644-1912), built China up to near its modern extent. Since 1912, internal revolution and periodic conflicts with the Japanese led to the creation of the "People's Republic of China" in 1949; at the same time, Nationalist China was established on the island of Formosa, now called Taiwan.

Since 1949 industry has been developed in a series of five-year plans. Coal reserves are believed to be the greatest in the world and it is estimated that about 300 million tons are mined each year. Manchuria and the Hwang Basin are the most important areas. Oil output is rising; rich iron ore deposits are worked in much of eastern China. Other important minerals include tin ore, wolfram, antimony, bauxite, copper and manganese. Manufacturing industries, textiles, chemicals, engineering and food processing are largely centred in the towns of the east.

China remains a mainly agricultural country; 85% of her people work on the land. Rice, wheat, maize and millet are the major cereals; other important crops include cotton, sweet potatoes, sugar (both cane and beet), tobacco, soya beans, tea and fruit. The plain areas of the east and some fertile basins elsewhere are the most important agricultural areas. The irrigated area is the largest for any one country in the world.

The rivers of the east are a major means of transport; new railways are still being built and existing ones improved; the motor car is far less important than it is in western countries. The Chinese written language has 30,000 ideographs (drawings); the spoken language has regional dialects and variations, of which Mandarin is the most important. More than one religion has been followed; Buddhism, Confucianism and Taoism being the strongest. *Capital: Peking. Population: probably over 750 million. Highest point: Kungur, 7,719 metres (25,337ft.). Principal river: Yangtse. Land area: 9,561,000 sq. km. (3,690,546 sq. miles).*

China. **A typical Chinese street scene. The little girl is eating rice, the staple food, with chopsticks.**

CYPRUS

Cyprus is an island republic within the Commonwealth, situated in the East Mediterranean. It is an important British military base. Cyprus has important mineral deposits and is famous for its copper. Other minerals include asbestos and iron pyrites. Besides minerals, citrus fruits, potatoes and wine are exported. About three quarters of the population are Greek-speaking members of the Eastern Orthodox Church; most of the remainder are Turkish Moslems. Cyprus came under British control in 1878 and was admitted to the Commonwealth. Recently a large proportion of the Greek population has agitated for union with Greece. *Capital: Nicosia. Population: 614,000. Land area: 9,251 sq. km. (3,572 sq. miles).*

Cyprus. **About three quarters of the population of this island are Greek-speaking members of the Eastern Orthodox Church; the remainder are Turkish Muslims.**

HONG KONG

Hong Kong is a British crown colony in S. China comprising the island of Hong Kong, Kowloon and the New Territories and adjacent islands. Hong Kong was ceded to Britain by China in 1841, Kowloon likewise in 1860 and the New Territories were leased in 1898 for 99 years. Since the mid 19th century, Hong Kong has become one of the leading commercial centres of S.E. Asia. There are more than 11,000 factories, most of them producing consumer goods. Since 1949 Hong Kong's population has been swollen by the influx of refugees from Communist China. Hong Kong is the only gateway to the Chinese mainland from the west. *Capital: Victoria. Population: 3.8 million. Land area: 1,013 sq. km. (398 sq. miles).*

INDONESIA

Indonesia is a republic of S.E. Asia, comprising the large islands of Java, Sumatra, the Celebes and most of Borneo, and more than 300 small islands and islets. On the mountain slopes are large plantations of tea, coffee, rubber, sugar cane and cinchona. Rice, spices, copra and palm oil are also produced. There are valuable mineral resources—tin, coal, bauxite and crude oil. Principal exports are rubber, petroleum, copra and tin. The population is predominantly of Malay stock. There is, however, quite a large Chinese community. The islands were under Dutch control from 1600 until the Second World War when they were occupied by the Japanese. Their independence was declared in 1945. Government is vested in the Provisional People's Consultative Assembly. *Capital: Djakarta. Population: 112 million. Land area: 1.9 million sq. km. (733,400 sq. miles).*

INDIA

India is a republic within the Commonwealth; it juts into the Indian Ocean as a large triangular peninsula in S.E. Asia. It is bounded to the north by the Himalayas; the peninsula itself is a large plateau of ancient rocks, the Deccan. Between these two, the Ganges flows for 2,510 km. (1,560 miles) from west to east, ending in the largest delta in the world, approximately 80,250 sq. km. (31,000 sq. miles). Most other major rivers flow from west to east. The coastal plains of the west are narrower than those of the east. Along with other countries of S.E. Asia, India is very dependent upon the monsoon climate.

The Indian peninsula, including modern Pakistan, has a long and rich history. The Indic civilisation of approximately 1500 B.C. was centred upon the Indus River basin. Buddhism was founded here in about 500 B.C. The Gangetic Empire of the 4th and 5th centuries united a large part of northern India. Then, from the late 15th century, European ideas were introduced and British control was established in the 18th and 19th centuries. This remained until independence was granted in 1947. Two separate nations were set up, India and Pakistan. The state of Jammu and Kashmir is disputed between India and Pakistan. The people are mainly Moslems, but it is legally part of India.

Mineral and industrial outputs are being increased in a series of five-year plans. Coal, iron ore, copper, manganese and gypsum are the most important minerals; crude oil production is also of growing value. The states of Bihar and West Bengal lead in mineral production. The most valuable industries are iron and steel, cotton textiles, silk, carpet making and wood and metal working.

Agriculture has always been the major occupation in India. 70% of the population are dependent on the land for their living. The most important crops are rice, wheat, jowar and bajra (grain crops), sugar cane, oilseed, groundnuts, cotton and jute. There are a large number of cattle but they are mainly used as draft animals, since the Hindu religion regards them as sacred.

Irrigation has been extended to more than 26 million hectares of land ($64\frac{1}{4}$ million acres), a figure which is second only to that of the People's Republic of China for any national total.

India trades very widely throughout the world—the U.S.A., U.K., U.S.S.R., Japan and West Germany are her leading trade partners. Tea and textiles are the major export item. Wheat is the most important import; other major imports include rice, raw cotton and machinery.

There are some 845 language groups, but English and Hindi are the official tongues. Most Indians are Hindus, but there are also some Moslems, Christians and Buddhists. *Capital: New Delhi. Population: 500 million. Principal river: Ganges. Land area: 3,053,600 sq. km. (1,178,700 sq. miles).*

India. **The Golden Temple at Benares, a typical example of the sumptuous and elaborate Indian art.**

IRAN

Iran (also known as Persia) is a kingdom between the Caspian Sea and the Persian Gulf. Wheat, barley, cotton, tobacco and fruit are grown and there is rice on the irrigated land. Sheep and goats are kept for wool and hides. In the south-west are large petroleum deposits—a major source of income. Other important exports are cotton, carpets, dried fruit, wool and hides. More than half the population are Persians who speak an Indo-European language. The remainder are Azerbaijan Turks, Kurds and various other groups. Iran is a hereditary monarchy, ruled by a Shah. Most wealth remains with a small minority and the standard of living of the rural population is very low. Religion is Shia Moslem. *Capital: Tehran. Population: 25.8 million. Highest point: Qolleh-ye Damavand, 5,775 metres (18,934 ft.). Land area: 1,621,860 sq. km. (626,038 sq. miles).*

IRAQ

Iraq is a S.W. Asian republic, centred on the fertile basin of the Tigris and Euphrates rivers. To the north-east are rugged highlands where the Kurdish people live; the Bedouin tribes roam the deserts of the south-west. One of the country's major sources of wealth is oil, the chief field being that around Kirkuk. Half the revenue from oil royalties is allocated for irrigation, land improvement and social welfare. Iraq is a major world exporter of dates and the date palm provides food, matting, textile fibres and building materials. Wheat, barley and rice are grown on irrigated land. The population is 75% Arabian, 15% Kurdish and there are some Persians. Religion is mainly Islam. *Capital: Baghdad. Population: 8.3 million. Principal river: Euphrates. Land area: 438,466 sq. km. (169,240 sq. miles).*

ISRAEL

Israel is a Jewish republic on the Mediterranean Sea. It consists of a coastal plain, a central highland area, part of the Jordan river valley and the Negev Desert. Oranges, olives and wine are the principal exports. Many farming areas are organised in Kibbutz (collective settlements), in which irrigation is important. Potash, copper and petroleum are the chief mineral resources. Most of the population live in the coastal plain. 90% are Jews, 223,000 Moslems and 60,000 Christians. Israel was established in 1948 as the result of Zionist agitation to establish an independent state in Palestine, the original home of the Jews. Since then, relations between Israel and its Arab neighbour states have been uneasy. *Capital: Jerusalem. Population: 2.66 million. Land area: 20,700 sq. km. (7,990 sq. miles).*

JAPAN

Japan is an island group in the Pacific. It is the most highly industrialised country in Asia and also has highly developed agriculture and fisheries. Tokyo (the capital) is one of the world's largest cities. Principal exports are textiles, steel, ships and motor cars. Japan is also well-known for optical instruments, radios and cameras. It has to import much foodstuff, iron ore and petroleum. Situated in the earthquake zone, she frequently experiences tremors. Like China, over-population is a major problem. Religion is Buddhism and Shintoism. The Emperor is the symbol of the state, legislative power resides in the Diet and executive power is vested in the Prime Minister and Cabinet. *Capital: Tokyo, Population: 98.3 million. Land area: 369,662 sq. km. (142,690 sq. miles).*

Jerusalem. **The Mount of Olives and the church in the Garden of Gethsemane.**

Japan. **A winter view of Mount Fujiyama. At its foot can be seen part of an agricultural village and the extensive rice paddies.**

JORDAN

The Arab state of Jordan is almost completely land-locked; Aqaba, in the southern desert, is its only port. 10% of the land is under cultivation; most of the country is desert, small areas of which are irrigated. Wheat and barley are the chief crops. Phosphates are the principal mineral and are mined for export. Jordan was created after the Arab-Israeli War (1948-9) out of two areas: the original kingdom of Transjordan and the east-central part of former Palestine (west of Jordan). Part of Jerusalem lies in Jordan. There are about half a million Israeli refugees in the country. Jordan is a constitutional monarchy. *Capital: Amman. Population: 2.1 million. Principal river: Jordan. Land area: 97,740 sq. km. (37,728 sq. miles).*

KOREA (North)

North Korea is officially known as the Korean People's Democratic Republic. The Korean peninsula (between the Sea of Japan and the Yellow Sea) was partitioned into north and south after the Second World War, with the 38th parallel as the boundary. North Korea is in the Communist bloc. Agriculture is collectivised and rice, maize and other grains are grown. There are considerable mineral resources—coal, iron ore and barytes are most important. Textile, chemical and steel industries flourish. Most industry is state-owned. North Korea is the chief supplier of ginseng, a medicinal root. Most trade is with the U.S.S.R. and other communist nations. *Capital: Pyong-yang. Population: 12.5 million. Land area: 122,370 sq. km. (47,235 sq. miles).*

KOREA (South)

South Korea is officially known as the Republic of Korea. Rice is grown in large quantities and other crops include cotton, hemp, ramie and tobacco. Anthracite, fish products, graphite, iron ore, rice, seaweed products, soya beans, raw silk and tungsten are exported. The major industries are cement, foodstuffs and silk fabrics. In 1950, after many incidents on the 38th parallel, the Korean War broke out. The United States and other United Nations members intervened on the South Korean side; Communist China supported North Korea. Tremendous destruction was caused throughout the peninsula but an armistice was signed in 1953. *Capital: Seoul. Population: 29.2 million. Land area: 98,431 sq. km. (37,994 sq. miles).*

Jordan. **Mules and horses are still an important means of transport in this rugged country, as they were in Biblical times.**

KUWAIT

Kuwait is an independent Arab sheikdom on the Persian Gulf. It was formerly under British protection. Since 1946, when oil production began, Kuwait has grown into the largest producer of petroleum in the Middle East. She is the fourth largest producer of petroleum in the world (after the United States, Venezuela and the Soviet Union). Some of the huge revenues from oil have been used in constructing schools, hospitals, roads and irrigation systems. Vegetables and citrus fruits are grown with irrigation. The ruler (Sheik) is head of state; the prime minister, cabinet of 14 ministers and National Assembly are elected by popular vote. *Capital: Kuwait. Population: 470,000. Land area: 24,280 sq. km. (9,375 sq. miles).*

MACAO

Macao is a very small Portuguese possession in southern China. It is situated to the south of Canton and consists of the town of Macao and a few small offshore islands. It has been under Portuguese control since 1557 and flourished as a port for China's foreign trade during the 18th century. Since the middle of the 19th century, however, it has been eclipsed by Hong Kong, its eastern neighbour. Macao has an important fishing industry, much of the fish being salted or dried and exported, especially to China. Its manufactures include textiles, clothes and firecrackers. Most of the Chinese population live in the capital, the town of Macao. *Capital: Macao. Population: 169,000. Land area: 16 sq. km. (6 sq. miles).*

LAOS

Laos is an independent kingdom on the Indo-Chinese peninsula. The country is wooded and mountainous and for the most part underdeveloped. Primitive agriculture is practised and rice is the chief food crop. Timber, coffee, leather and hides are major export items. Tin is also exported but other mineral resources have not been exploited. Laos is landlocked; her trade moves through Cambodia, South Vietnam and Thailand. Laos became a French Protectorate in 1893 and an independent member of the French Union in 1949. Buddhism is the dominant religion. *Capital: Vientiane is the administrative capital; Luang Prabang is the royal capital. Population: 2.3 million. Land area: 236,800 sq. km. (91,400 sq. miles).*

MALAYSIA

Malaysia is a federation of thirteen states in south-east Asia. It is divided into two parts, W. Malaysia on the Malay peninsula south of Thailand and E. Malaysia, some 400 miles away in Borneo. It is the chief world supplier of rubber and tin. Other exports include iron ore, palm oil, coconut oil and copra. About half the population are Malays, two-fifths Chinese and the rest Indian with some pre-Malay aborigines. Islam is the official religion. Malaysia is a constitutional monarchy. The King is chosen by and from nine Sultans and reigns for five years. *Capital: Kuala Lumpur. Population: 10 million. Highest point: Mount Kinabalu, 4,175 metres (13,455ft.). Principal river: Sungai Perak. Land area: 333,215 sq. km. (128,620 sq. miles).*

MALDIVE ISLANDS

The Maldive Islands are a six hundred mile long chain of two thousand coral atolls in the Indian Ocean, four hundred miles southwest of Ceylon. The Maldive Islanders, who inhabit about two hundred of the islands, live by trading, seafaring, fishing and agriculture. They grow coconut palms, millet, fruit and nuts. Large quantities of bonito (or the Maldive fish) are exported. Large numbers of dried fish are exported to Ceylon. The Maldives are an elective Sultanate with an elected parliament (Majlis). They were under British protection and linked with Ceylon from 1887 until 1965. They are now fully independent. All of the inhabitants are Moslems. Their language, Maldivian, is related to old Sinhalese. *Capital: Malé. Population: 98,000. Land area: 298 sq. km. (115 sq. miles).*

LEBANON

The Lebanon is an east Mediterranean republic. Only a quarter of the land is cultivated from which the Lebanon cannot grow enough food for her own population. To pay for imports of grain and sugar, she exports citrus and other fruits, tobacco, olives, wool and cement. Oil pipelines from Saudi Arabia and Iraq terminate at Lebanese ports. Unlike other Arab countries, Lebanon is 53% Christian (mainly the Maronite sect) and 47% Moslem. By tradition, the President is always a Maronite Christian and the Prime Minister a Moslem. It is sometimes called the Levant. *Capital: Beirut. Population: 2.2 million. Highest point: Qurnat Al-Sawda, 3,086 metres (10,131ft.). Principal river: Litani. Land area: 10,400 sq. km. (4,020 sq. miles).*

Hong Kong. **Kowloon and the New Territories seen from the main island. This European colony on the Asian mainland is tolerated by Communist China which uses it for commercial and financial contacts with the Western world.**

MONGOLIA

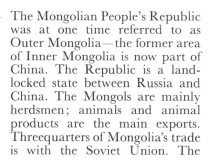

The Mongolian People's Republic was at one time referred to as Outer Mongolia—the former area of Inner Mongolia is now part of China. The Republic is a land-locked state between Russia and China. The Mongols are mainly herdsmen; animals and animal products are the main exports. Threequarters of Mongolia's trade is with the Soviet Union. The U.S.S.R. also supports small, growing industries in Mongolia. The only minerals found in the country are coal, gold and oil. Much of the land is desert. The Buddhist religion was suppressed in the 1930s; today only one monastery remains in the whole country. *Capital: Ulan Bator. Population: 1 million. Land area: 1,565,000 sq. km. (604,090 sq. miles).*

MUSCAT AND OMAN

Muscat and Oman is an independent sultanate in the Arabian peninsula. It is mainly a desert country with small fertile areas in the hills, oases and the eastern coastal plain. Dates and sugar cane are the most important products. Since 1967, crude oil has been exported from Saeh el Maleh, on the Gulf of Oman coast. The population is largely Arab, with significant Baluchi and Negro minorities. Since the early part of the nineteenth century the sultanate has enjoyed close ties with Great Britain. *Capital: Muscat. Population: 750,000. Highest point: Fabel ash Sham, 3,170 metres (10,400 ft.). Land area: 212,000 sq. km. (82,000 sq. miles).*

NEPAL

Nepal is a mountain kingdom in the Himalayas. Rice, maize, millet and wheat are the chief crops; timber, medicinal herbs and cattle are amongst the main export items. The population is part Mongolian and part Indian; the Gurkhas are the predominant group. Nepal is famous as the birthplace of Buddha in 560 B.C. Religion is Buddhist and Moslem. The illiteracy rate is believed to be about 90%. Government is by direct-rule monarchy. *Capital: Katmandu. Population: 9.4 million. Highest point: Mt. Everest, 8,848 metres (29,028ft.). Land area: 141,400 sq. km. (54,600 sq. miles).*

PAKISTAN

Pakistan is a Moslem republic created in 1947 consisting of two parts separated by 1,000 miles of Indian territory. Jute (80% of world production), rice and sugar cane are grown in E. Pakistan. W. Pakistan produces wheat, other cereals and cotton. Jute-manufacturing and textile plants are found in the east. Hydro-electricity and natural-gas industries are being developed in the west and there are also small textile and food processing industries. Bengali is spoken in the east; Urdu in the west. *Capital: Islamabad. Population: (W) 42.9 million; (E) 50.8 million. Land area: (W) 142,721 sq. km. (55,126 sq. miles); (E) 803.633 sq. km. (310,403 sq. miles).*

PERSIAN GULF TRUCIAL STATES

The Persian Gulf Trucial States comprise seven small independent sheikdoms under British protection; Abu Dhabi is the largest and most important. The country is mainly desert; Abu Dhabi is the only state with a large fertile area. Pearl fishing along the coast is not as important as it used to be. Oil production is the most important source of employment. Oil was discovered in the late 1950s and now more than 10,000,000 tons are produced each year. The United Kingdom is the leading trading partner; Japan and India are next in importance. *Principal city: Dubai. Population: 110,000. Land area: 83,660 sq. km. (32,300 sq. miles).*

PHILIPPINES

The Philippines are a group of 7,100 islands in the W. Pacific. The largest island, Luzon, has almost half the population. Principal food crops are rice, sugar cane, tobacco and maize. Minerals include chromite, iron ore, copper, gold and silver. Copra, Manila hemp, sugar, timber and copper are exported. Literacy is over 75% (25% of the budget is for education) and there are over 20 universities. The islands were discovered by Magellan in 1521 and after periods under Spanish control were ceded to the U.S.A. in 1898. They became an independent republic in 1946. About four fifths of the population are Roman Catholic. *Capital: Manila. Population: 30.6 million. Land area: 299,400 sq. km. (115,600 sq. miles).*

QATAR

Qatar, like Bahrain and the Persian Gulf Trucial States, is an independent sheikdom on the Persian Gulf, in special treaty relations with Britain. Some nomads graze livestock; pearl diving and fishing are carried out along the coast. Oil was discovered on the west coast in 1939 and production started in 1946. Apart from the capital city, almost all towns are associated with oil production and export. One quarter of the revenue from oil is reserved for the ruler; the rest is used for public development and welfare. Free education, health services and hospitals are provided. The population is of mixed origins. Qatar was under Persian rule for a long time but in 1868 an agreement was signed with Great Britain. The Sheik is an absolute monarch (which means he governs alone). *Capital: Doha. Population: 75,000. Land area: 10,360 sq. km. (4,000 sq. miles).*

Philippines. **Buffalos are very important domestic animals in these islands where they plough, harrow, draw loads and carry burdens on their backs.**

SINGAPORE

The Republic of Singapore is an island off the south of the Malay peninsula to which it is linked by a causeway carrying both a road and railway. It is an important commercial centre and one of the largest transit ports in the world. It also exports rubber and tin of Malaysian origin. Many processing industries have been established, including chemicals, timber and plastics. Chinese immigrants make up about three quarters of the population; 15% are Malays; and 8% are Indians and Pakistanis. Singapore became part of the Federation of Malaysia when it was set up in 1963 but she broke away and became independent in 1965. Singapore is a member of the Commonwealth. It was a wartime naval base and there are still important British service bases on the island. *Capital: Singapore. Population: 1.9 million. Land area: 581 sq. km. (224 sq. miles).*

Pakistan. **A street scene in the centre of Rawalpindi which is 1,710ft. above sea level. When under British rule, it was one of the greatest garrison towns in India.**

SOUTH YEMEN

The South Yemen People's Republic lies at the southern end of the Arabian peninsula. It comprises the former British colony of Aden and sixteen other sultanates and emirates. In its present form, it was proclaimed in 1967. Aden, at the entrance to the Red Sea, is an important bunkering port and the largest centre in the whole republic. In the other areas, most of the farming is conducted on a subsistence basis, although the output and export of long staple cotton which yields high quality thread is increasing. But for all the agricultural activities, irrigation is of the utmost importance to the farmers because rainfall is low and uncertain. *Capital: Madinet al-Shaab. Population: 1.5 million. Highest point: Qaured Audilla, 2,439 metres (8,200ft.). Land area: 160,300 sq. km. (61,890 sq, miles).*

SAUDI ARABIA

Saudi Arabia is an Arab kingdom covering most of the Arabian peninsula. It is a desert area with its economy originally based on oasis agriculture and nomadic animal rearing. These are still to be found, dates being most important. Oil was discovered in the late 1930s and today it is one of the world's leading producers of crude oil. A large proportion of the revenue from this source goes in grants to desert tribes. The country is socially and technically backward. Religion is Moslem. The religious centres of Mecca and Medina attract pilgrims, who are an important source of income. The country was established under its present name in 1932 by Ibn Saud, the then Sultan of Nejd. *Capital: Riyadh. Population: 7 million. Land area: 2,400,000 sq. km. (927,000 sq. miles).*

SYRIA

Syria is a primarily agricultural country in the Middle East. Cotton, cereals and tobacco are grown for export; cereals and sugar beet are raised for home consumption. Mineral exploration suggests that oil and natural gas may be extracted soon. Some revenue is received from petroleum companies whose pipelines cross Syria. Home industries include textiles and food processing. The predominantly Arab population is 85% Moslem and 13% Roman Catholic and orthodox Christian. Syria was under a French mandate until 1941 when she was granted independence. In 1958 she joined with Egypt in the United Arab Republic but in 1961 a coup aimed at restoring Syrian independence was successfully carried out by high-ranking army officers. *Capital: Damascus. Population: 4.8 million. Land area: 185,680 sq. km. (71,672 sq. miles).*

Turkey. **The 16th century Selimiye mosque at Edirne in Thrace.**

TAIWAN

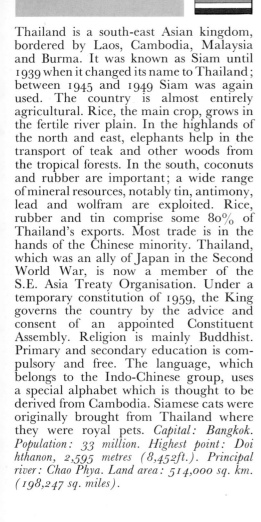

Taiwan is a large island off the coast of China, previously called Formosa (Portuguese for beautiful). Rice, sugar cane, pineapples, bananas and tea are grown on the western coastal plain. Camphor is produced from the trees in the mountain forests and supplies are sent all over the world. Coal is the most important mineral. There are aluminium, oil refining, food processing and cement industries. The island was discovered by the Portuguese in 1590, was under Chinese control from 1863, ceded to Japan in 1895 and returned to China after the Second World War. Since 1949, when mainland China became the People's Republic, Taiwan has been the refuge of Chiang Kai-shek's Nationalist Chinese regime which receives support from the U.S.A. *Capital: Taipei. Population: 12,990,000. Land area: 35,961 sq. km. (13,885 sq. miles).*

Bangkok. **A view of a floating market which forms a link between the people in the city and those living in the country districts.**

THAILAND

Thailand is a south-east Asian kingdom, bordered by Laos, Cambodia, Malaysia and Burma. It was known as Siam until 1939 when it changed its name to Thailand; between 1945 and 1949 Siam was again used. The country is almost entirely agricultural. Rice, the main crop, grows in the fertile river plain. In the highlands of the north and east, elephants help in the transport of teak and other woods from the tropical forests. In the south, coconuts and rubber are important; a wide range of mineral resources, notably tin, antimony, lead and wolfram are exploited. Rice, rubber and tin comprise some 80% of Thailand's exports. Most trade is in the hands of the Chinese minority. Thailand, which was an ally of Japan in the Second World War, is now a member of the S.E. Asia Treaty Organisation. Under a temporary constitution of 1959, the King governs the country by the advice and consent of an appointed Constituent Assembly. Religion is mainly Buddhist. Primary and secondary education is compulsory and free. The language, which belongs to the Indo-Chinese group, uses a special alphabet which is thought to be derived from Cambodia. Siamese cats were originally brought from Thailand where they were royal pets. *Capital: Bangkok. Population: 33 million. Highest point: Doi hthanon, 2,595 metres (8,452ft.). Principal river: Chao Phya. Land area: 514,000 sq. km. (198,247 sq. miles).*

TIMOR

Timor, an island in the Malay Archipelago, is the largest of the Lesser Sunda islands. Its eastern portion and two nearby islands comprise Portuguese Timor. The remainder of the island is a constituent part of Indonesia and here poor soil and soil erosion has hindered the establishment of permanent villages. The principal crops of Portuguese Timor are dry rice, maize and sweet potatoes. Terrace cultivation of wet rice by irrigation is also practised. Pigs, goats, horses, fowls and buffaloes are kept. Chief exports are coffee, sandalwood, copra, maize, rubber and wax. Most of the islanders are pagans, but Islam and Christianity have made some progress. Between 1586 and 1896 the territory was administered with Macao, another Portuguese possession in S.E. Asia. *Capital: Dili. Population: 517,000. Land area: 14,925 sq. km. (5,760 sq. miles).*

TURKEY

Turkey is a republic extending over the whole of Asia Minor and a small part of the Balkan Peninsula in Europe. Asian and European Turkey are separated by the Turkish Straits (the Bosporus, the Sea of Marmara and the Dardanelles). About 75% of the land is agricultural; cereals, cotton, fruit, nuts, oilseeds, sugar beet, tobacco, opium and wool are produced. Mineral wealth is varied; coal has by far the largest production. Iron ore, crude oil, chrome and manganese are exported. Heavy and light industries produce manufactured goods mainly for home use; many of these industries are new and expanding. 98% of the population are Moslems. In 1960 a military uprising overthrew the government, executing the Prime Minister and other Cabinet ministers. *Capital: Ankara. Population: 32.7 million. Land area: 780,576 sq. km. (301,300 sq. miles).*

South Vietnam. **A typical scene in a village street. Notice the girl in the foreground who is measuring rice, the staple food of this country.**

VIETNAM (North)

North Vietnam, officially known as the Democratic Republic of Vietnam, has a Communist government. Agriculture is collectivised. Rice is the major crop. Sugar cane, maize, cotton and silk are also important. Coal, non-ferrous ores, timber, tea and coffee are exported in exchange for manufactured goods and petroleum products. Industry is nationalised; food processing, textiles and mixed engineering are most important. Before the Second World War the whole of Vietnam was divided into three French protectorates. During the Second World War it was occupied by the Japanese. Local resistance to French rule in 1945 resulted in the Indo-Chinese war; the Geneva armistice of 1954 partitioned Vietnam pending elections which were to lead to reunification. However, these elections have not been held and a state of war still exists between north and south. *Capital: Hanoi. Population: 17 million. Land area: 164,100 sq. km. (63,340 sq. miles).*

VIETNAM (South)

South Vietnam, officially called the Republic of Vietnam, is governed by a President and National Assembly, both elected by the nation's vote. Rice is grown in the Mekong Delta for home consumption and export. Rubber, coffee and tea are also exported. Considerable financial aid is received from the U.S.A. Religion is predominantly Buddhist, although Taoism is the real religion of the country; there is also a strong Roman Catholic minority. In 1963 dissatisfaction among the Buddhists at the treatment they received from the Roman Catholics (the President was R.C.) led to an army coup and the overthrow and execution of the President. Pending the establishment of a reunified Vietnam, the efforts of the Vietcong (Communists) to dominate S. Vietnam have led to increased U.S. military aid since 1965. *Capital: Saigon. Population: 16 million. Land area: 171,665 sq. km. (66,263 sq. miles).*

YEMEN

The Yemen is an Arab state in the south-west of the Arabian peninsula. Much of the interior is mountainous, yet with irrigation the valleys and coastal plains provide fertile agricultural areas. Millet and maize are the main subsistence crops. Exports include coffee, hides and dried fruit. The country's population is mainly Moslem. Yemen is an Arabic word meaning "on the right hand" which is the equivalent of "lucky". In the 1960s there has been a series of disputes between the royalist and the republican elements in the state. The former, headed by the Imam, has enjoyed the support of Saudi Arabia; the latter, led by the army chiefs, has received support from Egypt (U.A.R.). The matter is unresolved. *Capital: Sana. Population: 4.5 million. Land area: 195,000 sq. km. (75,250 sq. miles).*

AFRICA

Africa is sometimes referred to as the "Dark Continent". This is because, until about a hundred years ago, Europeans knew very little about it. After the defeat of Carthage in 146 B.C. the Romans established a province on the North African coast, facing Sicily, but Europe's contacts with Africa came to an end when the Arabs conquered North Africa in 697 A.D. They resisted all European attempts to set foot on Moslem soil.

In fact, the interior of Africa remained virtually unknown to Europeans until the 18th century, although the Portuguese did a little coastal exploration and drew up a number of maps during the 15th century. The physical geography of the continent helped to promote Africa's aura of mystery, too. The Sahara desert provided a very effective barrier to exploration from the north and there were few natural harbours along the coast to provide shelter for shipping. In any case, progress to the interior was hampered by the dense, tropical forests which were difficult to penetrate, the hostility of the native population, the risk of catching tropical diseases or fevers and the difficulties of navigating the African rivers.

Two Scotsmen, James Bruce and Mungo Park, were among the first Europeans to travel far into the interior. Then, starting in 1849, David Livingstone went there to carry out missionary work among the native peoples and to put an end to the slave trade. Livingstone died of fever in 1873 whilst trying to find the source of the Nile.

Henry Stanley, a journalist, was sent out to find Livingstone and he carried on this work, also managing to trace the course of the River Congo. Other explorers from all over Europe and from America then came to Africa and rapid progress was made in man's knowledge of the continent. Then, when the Suez Canal was opened in 1869 and diamonds were discovered in South Africa, a number of European powers frenziedly scrambled to claim colonial territories in this rich continent.

Africa is the second largest continent with a total area of over 31 million sq. km. (12 million sq. miles). It is physically separated from all the other continents except Asia to which it is joined by the narrow isthmus of Suez.

Much of Africa is ancient plateau land at heights in excess of 305 metres (1,000ft.); in the south and east heights of 1,525 metres (5,000ft.) and more are reached on these plains. Yet there are few high mountain ranges; only in Ethiopia, Kenya, Tanzania, Uganda, Ruanda, Lesotho, Morocco and Chad does the continent rise above 3,050 metres (10,000ft.). The Great Rift Valley, consisting of a number of large, deep valleys extending from Syria to Mozambique, is another striking physical feature of the continent. Many of Africa's major lakes are in this region.

All of Africa's important rivers rise in the interior plateau and usually descend to sea level in a series of

Continued on page 54

EUROPEAN EXPLORATIONS AND SETTLEMENTS IN AFRICA

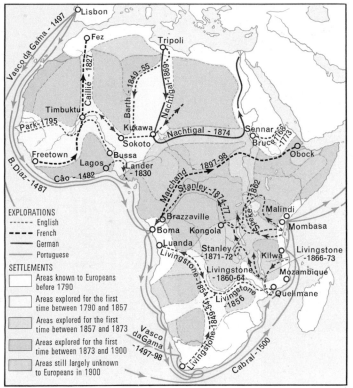

EXPLORATIONS
- - - - English
▬ ▬ ▬ French
▬▬▬ German
▬▬▬ Portuguese

SETTLEMENTS
- Areas known to Europeans before 1790
- Areas explored for the first time between 1790 and 1857
- Areas explored for the first time between 1857 and 1873
- Areas explored for the first time between 1873 and 1900
- Areas still largely unknown to Europeans in 1900

DISTRIBUTION OF AFRICAN PEOPLES

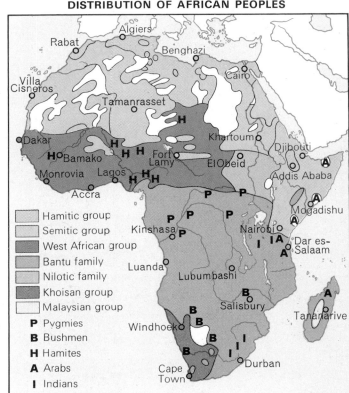

- Hamitic group
- Semitic group
- West African group
- Bantu family
- Nilotic family
- Khoisan group
- Malaysian group
- **P** Pygmies
- **B** Bushmen
- **H** Hamites
- **A** Arabs
- **I** Indians

ATLANTIC OCEAN

MEDITERRANEAN SEA

Black Sea · Caspian Sea · Aral Sea

S a h a r a

S u d a n

Gulf of Guinea

Congo Basin

Equator

ATLANTIC OCEAN

INDIAN OCEAN

Tropic of Cancer

Tropic of Capricorn

Red Sea · Gulf of Aden · Arabian Peninsula · Rub' al Khali

Madagascar

Kalahari Desert

Cape of Good Hope · C.Agulhas

ALTITUDES

Metres / Feet
4000 / 13123
3000 / 9843
2000 / 6562
1000 / 3281
500 / 1640
200 / 656
0 Sea level
Depression

DEPTHS

0
200 / 656
2000 / 6562
4000 / 13123
More than

Scale 1:34 000 000

0 250 500 750 1000 1250 1500 Kms.

0 250 500 750 1000 St.mls.

10 West from Greenw. 0 East from Greenw. 10

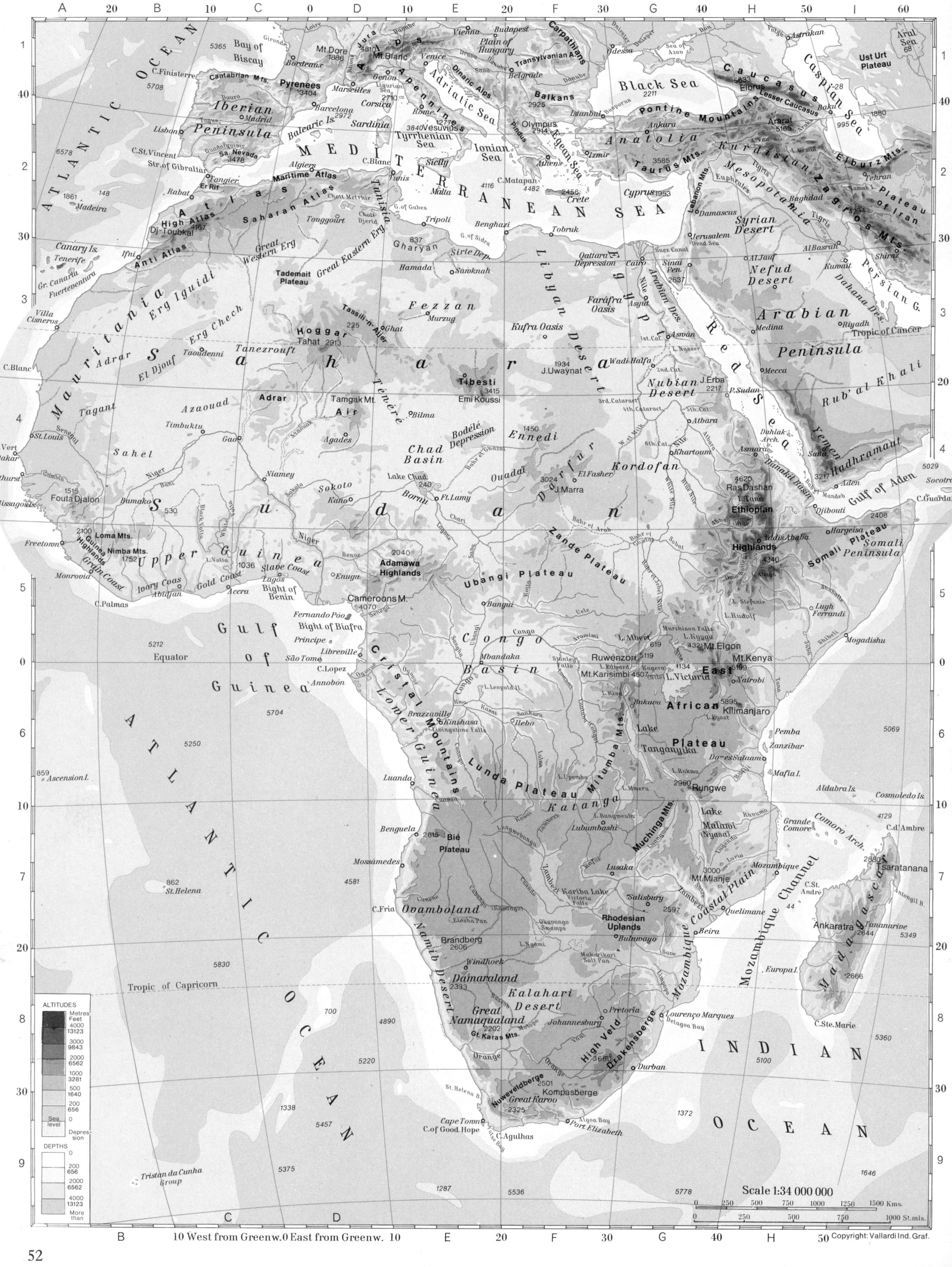

Copyright: Vallardi Ind. Graf.

Scale 1:34000000

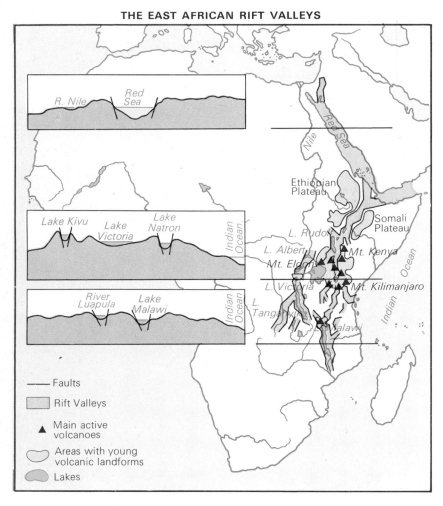

of the River Congo is typical of this type of climate; the total rainfall for the year may reach 2,000 mm. (80in.) whilst the average monthly temperature is always above 24°C. (75°F.). In the east, the nights are much cooler because of the height of the plateau. At Nairobi, for example, daytime temperatures average 24-26°C. (75-80°F.) while the temperature at night often falls to 7-10°C. (45-50°F.).

On either side of the equatorial belt lies a zone where there is a marked wet season, which arrives slightly after the time when the sun is directly overhead. A cooler season prevails when the sun is overhead in the opposite hemisphere. The resulting savanna climate of summer rain is found over more than one third of Africa. To the north of the equatorial zone the savanna region stretches from east to west but in the south it is less continuous on the higher plateaux of the interior.

Beyond these savanna belts are the desert regions. In the north the Sahara extends from the Atlantic Ocean to the Red Sea and the Desert of Arabia and it has an average north-south extent of some 1,300 km. (800 miles). There is almost no rainfall at all in this area. For example, there is only an appreciable amount of rain on an average of five days during the year at Cairo and the average annual rainfall is barely 25 mm. (1in.).

Temperatures in the desert zones are extreme because there are no clouds to moderate the heat of the sun during the day and when the sun sets there are no clouds to retain the heat during the night. Day temperatures in Cairo usually rise to 38°C. (100°F.) during five months of the year and even in winter they reach 31°C. (88°F.). But night temperatures often fall in winter to 5°C. (40°F.)—a difference of almost 26°C. (48°F.) in 24 hours.

The corresponding desert area in the southern hemisphere includes the Kalahari desert which is the home of the Bushmen.

Finally, beyond the desert zones are areas of Mediterranean climate. Africa's north coast is on the Mediterranean Sea and in places shares the climate of most Mediterranean lands—summer rain and winter drought. In the southern hemisphere, in a region stretching 240 km. (about 150 miles) north from Cape Town, a Mediterranean climate also prevails. Here it is always warm and even in winter the average temperature at Cape Town rises to 14°C. (58°F.).

The natural vegetation and cultivated crops of Africa are closely related to these climatic regions.

In the Mediterranean area of the north and in South Africa, vegetation is characteristic of the warm, temperate climate. Wheat, barley, cotton, citrus fruits, grapes, date palms and olives are grown; in places, irrigation is used.

Further south, in the desert areas, only the oases support any kind of vegetation.

Grassy plains cross the sub-tropical savanna regions and these are rich in animal life. Here some trees are found and

rapids and waterfalls. For instance, the Zambezi River cascades 108 metres (355ft.) over Victoria Falls. After cascading down from Lake Victoria and the Ethiopian mountains, the River Nile still has six sets of falls to negotiate as it flows through the desert to the sea. Such falls and rapids make African rivers difficult to navigate, yet they are valuable for installing power stations. Again, a number of African rivers flow out to sea in deltas which do not provide natural harbours for shipping.

Africa is the most tropical of all the continents. The equator runs practically through its centre and the Tropics of Cancer and Capricorn pass through it as well. This means that 23.3 million sq. km. or more than nine million sq. miles of its area—three times the size of Australia—are in the Tropics with the sun high overhead all the year round. In the area around the equator is a belt, occupying about one tenth of Africa's total area, which has uniformly high temperatures, great humidity and heavy daily rain in most months. The basin

THE COURSE OF THE NILE

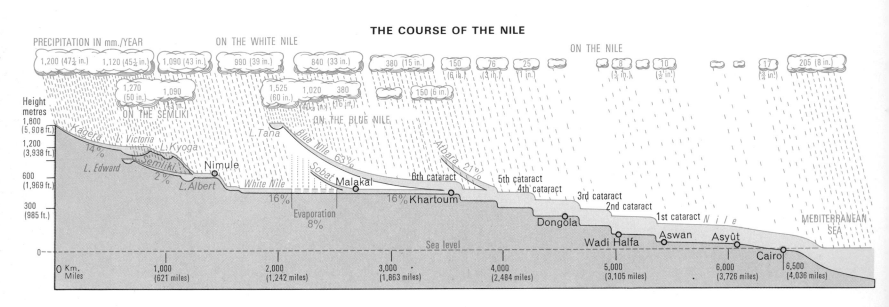

The pyramids and sphinx of ancient Egypt. Since these were built, the climate has become very dry; thus they have not been destroyed by the rain and wind. Modern Egypt (the United Arab Republic) is in strong contrast with its predecessor.

the grass often grows as high as 2 metres (6ft.).

In the equatorial zones the luxuriant vegetation of the rain forests is almost impenetrable. Mahogany and ebony trees, both valuable for the hard woods they provide for furniture making, are found here. Oil palms, cocoa, coffee, rubber trees and sugar cane also grow.

Most of the native population of Africa either cultivate the land or raise cattle. For instance, the Hamitic Berbers in the Atlas mountains are primarily cultivators but on the fringes of the desert, where the climate does not favour cultivation, they herd cattle.

The principal cereal grown by the Africans is millet but maize was introduced from America along with ground nuts, yams and cassava. In the forests of West Africa, cocoa and oil palm growing is very important.

Industrialisation in the Republic of South Africa and Rhodesia has changed the economy. Here some Africans have been attracted to the towns to work in the mines or in domestic service for the Europeans. But in most parts of Africa industrialisation is only just beginning.

Cocoa is Africa's most important food export, West Africa producing more than two thirds of the world output. Another important crop in the forest belt is the oil palm whose products are so important in the manufacture of margarine and soap. Cotton from Uganda and groundnuts from the savanna regions are also important in world trade.

Africa's mineral resources are not well exploited because of transport difficulties. Pipelines now bring oil and natural gas from the Sahara to the coast. In South Africa, the Rand, with Johannesburg at its centre, produces about three quarters of the world's gold. Zambia and the Katanga region of the Congo together produce about a quarter of the world's copper.

Africa's total population is over 280 million. Nevertheless, the average density is lower than any other continent, apart from Australia and Antarctica. However, some parts of Africa, like

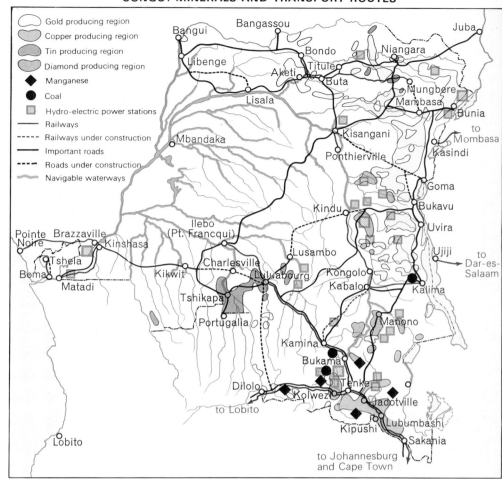

CONGO: MINERALS AND TRANSPORT ROUTES

the Nile valley, are heavily peopled, whilst others, like the Sahara, are almost deserted.

There are many different races of Africans. In the eastern Congo region live the tiny pygmies who seldom grow taller than five feet. Not far away, in Burundi, live the Watusi who often grow as tall as seven feet. In between these extremes are many other negro people such as the Bushmen and Zulus of South Africa, the Bantu and Masai from the east, the Ibo and Yoruba of Nigeria and the Hottentots, now largely confined to south-west Africa. All of these groups have their own rich cultures and traditions, yet many of them have adopted non-African religions, such as Christianity or Islam.

In the north of the continent—from Morocco to Egypt—are another large group—the Arabs. Because they live so close to Europe, their ways of life have tended to be influenced by European ideas. They are mostly Moslems and speak Arabic.

Most of Africa's large animals such as the elephant, zebra, rhinocerous, antelope, hippopotamus and giraffe are found in the savanna grasslands. For many years people used to hunt these animals for sport. But, now it is realised that many of these beautiful creatures are in danger of becoming extinct, many more people take cameras instead of guns on safari with them. Africa also has some spectacular snakes, some of the pythons growing as long as 7 metres (21ft.). Crocodiles are found in most rivers and lakes—the largest of them, the Nile crocodile, growing up to 5 metres (16ft.).

When colonisation of Africa began less than a hundred years ago, the native peoples whom the Europeans encountered seemed primitive and uneducated. But although many aspects of their ways of life have been preserved, the Europeans had a tremendous impact on them. Their knowledge of medicine helped to bring disease under control with the result that the population has grown rapidly. They have built modern cities, established plantations and built railways across the country. And they are now harnessing Africa' rivers to provide hydro-electric power for the new industries.

Having done all this work, and sampled the rewards that this rich continent has to offer, the Europeans are now tending to take a back seat and, in many cases, have granted self-government to their colonies. This has not always been achieved without a certain degree of internal friction, notably in the Congo

But in most cases it has been carried through satisfactorily and the African peoples are working harder for the nations which generally now belong exclusively to them.

AFRICA: TYPES OF SUBSISTENCE ECONOMY

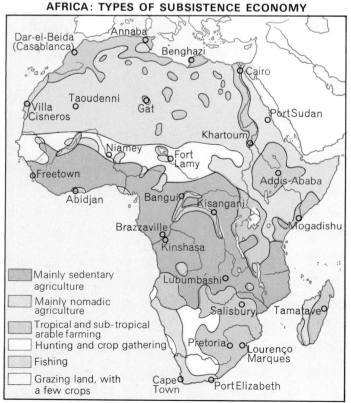

THE RESOURCES OF THE SAHARA

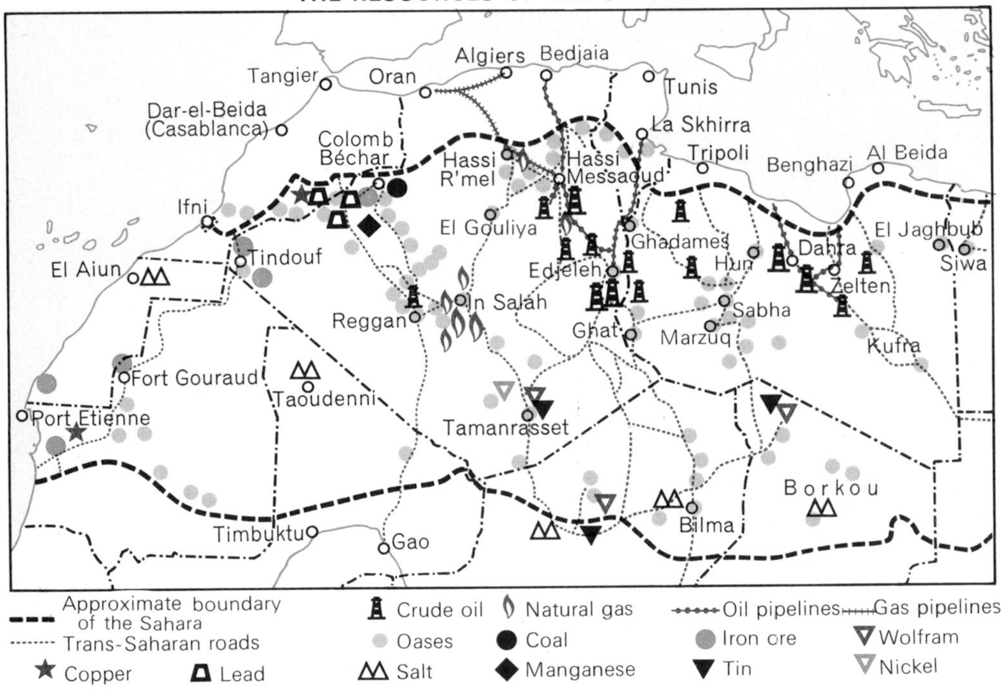

Tangier
Oran
Algiers
Bedjaia
Tunis
Dar-el-Beida (Casablanca)
Colomb Béchar
Hassi R'mel
Hassi Messaoud
La Skhirra
Tripoli
Benghazi
Al Beida
Ifni
El Gouliya
Ghadames
Dahra
El Jaghbub
Siwa
El Aiun
Tindouf
Edjeleh
Hun
Zelten
In Salah
Sabha
Reggan
Ghat
Marzuq
Kufra
Fort Gouraud
Taoudenni
Port Etienne
Tamanrasset
Borkou
Bilma
Timbuktu
Gao
Approximate boundary of the Sahara
Trans-Saharan roads
Copper
Lead
Crude oil
Oases
Salt
Natural gas
Coal
Manganese
Oil pipelines
Gas pipelines
Iron ore
Tin
Wolfram
Nickel

BOTSWANA

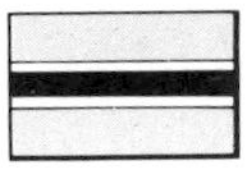

Botswana is an independent republic within the Commonwealth. From 1895 to 1966 it was the British protectorate of Bechuanaland. Cattle rearing and dairying is the most important activity. Animal products, some manganese and a small amount of asbestos are exported. The population live in villages some way from their ploughed lands and communal cattle grazing areas. The people belong to eight main tribes, of which the Bamangwato are the largest. *Capital: Gaberones. Population: 576,000. Land area: 575,000 sq. km. (222,000 sq. miles).*

BURUNDI

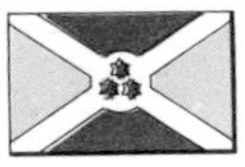

Burundi is a republic in central Africa. It was formerly part of the Belgian Congo and later, as Ruanda-Urundi, under German administration. It was granted independence in 1962. It is wholly agricultural with over half the farming organised on a subsistence basis. Coffee is the main export, going chiefly to the U.S.A. Other crops include cotton, vegetable oil and tobacco. Stock-rearing is important with a large output of hides. *Capital: Burumbura. Population (largely Hutu and Tutsi): 2.8 million. Land area: 27,834 sq. km. (10,747 sq. miles).*

AFARS and ISSAS

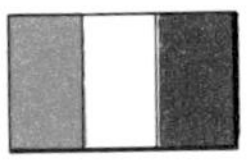

The Afars and Issas is an overseas territory of France in east Africa. It was formerly called French Somaliland. In March 1967 a referendum favoured continuance of the association with France, rather than independence. The sparse population outside the capital is mainly engaged in nomadic pastoralism — goats, sheep and camels — or fishing for pearls, sponges and shellfish. Djibouti has been the terminus since 1897 of the Franco-Ethiopian railway from Addis Ababa. *Capital: Djibouti. Population: 108,000. Land area: 21,980 sq. km. (8,490 sq. miles).*

CAMEROUN

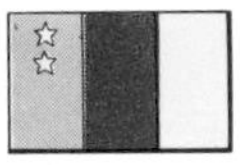

Cameroun is a federal republic on the Gulf of Guinea. The Cameroons were a German colony until the First World War when they were mandated to France and Britain. Since 1960 the French (Cameroun) has been independent. In 1961, part of the British Cameroun joined the federation. It is primarily an agricultural country; cacao is widely grown, much of it for export. Coffee, bananas, aluminium and tropical hardwoods are also sent abroad. There are small metallurgical, chemical and textile industries. *Capital: Yaounde. Population: 5.2 million. Land area: 474,000 sq. km. (182,964 sq. miles).*

ALGERIA

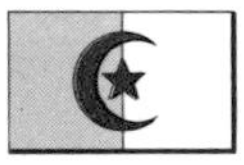

Algeria is an independent north African republic between Morocco, Tunisia and Libya and stretching southwards into the heart of the Sahara desert. A narrow coastal belt is highly fertile; vineyards, cereals and citrus fruits are important here. Some of the mountain areas of the north are valuable for grazing and forestry. Industry is being developed and there are rising exports of iron and zinc ores, natural gas, phosphates and petroleum. About a third of the land under cultivation is owned by European farmers. The large, rural native population is, for the most part, illiterate and barely self-supporting. The birth rate is very high. Only about 10% of Algeria's population, is non-Moslem. Algeria was ruled by France from 1830 until 1962 when she gained independence. France still has military and naval bases there and she lends a considerable amount of economic aid. *Capital: Algiers. Population: 10.5 million. Land area: 2,466,833 sq. km. (952,200 sq. miles).*

ANGOLA

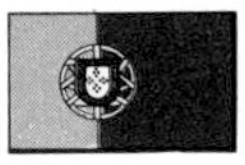

Angola is a Portuguese overseas territory in S.W. Africa. The native Bantu grow maize, groundnuts and rice for their own consumption. The Portuguese settlers have plantations of coffee, sugar and cotton. Coffee, diamonds and iron ore are the major exports. There is some oyster fishing off the south coast. Lobito on the Atlantic coast is the western terminal of the only coast to coast railway in south central Africa. Angola was discovered by the Portuguese in 1482 and for two centuries native slaves were shipped from there to Brazil. The present government's official policy is racial assimilation and since 1962 Africans have been able to qualify as Portuguese citizens. However, Africans can vote only if they are of comparable social and educational standard to the Portuguese. Lack of schools has meant that the literacy rate is low but educational facilities for the Africans are being extended at present. *Capital: Luanda. Population: 5 million. Land area: 1,246,700 sq. km. (481,300 sq. miles).*

AFRICA: ROCKS AND ASSOCIATED MINERAL DEPOSITS

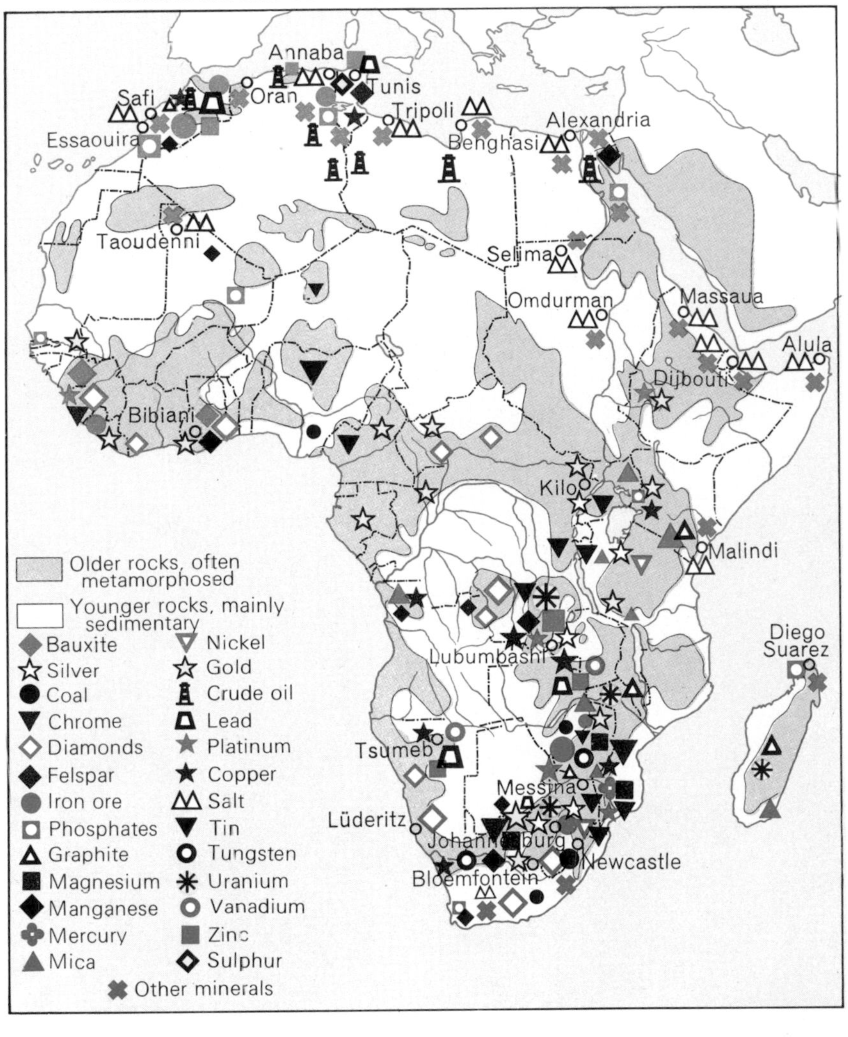

Annaba
Tunis
Safi
Oran
Tripoli
Alexandria
Essaouira
Benghasi
Taoudenni
Selima
Omdurman
Massaua
Alula
Djibouti
Bibiani
Kilo
Malindi
Lubumbashi
Diego Suarez
Tsumeb
Messina
Lüderitz
Johannesburg
Newcastle
Bloemfontein
Older rocks, often metamorphosed
Younger rocks, mainly sedimentary
Bauxite
Silver
Coal
Chrome
Diamonds
Felspar
Iron ore
Phosphates
Graphite
Magnesium
Manganese
Mercury
Mica
Nickel
Gold
Crude oil
Lead
Platinum
Copper
Salt
Tin
Tungsten
Uranium
Vanadium
Zinc
Sulphur
Other minerals

CAPE VERDE ISLANDS

The Cape Verde Islands are a Portuguese overseas territory. The fifteen islands form a crescent-shaped archipelago off the West African coast. They fall into two groups called the Windward (Barlavento) and Leeward (Sotavento) islands. The islands are mountainous and volcanic but coffee, bananas and manioc are grown in the fertile valleys; livestock are also important. Because the islands are separated by rough seas, each has developed its own dialect, customs and individuality. Roman Catholicism is the official religion but due to the shortage of priests, pagan customs survive. *Capital: Praia. Population: 202,000. Land area: 4,033 sq. km. (1,557 sq. miles).*

CENTRAL AFRICAN REPUBLIC

The Central African Republic has been a land-locked independent state since 1960; it is just north of the equator, bordered by the Congolese Republic, Congo, Cameroun, Chad and Sudan. It was formerly the region of Ubangi-Shari in French Equatorial Africa but has been independent since 1960. The land is mainly savanna and exports include cotton, diamonds, coffee and groundnuts. It is a member of the French Community. The population comprises largely Bantu or Sudan negroes. *Capital: Bangui. Population 1.47 million. Land area: 624,930 sq. km. (241,223 sq. miles).*

CHAD

Chad is a central African republic, south of Libya and between Niger and the Sudan. It was formerly part of French Equatorial Africa, has been a member of the French Community since 1958, and self-governing since 1960. A mainly desert land, it includes the Tibesti mountains in the northern part of the country, which are the highest peaks in the Sahara. Principal exports are cotton and animal products. The population is mainly Arabs and Sudan negroes. *Capital: Fort Lamy. Population: 3.4 million. Highest point: Emi Koussi, 3,415 metres (11,201 ft.). Land area: 1,284,000 sq. km. (495,624 sq. miles).*

COMORO ARCHIPELAGO

The Comoro Archipelago lies between Malagasy and Mozambique, in the Mozambique channel. The islands are an overseas territory of France which were granted self-government in 1961. Cassava, sweet potatoes and other vegetables are grown on small plots of cultivatable land but most foodstuffs for the population are imported. Plantations, which cover 35% of the total area, produce vanilla, coffee and cocoa for export. The population speaks mainly Arabic. About half of them live on Grand Comore. *Capital: Moroni. Population: 244,000. Land area: 2,170 sq. km. (838 sq. miles).*

CONGO (The Republic of)

Formerly the French Congo, Congo (Brazzaville) has been an independent republic within the French Community since 1960. The country is bisected by the Equator and is largely rain forest. Its boundary with the Congo Republic (Kinshasa) is formed by the mighty Congo and Ubangi rivers. Principal exports are timber, palm oil, copra, peanuts and lead ore. The population, which is largely Bantu, is mainly found in the south-west, near to the Congo river or the coast. *Capital: Brazzaville. Population: 870,000. Principal river: Congo. Land area: 331,850 sq. km. (128,094 sq. miles).*

CONGO REPUBLIC

The Congo Republic (Kinshasa), formerly the Belgian Congo, lies in the vast equatorial forest of the Congo Basin. In the extreme south, Katanga is an important mining district for copper, diamonds, manganese, cobalt, tin, gold and uranium. Copper accounts for more than half of the country's exports. Leading agricultural exports include palm oil, palm kernels, cotton and coffee. The African population grow maize, sweet potatoes and cassava. *Capital: Kinshasha (formerly called Leopoldville). Population: 14 million. Principal river: Congo. Land area: 2,345,409 sq. km. (905,328 sq. miles).*

Old and new come face to face in Uganda. On one side of the road is a modern petrol filling station; on the other, a traditional roadside market.

DAHOMEY

Dahomey is a small republic on the Gulf of Guinea, between Niger, Nigeria, Togo and the Upper Volta. It was a French colony from 1904 until 1960 when it became self-governing. In 1958 Dahomey became a member of the French Community. Most of the population is engaged in agriculture. Maize and cassava are the main crops and 80% of the country's palm products are exported. Coffee and nuts are also sent abroad. Recently, cotton growing has been successfully started in the northern areas. There are small deposits of chromium, gold and iron ore. The principal port and commercial city is Cotonou. Since independence in 1960, the constitutional government has been replaced by two military uprisings, one in 1963 and the other in 1967. *Capital: Porto Novo. Population: 2.4 million. Land area: 115,672 sq. km. (44,684 sq. miles).*

EQUATORIAL GUINEA

Equatorial Guinea is a Spanish province just north of the equator. It was granted internal self government in 1964. It consists of Rio Muni, between Cameroun and Gabon, and the islands of Fernando Poo, Annobon and three smaller islets. Mahogany and okoume are grown in Rio Muni's forests and the logs are floated down the Benito and Muni rivers to the sea. Local Africans grow coffee on the central uplands and the Fang, who live in the east, grow rather more cocoa. Fernando Poo is of volcanic origin. There are large cocoa and coffee plantations and small African farms on the coastal plains. The central highlands have been partly cleared of forest for pasture. The population is largely Nigerian and Bubi. *Capitals: Bata (Rio Muni); Santa Isabel (Fernando Poo). Population: 260,000. Land area: 28,050 sq. km. (10,830 sq. miles).*

Congo Republic. **A scene on the shores of the River Congo, close to Kinshasa. On the opposite bank is Brazzaville, capital of the Republic of the Congo.**

ETHIOPIA

Ethiopia is an independent empire in N.E. Africa, formerly known as Abyssinia. It has a long and partly legendary history, which is said to originate with King Solomon and the Queen of Sheba. Most people live in the central highlands where they breed cattle and grow coffee, cane sugar, barley, maize, oilseeds, potatoes and tobacco. Coffee is the chief export. Italy invaded Ethiopia in 1935 and incorporated it in Italian East Africa but was ousted in 1941. The former Italian colony of Eritrea became part of the Federation of Ethiopia and Eritrea in 1952 and now has provincial status. Religion is Christian and Moslem. *Capital: Addis Ababa. Population: 21.8 million. Principal river: Blue Nile. Land area: 1,022,660 sq. km. (395,000 sq. miles).*

GHANA

Ghana (formerly called the Gold Coast) is an independent republic within the Commonwealth. It lies between the Ivory coast, Togo, Mali and Upper Volta. It is predominantly agricultural and is the world's largest producer of cocoa beans. Amongst other activities, coffee, timber production and fisheries are important. There are also rich mineral resources, especially bauxite, gold, diamonds and manganese. A new dam on the Volta River provides hydro-electric power for industry and homes, a rich fishing lake and easier transport. The expanding artificial harbour at Takoradi handles most of Ghana's trade. *Capital: Accra. Population: 8 million. Principal river: Volta. Land area: 238,537 sq. km. (92,075 sq. miles).*

GABON

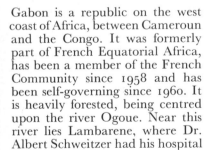

Gabon is a republic on the west coast of Africa, between Cameroun and the Congo. It was formerly part of French Equatorial Africa, has been a member of the French Community since 1958 and has been self-governing since 1960. It is heavily forested, being centred upon the river Ogoue. Near this river lies Lambarene, where Dr. Albert Schweitzer had his hospital for the treatment of lepers. The country is largely underdeveloped but valuable deposits of iron ore, manganese, petroleum and uranium have been found and are being worked. Timber, rubber, uranium, oil and iron ores are exported. *Capital: Libreville. Population: 470,000. Principal river: Ogoue. Land area: 267,000 sq. km. (103,060 sq. miles).*

GAMBIA

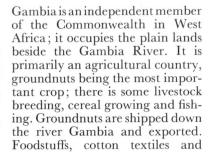

Gambia is an independent member of the Commonwealth in West Africa; it occupies the plain lands beside the Gambia River. It is primarily an agricultural country, groundnuts being the most important crop; there is some livestock breeding, cereal growing and fishing. Groundnuts are shipped down the river Gambia and exported. Foodstuffs, cotton textiles and petrol are the main imports. The capital, Bathurst, is situated on an island at the mouth of the river. Gambia was discovered by the Portuguese in the 15th century, and colonised by the British in the 17th century. Full self-government was achieved in 1965. *Capital: Bathurst. Population: 316,000. Principal river: Gambia. Land area: 10,369 sq. km. (4,000 sq. miles).*

Ghana. **Women do most of the work of growing, gathering, preparing and cooking the food in this predominantly agricultural country.**

Kenya. **A Kikuyu hut village built upon the tropical red soil (called Laterite) which tends to be infertile.**

GUINEA

Guinea (formerly part of French West Africa) is an independent republic bordering on the Ivory Coast, Senegal, Mali, Portuguese Guinea, Liberia and Sierra Leone. The country is the most mountainous in West Africa. Cattle rearing, rice and tropical fruit growing are important. There are bauxite and iron-ore deposits and large scale mining. Principal exports are bauxite, iron ore, diamonds, palm kernels, coffee, bananas and pineapples. The country is dominated and run by the Parti Democratique de Guinea, founded in 1961. Guinea has pursued a neutral policy in world affairs; it has received financial and military aid from Russia, and is pledged to the cause of African unity. *Capital: Conakry: Population: 3.5 million. Principal river: Niger. Land area: 245,857 sq. km. (94,900 sq. miles).*

IFNI

Ifni is a very small overseas province of Spain on the Atlantic coast of Morocco between the Atlas Mountains and the coast. Together with the Spanish Sahara, it is governed from the Canary Islands. Its activities are mainly pastoral with the rearing of camels, horses, asses and mules, but there are also fisheries, particularly for lobsters. Small amounts of cereals (mainly barley) and early vegetables are grown. Although the territory was ceded to Spain by Morocco in 1860, occupation was purely nominal until the Spanish flag was raised there in 1934. The capital, Sidi Ifni, is a free port and has a population of about 15,000. *Capital: Sidi Ifni. Population: 51,500. Land area: 1,500 sq. km. (580 sq. miles).*

GUINEA (Portuguese)

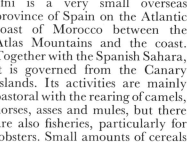

The Portuguese overseas territory of Guinea is on the Atlantic coast between Senegal and Guinea. It includes the islands of Bijagoz and Bolama. On the interior plateau the population herd cattle and grow millet and groundnuts. The coastal areas are very humid and swampy and here the people have cleared stretches of mangroves so that they can grow rice. On the higher, drier ground, coconut palms are grown. It is a country of hamlets and villages, Bissau, the capital, being the only town of any size. There is no railway and the few roads are poor. The coast was discovered in 1446 and the country has belonged to Portugal since 1879 but most of the original settlements are in decay. *Capital: Bissau. Population: 519,000. Principal river: Geba. Land area: 36,125 sq. km. (13,950 sq. miles).*

IVORY COAST

The Ivory Coast is a republic in W. Africa, formerly part of French West Africa (from 1893-1958). The name was given by early traders to the coast along the Gulf of Guinea, between Liberia and Ghana. At that time, ivory was important but although elephants are still found, ivory is no longer important commercially. Today, most of the population relies on subsistence agriculture—yams, manioc, maize and rice are most important. Coffee is the most valuable export; cocoa, timber and bananas are also sent abroad. Diamonds and manganese ore are increasing in importance. Complete executive powers are vested in the President who dominates the country through his highly organised party. *Capital: Abidjan. Population: 3.9 million. Land area: 322,463 sq. km. (124,471 sq. miles).*

KENYA

Kenya is an independent East African republic within the Commonwealth. It is situated astride the equator. The land is mainly agricultural; livestock, coffee, tea, wheat and maize are important on the western highlands; whilst coconuts, cotton and sugar are important in the hotter and lower eastern areas. Many tourists come to Kenya on safaris. The population is mostly African, the Kikuyu and Luo being the largest groups. There are Asian, Arab and European communities. A desire for majority rule and discontent with European monopoly of farm land led to the Mau Mau rebellion of 1952-56. Independence was granted in 1963. *Capital: Nairobi. Population: 8.6 million. Highest point: Mt. Kenya, 5,199 metres (17,040ft.). Land area: 582,600 sq. km. (224,960 sq. miles).*

LESOTHO

Lesotho is the former British protectorate of Basutoland. It is a small land-locked kingdom, surrounded by the Republic of South Africa. It is mainly an agricultural country producing maize, wool and mohair. Soil erosion, now being counteracted, has meant that agriculture cannot support the entire population. Some of the population (who are largely Bantu) work in the mines and cities of South Africa and many have settled there. In 1966 the country became an independent state within the Commonwealth and decided to adopt the name Lesotho. *Capital: Maseru. Population: 970,000. Land area: 30,350 sq. km. (11,716 sq. miles).*

LIBERIA

Liberia is an independent country on the coast of West Africa between the Ivory Coast and Sierra Leone. It was founded in 1822 by the American Colonization Society as a settlement for freed slaves. It became independent in 1847 and administration remained in the hands of the descendants of the original settlers. Christianity is the main religion. The chief sources of wealth are iron ore and rubber. Other exports are cocoa, coffee, palm kernels, gold and diamonds. The constitution is similar to that of the U.S.A. *Capital: Monrovia. Population: 1.25 million. Land area: 111,000 sq. km. (42,850 sq. miles).*

Libya. **Mosques in the skyline of Benghazi, joint capital of Libya and capital of the province of Cyrenaica.**

LIBYA

Libya is a North African kingdom fringing on the Mediterranean between Egypt and Tunisia. The land is mostly desert and agriculture confined to the coastal strip, oases and some irrigated areas. From there, agricultural products include dates, olive oil and cereals. Crude oil output is rapidly increasing and accounts for most of Libya's exports. The three provinces of Tripolitania, Cyrenaica and Fezzan which now make up the kingdom were under British and French administration 1945-51. They were united as the first independent state to be created by the U.N. Religion is Moslem and the language is Arabic. *Capitals: Tripoli and Benghazi. Population: 1.5 million. Land area: 1,759,540 sq. km. (679,183 sq. miles).*

MALAGASY REPUBLIC

Malagasy is an island (the fifth largest in the world) in the Indian Ocean, off the south-east coast of Africa. The island was known as Madagascar until its independence in 1960; it is a member of the French Community. Its economy is mainly agricultural, chief exports being coffee, vanilla, rice, sugar, cloves, sisal, tobacco, pepper, spices, ground nuts and raffia. Exploited mineral deposits include graphite, phosphates and mica. The main tribe in the east are the Hova who are wealthy and educated; they make up one quarter of the population. On the west smaller negroid groups predominate. *Capital: Tanarive. Population: 6.4 million. Highest point: Maromokotro, 2,884 metres (9,436ft.). Land area: 594,180 sq. km. (229,350 sq. miles).*

MALAWI

Malawi is an independent country in S.E. Africa, formerly called Nyasaland. It is a member of the Commonwealth. It is mainly agricultural, the chief crops being tobacco, tea, cotton, sisal and groundnuts. Some of these are exported. In return, imports include metals, machinery, textiles and oil products. There are few known mineral deposits. It is a land-locked state, and so relies on its neighbours for sea ports. The population is largely Bantu, the Chewa and Nguru being the largest racial groups. Nyasaland became a British protectorate in 1891, became part of the Federation of Rhodesia and Nyasaland in 1953, was granted self-government in 1963 and gained full independence, as Malawi, in 1964. *Capital: Zomba. Population: 4.05 million. Land area: 93,600 sq. km. (36,130 sq. miles).*

Libya. **The Zelten oil wells in the desert are an important feature, bringing new wealth into the country.**

MALI

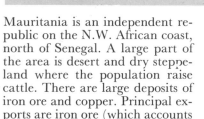

Mali is an independent republic in N. W. Africa. It is a desert and semi-desert area in which farming is being organised on a collective basis, with new irrigation schemes. The country's chief export are groundnuts, fish, cotton, rice and cattle. Her mineral resources (iron ore, manganese and phosphates) are largely unexploited. The country was annexed by the French and named French Sudan in 1895.

In 1958 it became the autonomous Sudanese Republic, within the French Community. It united with Senegal in 1959 as the Mali Federation but in 1960 the union was dissolved and it declared itself the independent Mali Republic. Religion is mainly Moslem. *Capital: Bamako. Population: 4.7 million. Principal river: Niger. Land area: 1,204,021 sq. km. (464,752 sq. miles).*

MOROCCO

Morocco is an independent kingdom in N.W. Africa. It was under French and Spanish protection until 1956. The interior is dominated by the Atlas Mountains; most of the people live along the coastal lowlands. Principal exports are citrus fruits, cork, fish, vegetables, iron ore, lead and phosphates. Dams have been built for irrigation and to provide hydroelectric power and a number of

industries, including fish canning, textile manufacturing and fruit and vegetable processing have been established. There are also deposits of crude oil. The people living along the coast are mainly Arabs while those living in the Atlas Mountains are chiefly Berbers. Religion is Moslem. *Capital: Rabat. Population: 13.3 million. Land area: 430,000 sq. km. (165,980 sq. miles).*

MAURITANIA

Mauritania is an independent republic on the N.W. African coast, north of Senegal. A large part of the area is desert and dry steppe-land where the population raise cattle. There are large deposits of iron ore and copper. Principal exports are iron ore (which accounts for over 90% of the total), copper ore, fish, cattle and salt. The population is largely Moorish with

a negroid mixture in the south. They are partly nomadic and partly settled. Their religion is mainly Islam. Mauritania became a French protectorate in 1903, a colony in 1920 and since 1960 has been an independent republic within the French Community. *Capital: Nouskchott. Population: 1.1 million. Land area: 1,085,805 sq. km. (419,120 sq. miles).*

MOZAMBIQUE

Mozambique is a Portuguese overseas territory on the Indian Ocean. The principal crops are sugar cane, coconuts, cotton, tea and sisal, all of which are exported. There are few minerals. Along the north coast and in the valleys of the Zambezi and Limpopo are plantations run by Indians, Chinese and Europeans. Mozambique was discovered by Vasco da Gama in 1498. Today

there are about 100,000 Portuguese settlers. The country is commercially important for its entrepot ports (Beira, Lourenço Marques and Mozambique) which handle the trade of Malawi, Zambia and part of South Africa. *Capital: Lourenço Marques. Principal river: Zambezi. Population: 7 million. Land area: 783,030 sq. km. (302,250 sq. miles).*

MAURITIUS

Mauritius is an island in the Indian Ocean, 885 kilometres (550 miles) east of the Malagasy Republic. It is a member of the Commonwealth; independence was gained in 1968. Two thirds of the population are descended from Indians brought to the island during the last century to work on the sugar plantations. Sugar is the only commercial crop and the islanders

suffer when the yield is poor or when a tropical hurricane hits the island. Forestry, tea and tobacco growing are of minor importance. Mauritius was held by France from 1715 to 1810 but it became British after the Napoleonic Wars. Both French and English are spoken on the island. *Capital: Port Louis. Population: 790,000. Land area: 1,865 sq. km. (720 sq. miles).*

NIGER

Niger is a land-locked republic in central Africa consisting of savanna and desert. The Aïr Mountains dominate the centre of the country. Principal exports are tin, groundnuts, gum arabic, salt and cattle. Deposits of copper, iron, uranium and crude oil are being investigated. The population is principally of the Hausa, Tuareg, Peulh and Jerma peoples and there are

also some 3,000 Europeans; most are engaged in agriculture. The country was first explored in the 1890s. It became a French protectorate in 1903, and a colony in 1920. In 1958 it voted for independence within the French Community which it obtained in 1960. *Capital: Niamey. Population: 3.4 million. Land area: 1,188,794 sq. km. (458,875 sq. miles).*

Morocco **tends to be rather a backward country. This is borne out by the nomadic way of life followed by these farmers as they wander from oasis to oasis with their herds of livestock.**

NIGERIA

Nigeria is a federal republic in W. Africa and a member of the Commonwealth. The country is wholly tropical; the natural vegetation ranges from mangrove swamp forest in the south to semi-desert in the north. A wide range of tropical crops are grown. Cocoa, groundnuts, hides, palm kernels and palm oil are the main exports. Nigeria is one of the few African countries which produce coal; tin and columbite are also important. There is a wide range of industries and roads railways and civil aviation are well developed by African standards. The population comprises the Hausa, Ibo and Yoruba tribes. *Capital: Lagos. Population: 56.4 million. Principal river: Niger. Land area: 923,772 sq. km. (356,669 sq. miles).*

REUNION

Reunion is an island in the Indian Ocean, south-west of Mauritius. It is an overseas department of France; as such, it is represented at the French National Assembly. It is much more mountainous than Mauritius and several volcanoes rise sharply from the coast. Most of the population, which is of mixed French and African descent, is distributed in small towns around the coast. The economy is based on sugar and production has risen to more than 200,000 tons annually. Rum, oils for perfumes and vanilla are also produced. *Capital: Saint-Denis. Population: 408,000. Land area: 2,512 sq. km. (970 sq. miles).*

RHODESIA

Rhodesia is an area in southern Africa, named after Cecil Rhodes who took possession of it for Britain in 1888. Maize, tobacco, sugar, oranges, cotton, tea and coffee are grown; it is also rich in minerals, gold, asbestos, copper, coal and chrome being exported. From 1953 to 1963, as Southern Rhodesia, the country was part of the Central African Federation. Then Nyasaland became the independent state of Malawi and Northern Rhodesia became Zambia. In 1965 Rhodesia severed its remaining connections with the United Kingdom by unilateral action. *Capital: Salisbury. Population: 4.5 million. Land area: 390,622 sq. km. (150,780 sq. miles).*

Morocco. **A typical scene in one of the many casbahs or street markets.**

Rhodesia. **Part of the Victoria Falls. Situated 800 miles up the Zambezi River, these falls are over a mile wide in April, May and June when the volume of water is greatest, and over 350ft. high.**

RWANDA

Rwanda is a republic in central Africa, formerly part of the Belgian Congo. Apart from the Nile Delta area, it is the most densely populated part of Africa. Most of the people live by subsistence agriculture. A little coffee, hides and cotton are exported. Tin is the most important mineral. For many years the Tutsi (a Nilotic tribe) ruled with the Hutu (a Bantu tribe) and pygmies as their slaves. In 1946 the country became a Belgian trusteeship under the U.N. and was called Ruanda-Urundi. When this ended it was split into Burundi and Rwanda. Burundi kept a monarchy but Rwanda voted to abolish the Tutsi rule and became a republic. *Capital: Kigali. Population: 3 million. Land area: 26,330 sq. km. (10,169 sq. miles).*

ST. HELENA

St. Helena is a British island dependency in the South Atlantic Ocean, 3,060 kilometres (1,900 miles) north-west of Cape Town. There is some flax-fibre production and a lace-making industry but most of the population live by subsistence agriculture. The island was discovered by Portugal in 1502 and was used as a general port of call for sailing ships bound for the Orient. It was annexed in 1633 by the Dutch and in 1659 by the British to the East India Company who loaned it to the Crown in 1815 as a place of exile for Napoleon. He remained there until his death in 1821. The island has two dependencies: Ascension and Tristan da Cunha. *Capital: Jamestown. Population: 4,700. Land area: 122 sq. km. (47 sq. miles).*

ST. TOME AND PRINCIPE ISLANDS

The islands of St. Tome and Principe are a Portuguese overseas territory in the Gulf of Guinea. Both are mountainous and of volcanic origin. These two islands were the world's principal producers of cocoa at the beginning of this century but reports of slave labour scared away British chocolate manufacturers. Cocoa still accounts for three quarters of the exports but oil-palm products, coffee and copra are also important. Both the islands are very fertile and cultivation is intense. Despite the fact that they are heavily populated, additional labour is required and contract workers, mainly from Mozambique, come to work on the plantations. St. Tome is the larger island. *Capital: St. Tome. Population: 63,500. Land area: 964 sq. km. (372 sq. miles).*

SEYCHELLES ISLANDS

The Seychelles are a group of about ninety volcanic islands in the Indian Ocean. The main crops, grown on plantations run by Europeans, are coconuts, cinnamon and vanilla. These are exported to pay for imported foodstuffs such as rice, flour and sugar. There is no airport and boats call twice each month. The largest island, Mahe, supports about three quarters of the population of the Seychelles and Victoria, the capital, is the headquarters of the British colonial administration. French settlers came from Mauritius in 1777 and brought with them slaves. By the time that the islands were ceded to Britain in 1814, the French language was well established. A creole language is now spoken by about 94% of the population. *Capital: Victoria. Population: 48,000. Land area: 259 sq. km. (100 sq. miles).*

SENEGAL

Senegal is an independent republic on the west coast of Africa. Groundnuts are most important and production totals over a million tons annually; millet, rice and cattle are also significant. Senegal's coast is one of the richest fishing grounds around Africa and much fish is dried and exported. Mineral production is confined mainly to salt and phosphates. Senegal's industries are mainly concerned with the processing of groundnuts but there are cement and cotton factories, a large oil refinery and a fertiliser industry. Senegal is the oldest French colony in Africa and became self-governing within the French Community in 1960. It was finally federated with Mali. *Capital: Dakar. Population: 3.5 million. Principal river: Senegal. Land area: 197,161 sq. km. (76,105 sq. miles).*

SIERRA LEONE

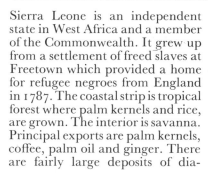

Sierra Leone is an independent state in West Africa and a member of the Commonwealth. It grew up from a settlement of freed slaves at Freetown which provided a home for refugee negroes from England in 1787. The coastal strip is tropical forest where palm kernels and rice, are grown. The interior is savanna. Principal exports are palm kernels, coffee, palm oil and ginger. There are fairly large deposits of diamonds, iron ore and chromite in the interior which are mined and exported. The interior is administered in three provincial regions and here the population maintains its traditional, tribal way of life. When Sierra Leone became an independent state in 1961, it was admitted to the U.N. as the one hundredth member. *Capital: Freetown. Population: 2.4 million. Land area: 72,326 sq. km. (27,925 sq. miles).*

South Africa. **The city of Cape Town, dominated by the Table Mountain. This is one of South Africa's three major ports, and its second largest city.**

African women traditionally carry young children on their backs and their shopping (even in plastic hold-alls) on their heads.

SOMALI REPUBLIC

The Somali Republic is an independent state in East Africa. It was created in 1960 when British Somaliland and the International Trust Territory of Somaliland (administered by Italy) joined together to form the new State. About three quarters of the population are pastoral nomads or semi-nomads, living mainly on milk, blood and a little corn. They speak the Somali tongue and often claim descent from immigrant Arabs. Between the two world wars, the Italians established plantations in river valleys in the south where cotton, sugar cane, bananas and maize are grown. The fisheries yield tunny and mother of pearl. No minerals are extracted, though iron ore, columbite and beryl have been discovered. Principal exports are bananas, hides and cattle. Religion is Moslem. *Capital: Mogadishu. Population: 2 million. Land area: 637,660 sq. km. (246,135 sq. miles).*

SOUTH-WEST AFRICA

South-west Africa is a former German colony, officially administered as a mandate under the Treaty of Versailles (from 1919) and now a United Nations trusteeship by the Republic of South Africa. The native Hottentots, Bushmen, Ovambo and Herero raise sheep and cattle. Karakul sheep pelts are an important export product. Pilchards and rock lobsters are also important. The country is rich in minerals. Diamonds are washed near Luderitz and the mouth of the Orange River; other minerals include lead, zinc, gold, iron, copper and salt. The population includes some 75,000 Europeans. The Namib Desert occupies the western coastal strip of the country. *Capital: Windhoek. Population: 530,000. Highest point: Brandberg, 2,616 metres (8,556 ft.). Principal river: Orange. Land area: 823,975 sq. km. (318,260 sq. miles).*

SOUTH AFRICA (Republic of)

South Africa is an independent republic at the tip of Africa. It has the most advanced economy of any country in Africa. Principal exports are foodstuffs, gold, diamonds and wool. Coal, iron and uranium are also important. Maize, wheat, sugar cane, tobacco, temperate and tropical fruits are grown. About 3.5 million of the population are of European origin (60% being of Dutch origin); the remainder are largely Bantu. Since the early 1950s a policy of apartheid (separate racial development) has been adopted; this led to South Africa's withdrawal from the Commonwealth in 1961. *Capitals: Pretoria and Cape Town. Population: 18.5 million. Principal river: Orange. Land area: 1,224,090 sq. km. (472,500 sq. miles).*

SPANISH SAHARA

The Spanish Sahara is a Spanish desert province on the north-west coast of Africa, between Morocco and Mauritania. The territory comprises a coastal strip and an interior plateau. Much of the area is desert. The climate is very hot and dry. Enormous phosphate deposits, said to be the largest in the world, were discovered in 1963. The population is mostly nomadic Berber herdsmen, travelling from oasis to oasis with their camels, goats and sheep. There is also some oasis agriculture and salt mining. Trawl-fisheries are another important source of revenue. Two ports have recently been established on the coast; Villa Cisneros and Playa El Aaiun. *Population: 36,000. Land area: 266,000 sq. km. (102,680 sq. miles).*

SUDAN

The Sudan is a north African republic, lying astride the Nile Valley. Much of the country is desert or poor grassland. Yet the economy is largely agricultural. The Sennar Dam on the Blue Nile irrigates the Gezira area which produces high-quality cotton. Nomadic tribes raise sheep and cattle. Cotton, gum arabic, groundnuts, oilseeds, millet and livestock are the major exports. Arabic-speaking Moslem whites inhabit the north of the country while various negro tribes (mainly Christian) inhabit the south. The country has an outlet to the Red Sea at Port Sudan; most of the population live close to the main river valleys. Between 1899 and 1955 the Sudan was governed by Britain and Egypt but then she voted for independent sovereignty. In 1958 the Sudanese army seized control by a coup d'etat. *Capital: Khartoum. Population: 13 million. Principal river: Nile. Land area: 2,505,800 sq. km. (967,250 sq. miles).*

Egypt. **Alexandria, a general view of one of the main thoroughfares of this busy port.**

SWAZILAND

Swaziland is a member of the Commonwealth; it achieved independence in September 1968. It is a land locked country, being surrounded by the Republic of South Africa and Mozambique and lying to the east of the Drakensberge Mountains. The principal agricultural products are citrus fruits, cotton, rice, sugar and tobacco. Softwood plantations have been established on the slopes of the mountains in the west and pulp mills and box factories have been set up. The chief earners of revenue are Swaziland's mines. Iron ore and asbestos are the two major minerals exported. Coal is mined and used for the local factories and railways, as well as being exported. Although the country is thriving economically, half of the people remain subsistence cultivators. *Capital: Mbabane. Population: 390,000. Land area: 17,400 sq. km. (6,705 sq. miles).*

TANZANIA

The United Republic of Tanzania is in eastern Africa and consists of Tanganyika, independent since 1961, and Zanzibar, independent since 1963. The climate varies from hot tropical on the coast to cooler and drier in the interior. Much of the land is savanna with some parts of the interior (and the coastal strip) being tropical forest. Hardwoods are a valuable export, as are sisal, cotton and coffee. Gold and diamonds are the most important minerals. Zanzibar island and Pemba lie off the Tanzanian coast—2,642 sq. km. (1,020 sq. miles) in extent. Their chief importance is as the world's largest producer of cloves. The area was first explored in the 1850's and was claimed by Germany in 1885 and called German East Africa. It was taken by Britain during the First World War. The Serengeti Park is a game reserve and sanctuary. *Capital: Dar-es-Salaam. Population: 12,250,000. Highest point: Mt. Kilimanjaro, 5,895 metres (19,340ft.) Land area: 937,060 sq. km. (361,700 sq. miles).*

Tunisia. **Tunis, a typical view of one of the streets in this Arab city.**

A typical North African market scene.

TOGO

Togo is a republic in west Africa, between Dahomey and Ghana. It is an independent member of the French Community. It is mainly agricultural, principal export crops being cocoa, coffee, copra, cotton, groundnuts and palm kernels. For home consumption, manioc, maize and yams are most important. Some teak plantations have been established in recent years. There are rich deposits of phosphates, iron ore and bauxite. Togo was a German colony until the First World War and was then mandated to Britain and France. From 1946 it was a United Nations Trust Territory. In 1960 it achieved independence. *Capital: Lomé. Population: 1.7 million. Principal river: Oti. Land area: 56,000 sq. km. (21,600 sq. miles).*

TUNISIA

Tunisia is an independent Arab-speaking republic in north Africa, on the Mediterranean Sea, between Algeria and Libya. It is mainly agricultural, producing cereals, citrus fruits, dates, olive oil, wine and flowers (for perfume), most of them for export. There are large deposits of phosphates which are sent abroad and there are smaller deposits of iron ore and lead. It is more prosperous than its neighbours. The French established a protectorate in Tunisia in 1881 which lasted for 75 years. Independence was granted in 1956 and in 1957 the Bey (ruler) was deposed and the monarchy abolished. Tunis is near the site of ancient Carthage. *Capital: Tunis. Population: 4.5 million. Land area: 164,150 sq. km. (63,362 sq. miles).*

UGANDA

Uganda is a land locked country in east central Africa, between Sudan, Kenya, Tanzania and Rwanda. It is a member of the Commonwealth, has been independent since 1962 and a republic since 1967. The country occupies a high plateau and is mainly natural savanna land. The principal commercial crops are coffee, cotton, tea, maize, groundnuts, oilseeds, sisal, sugar and hardwoods. There are some mineral resources and beryl, copper and tin are exported. The Owen Falls hydro-electric scheme at Jinja has encouraged the development of various industries. Uganda's population includes about 88,000 Asians and 10,000 Europeans. The Africans include about one million Baganda, who were the most advanced tribe when Europeans first explored the country. *Capital: Kampala. Population: 7.75 million. Highest point: Mt. Ruwenzori, 5,109 metres (16,763ft.). Principal river: Nile. Land area: 236,037 sq. km. (91,110 sq. miles).*

UPPER VOLTA

The Upper Volta is an independent republic in west Africa, north of Ghana. It was formerly a French colony but gained independence in 1960. Most of the population are farmers. The principal occupation for home and export is livestock breeding; much millet is grown for home use, whilst cotton and groundnuts are grown for export. The chief mineral is gold; diamonds and manganese are also extracted. The country's outlet to the sea is through Abidjan in the Ivory Coast. The area was part of the Mossi empire until it was annexed by France in 1896. It was part of the Niger and Upper Senegal colony in 1904 and took its present shape and name in 1919. From 1932 until 1947 it was divided between Ivory Coast, Sudan and Niger and was re-established as Upper Volta in 1947. *Capital: Ouagadougou. Population: 5 million. Principal river: Volta: Land area: 274,122 sq. km. (105,811 sq. miles).*

UNITED ARAB REPUBLIC

The countries of Egypt and Syria united in February 1958 to form the United Arab Republic under President Nasser of Egypt. In March 1958 the Yemen joined and Iraq joined in 1961 when Syria left the U.A.R. In 1962 the union was dissolved completely and the United Arab Republic is now Egypt alone. The country is mainly desert but huge irrigation schemes along the length of the Nile valley provide water all the year round for intensive farming. Principal crops, grown mainly for export, are cotton and sugar cane: for home consumption, wheat, maize and millet are most important. To help maintain Egypt's trade balance a number of industries have been established in Cairo and Alexandria, including cigarette making, date drying and sugar milling. There are deposits of coal, manganese and oil. Tourists to the remains of ancient Egypt are an important source of income. *Capital: Cairo. Population: 27 million. Principal river: Nile. Land area: 1 million sq. km. (38,110 sq. miles).*

ZAMBIA

Zambia is an independent country in central Africa and a member of the Commonwealth. It is land locked and was formerly called Northern Rhodesia. Zambia is the world's second largest producer of copper. Huge quantities are mined in the north, along the border with the Congo, and then smelted and refined for export. Cobalt, zinc, lead and manganese are also mined. The main crops are maize, tobacco, cassava and groundnuts. The capital, now at Lusaka, was once at Livingstone, near Victoria Falls. David Livingstone first came to this area in 1851, discovered the Victoria Falls in 1855 and died in a native village near Lake Bangweulu in 1873. In 1953 the former British protectorate of Northern Rhodesia became part of the Federation of Rhodesia and Nyasaland. The Federation was dissolved in 1963 and full independence, as Zambia, was achieved in 1964. *Capital: Lusaka. Population: 3.8 million. Principal river: Zambezi. Land area: 752,262 sq. km. (290,375 sq. miles).*

A herd of elephants making their way through the tall grasses of the savanna in Zambia.

NORTH AMERICA
INCLUDING CENTRAL AMERICA

The great expanse of land which we call America is often subdivided into constituent parts; sometimes it is divided into three—north, central and south. Sometimes we want to refer to those parts which are dominated by the Latin races as Latin America. At other times we may refer to those parts which speak the English language as Anglo America. But here, we are simply dividing the continent into two parts, the division being the boundary between the states of Panama and Colombia.

North America has a land area of 23,042,000 sq. km. (8,900,000 sq. miles) making it the third largest continent. To the north, Arctic Canada and Greenland stretch to within 800 km. (500 miles) of the North Pole and to the south the isthmus of Panama is within 800 km. (500 miles) of the Equator. From east to west the continent stretches some 5,800 km. (3,600 miles) and embraces eight time zones. For instance, when it is 1 a.m. in Alaska, it is 9 a.m. in Newfoundland. But the continent narrows southwards and in Mexico there is only one time zone.

The continent becomes so narrow that at one point it forms little more than a land bridge to South America. It was here, in 1914, that the Panama Canal was cut to connect the Atlantic and Pacific oceans. Before the opening of the canal, ships bound east or west had to take the long journey around Cape Horn.

After the discovery of North America by Columbus in 1492, the New World, as it was called, was settled by those European countries who had been so active in exploring it—Spain, France and Britain. Britain and France established settlements in the central and northern areas while the Spanish penetrated Mexico and central America.

The Spanish conquistadores, searching for gold, made inroads into Mexico and pushed northwards to Colorado and north-westwards to California. But they did not gain permanent control of any land north of the Rio Grande.

The French settled mainly in Quebec and Canada, along the River St. Lawrence. Today, this part of Canada is still predominantly French-speaking. Towards the end of the 17th century the French pushed deeper into the continent, following the Mississippi south to the Gulf of

Continued on page 72

NORTH AMERICA: INDIAN TRIBAL AREAS AND LANGUAGES AND EARLY EUROPEAN EXPLORATION

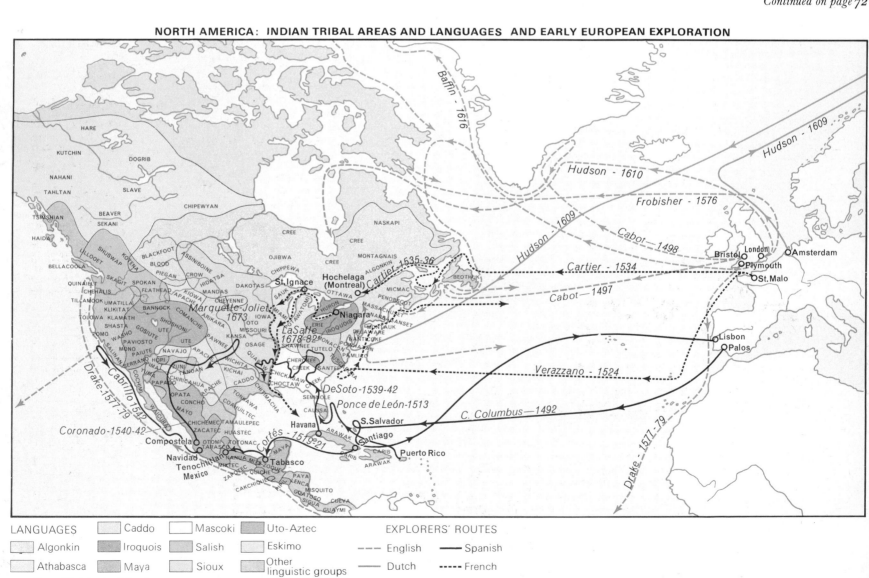

LANGUAGES: Caddo, Mascoki, Uto-Aztec, Algonkin, Iroquois, Salish, Eskimo, Athabasca, Maya, Sioux, Other linguistic groups

EXPLORERS' ROUTES: English, Spanish, Dutch, French

(Names of North American Indian tribes are printed in red)

A typical example of modern town planning in the United States of America. This is a view of the area surrounding George Washington bridge which connects New Jersey with New York.

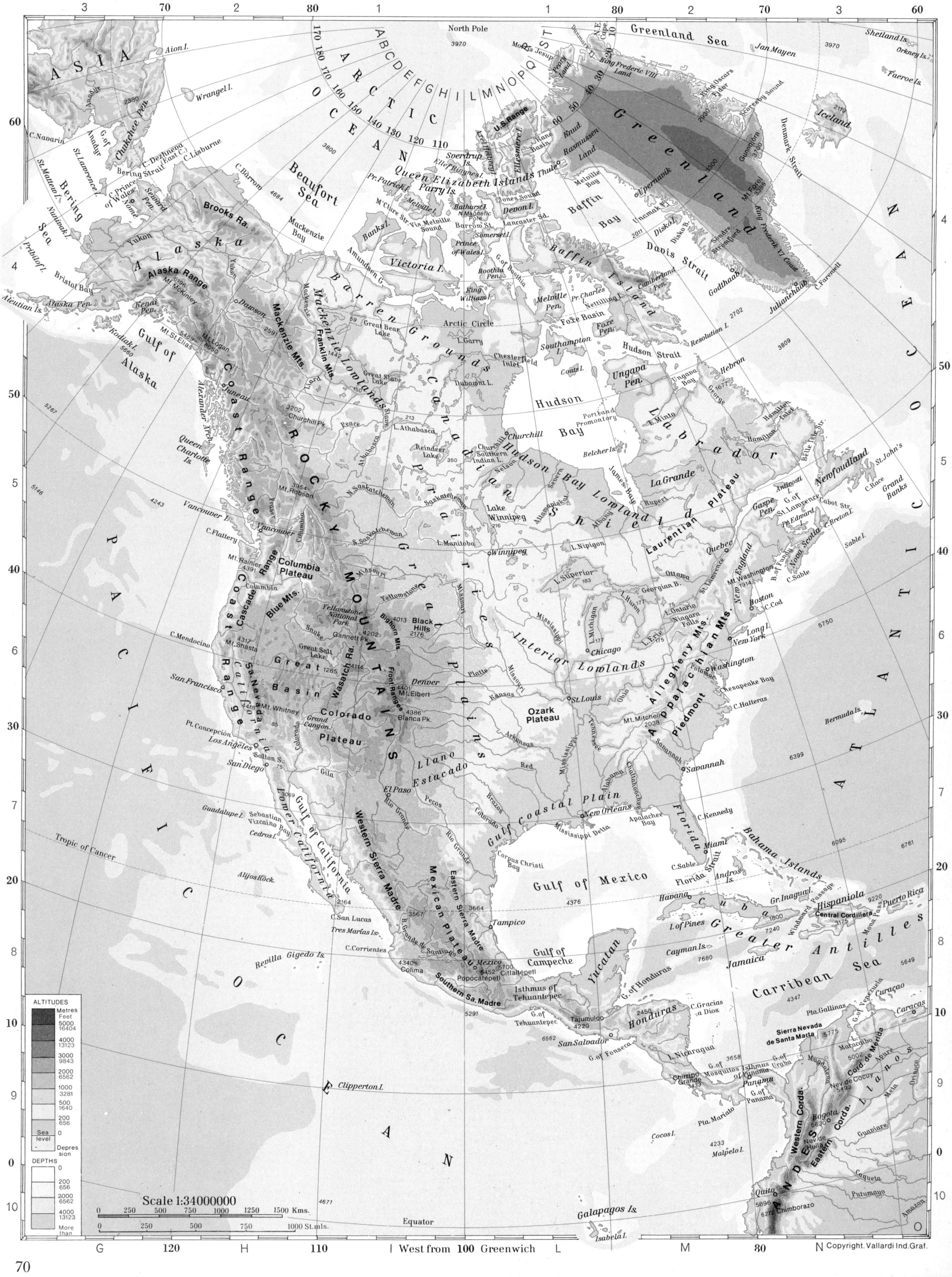

ASIA

ARCTIC OCEAN

Beaufort Sea

Bering Sea

Greenland Sea
Greenland
Iceland
Jan Mayen
Shetland Is.
Orkney Is.
Faeroe Is.

North Pole
Arctic Circle

Queen Elizabeth Islands
Parry Is.
Victoria I.
Banks I.
Baffin Island
Baffin Bay
Davis Strait

Brooks Ra.
Alaska
Alaska Range
Mt. McKinley
Mackenzie Mts.
Franklin Mts.

Barren Grounds
Canadian Shield
Prairies
Great Plains

Rocky Mountains
Coast Range
Cascade Range
Sierra Nevada
Great Basin
Colorado Plateau
Columbia Plateau

Gulf of Alaska
PACIFIC OCEAN

Hudson Bay
Hudson Strait
Labrador
Newfoundland
Laurentian Plateau
Interior Lowlands
Appalachian Mts.
Allegheny Mts.
Piedmont

L. Superior
L. Michigan
L. Huron
L. Erie
L. Ontario
Chicago
New York
Washington
Boston

Great Salt Lake
Denver
Mt. Elbert
St. Louis
Ozark Plateau

Los Angeles
San Diego
San Francisco

Llano Estacado
Gulf Coastal Plain
New Orleans
Mississippi Delta
Florida

Gulf of Mexico
Gulf of California
Lower California
Western Sierra Madre
Eastern Sierra Madre
Mexican Plateau
Mexico
Popocatepetl
Southern Sa. Madre
Isthmus of Tehuantepec

Tropic of Cancer

Bahama Islands
Cuba
Havana
Jamaica
Hispaniola
Puerto Rico
Greater Antilles
Caribbean Sea

Yucatan
Gulf of Campeche
Honduras
Nicaragua

ATLANTIC OCEAN

Bermuda Is.
Galapagos Is.
Clipperton I.
Cocos I.
Malpelo I.

Andes
Western Cord.
Eastern Cord.
Central Cordillera
Sierra Nevada de Santa Marta
Bogota
Quito
Chimborazo
Caracas

Equator

ALTITUDES
Metres Feet
5000 16404
4000 13123
3000 9843
2000 6562
1000 3281
500 1640
200 656
Sea level 0
Depression

DEPTHS
0
200 656
2000 6562
4000 13123
More than

Scale 1:34000000
0 250 500 750 1000 1250 1500 Kms.
0 250 500 750 1000 St.mls.

West from 100 Greenwich

Copyright. Vallardi Ind. Graf.

70

U.S.S.R.

ARCTIC OCEAN

North Pole

Wrangel I.
G. of Anadyr
Chukchee Pen.
C. Dezhneva (East C.)
Bering Strait
C. Pr. of Wales
Seward Pen.
Nome
Kotzebue
Pt. Barrow
C. Barrow

Beaufort Sea

Queen Elisabeth Islands
Pr. Patrik I. Parry Is.
Melville I. Bathurst I.
Banks I.
Viscount Melville Sound
Prince of Wales I.
Somerset I.
Lancaster Sound
Devon I.

Greenland (Den.)

Peary Land
King Frederik VIII Land
King Christian X Land
King Frederik VI Coast
Knud Rasmussen Land
Thule
Upernavik
Disko
Godhavn
Godthaab
Julianehaab
C. Farewell

Jan Mayen (Nor.)
Shetland Is.
Orkney Is.
Faeroe Is. (Den.)
ICELAND
Reykjavik
Denmark Strait
Scoresby Sound

Bering Sea
St. Lawrence I.
Nunivak I.
Pribilof I.
Aleutian Is.
Alaska Peninsula
Kodiak I.
Anchorage
Mt. McKinley
Gulf of Alaska
Alexander Arch.
Seward
Fairbanks
Yukon
Alaska (U.S.A.)
Fort Yukon
Dawson
Mt. Logan 6050
Whitehorse
Skagway
Juneau
Yukon Territory

Prince of Wales I.
Boothia Pen.
G. of Boothia
Melville Pen.
Coppermine
Great Bear Lake
Port Radium
Fort Norman
Norman Wells
Mackenzie
Aklavik
Great Slave Lake
Fort Simpson
Fort Resolution
L. Athabasca
Uranium City

Baffin Bay
Baffin Island
Foxe Basin
Foxe Pen.
Southampton I.
Fore Basin
Hudson Strait
Resolution I.
Davis Strait

Northwest Territories
Arctic Circle

CANADA

British Columbia
Queen Charlotte I.
Pr. Rupert
Prince George
Dawson Creek
Peace
Athabasca
Edmonton
Alberta
Calgary
Lethbridge
Medicine Hat
Saskatchewan
Saskatoon
Prince Albert
Regina
Manitoba
Reindeer L.
Churchill
L. Winnipeg
Winnipeg

Hudson Bay
Port Nelson
Churchill
Belcher I.
Fort George
Port Harrison
Fort Chimo
Ungava Bay
Ungava Pen.
Hebron
Labrador
Schefferville
Battle Harbour
Newfoundland
Sept Iles
Anticosti I.
Gaspé
G. of St. Lawrence
St. John's
Newfoundland I.
Cabot Str.
St. Pierre & Miquelon (Fr.)
Sydney
Cape Breton I.
New Brunswick
Charlottetown
Pr. Edward I.
Halifax

Vancouver I.
Vancouver
Victoria
SEATTLE
Spokane
Tacoma
Portland
Salem
Oregon
Medford
C. Mendocino
Idaho
Boise
Butte
Montana
North Dakota
Bismarck
Missouri
South Dakota
Wyoming
Nebraska
Cheyenne
Great Salt Lake
Ogden
Salt Lake City
Utah
Nevada
Sacramento
Oakland
SAN FRANCISCO
Fresno
California
Mt. Whitney 4418
Las Vegas
LOS ANGELES
Long Beach
SAN DIEGO
Mexicali
Arizona
Phoenix
Tucson
El Paso
Colorado
Denver
Santa Fe
Albuquerque
New Mexico
Amarillo
Trinidad
Pueblo

UNITED STATES

Minnesota
St. Paul
Minneapolis
Wisconsin
Iowa
Des Moines
Omaha
Kansas
Kansas City
Wichita
Oklahoma
Oklahoma City
Tulsa
Missouri
St. Louis
Fort Worth
DALLAS
Texas
Austin
San Antonio
Corpus Christi
Laredo
Galveston
HOUSTON
Rio Grande

L. Superior
Duluth
Fort William
L. Nipigon
Ontario
Sudbury
Cochrane
Moosonee
North Bay
Ottawa
MONTREAL
Quebec
Chicoutimi
Maine
Portland
BOSTON
C. Cod
New Haven
NEW YORK
Albany
New York
PHILADELPHIA
BALTIMORE
WASHINGTON
Richmond
Virginia
North Carolina
C. Hatteras
Charlotte
South Carolina
Charleston
Georgia
Atlanta
Montgomery
Savannah
Jacksonville
Alabama
Mississippi
Jackson
Baton Rouge
Louisiana
NEW ORLEANS
Tampa
Miami
Florida
Key West

Michigan
L. Huron
L. Michigan
MILWAUKEE
CHICAGO
Indiana
Indianapolis
Illinois
L. Erie
DETROIT
Toledo
Ohio
CLEVELAND
Columbus
Cincinnati
PITTSBURGH
Kentucky
Nashville
Tennessee
Memphis
Little Rock
Arkansas
L. Ontario
TORONTO
BUFFALO

Bermuda (Br.)

MEXICO
Gulf of California
Lower California
Guadalupe I. (Mex.)
Cedros I.
Revilla Gigedo Is. (Mex.)
Hermosillo
Guaymas
Chihuahua
Ciudad Juarez
Torreon
Durango
La Paz
Mazatlán
Culiacan
Saltillo
MONTERREY
Nuevo Laredo
San Luis Potosi
Tampico
Leon
GUADALAJARA
Manzanillo
MEXICO
Puebla
Veracruz
Coatzacoalcos
Acapulco
Oaxaca
Tehuantepec
G. of Tehuantepec
Mérida
Campeche
G. of Campeche
Yucatan Str.

Gulf of Mexico

HAVANA
Pinar del Rio
Sta. Clara
CUBA
Camagüey
Santiago de Cuba
Guantanamo
I. of Pines
Cayman Is. (Br.)
JAMAICA
Kingston
HAITI
Port au Prince
DOMINICAN
Santo Domingo
San Juan
Puerto Rico (U.S.A.)
Virgin Is.
Gr. Bahama I.
Gt. Abaco I.
Nassau
Eleuthera I.
S. Salvador or Watlings I.
Long I.
Gt. Inagua I.

Bahamas

Caribbean Sea

British Honduras
Belize
GUATEMALA
Guatemala
San Salvador
EL SALVADOR
HONDURAS
Tegucigalpa
NICARAGUA
Managua
L. Nicaragua
Bluefields
COSTA RICA
San Jose
Colon
PANAMA
Panama
Panama Canal Zone
Las Tablas

Cocos I. (Cost.)

Clipperton (Fr.)

PACIFIC OCEAN

Malpelo I. (Col.)

VENEZUELA
CARACAS
Maracaibo
Barranquilla
Cartagena
Barquisimeto
Bucaramanga
S. Fernando de Ap.
COLOMBIA
BOGOTA
Medellin
Manizales
Cali
Ibagué
Pasto
Quito
ECUADOR
Guayaquil
Galapagos Is. (Ec.)
Isabela
PERU
Iquitos
BRAZIL

ATLANTIC OCEAN

Tropic of Cancer

Equator

West from 100 Greenwich

Scale 1:34 000 000

0 250 500 750 1000 1250 1500 Kms.
0 250 500 750 1000 St. mis.

Copyright: Vallardi Ind. Graf.

THE UNITED STATES AND CANADA: AGRICULTURAL REGIONS

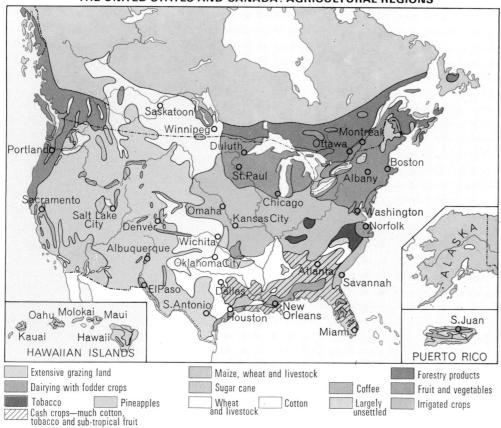

Extensive grazing land
Dairying with fodder crops
Tobacco
Pineapples
Cash crops—much cotton, tobacco and sub-tropical fruit
Maize, wheat and livestock
Sugar cane
Wheat and livestock
Cotton
Forestry products
Coffee
Fruit and vegetables
Largely unsettled
Irrigated crops

HAWAIIAN ISLANDS

PUERTO RICO

THE ST. LAWRENCE SEAWAY

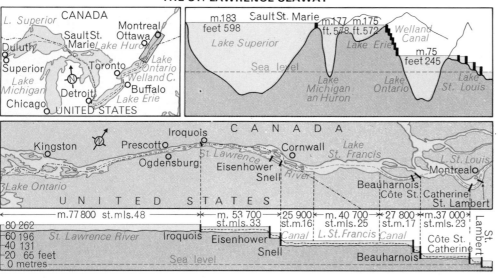

UNITED STATES – CANADA: MINERALS AND INDUSTRIAL AREAS

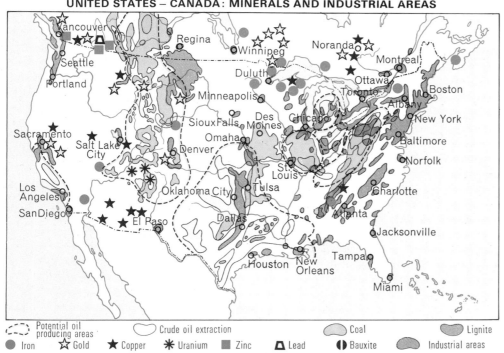

Potential oil producing areas
Crude oil extraction
Coal
Lignite
Iron
Gold
Copper
Uranium
Zinc
Lead
Bauxite
Industrial areas

Mexico and claimed the whole of the Mississippi valley for France, naming it Louisiana after their king, Louis XIV.

The British established settlements in Massachusetts and Virginia on the east coast and from these were to grow up the original thirteen states of the Union.

Friction between Britain and France led to the Indian War in 1754 and when France was defeated she surrendered her Canadian territories to Britain.

With the end of French power in North America, the colonials began to resent Britain's restrictions and in 1776 the American Revolution broke out. On gaining independence the thirteen states established a central government. The area within the Union soon grew westwards, especially with the purchase of the French Mississippi lands from Napoleon in 1803.

In this way much of the North American continent developed into the three major countries which we know today—Canada, the United States and Mexico. And there are also a number of small independent republics in Central America and a few countries with European ties—British, French or Dutch.

Great mountain ranges run down both coasts of the continent. On the west, from Alaska in the extreme north to the Panama Canal in the south run the American cordilleras which include the famous Rocky Mountains. Within these mountain ranges there are a series of basins which are very dry and barren. The whole of the area is renowned for its attractive scenery, much of which is preserved as National Parks, which are favourite holiday resorts. In the east, from the Gulf of St. Lawrence to the Gulf of Mexico, are smaller and lower mountain ranges, the most notable of which are the Appalachians.

Between these two mountain blocks are the lowlands. To the north is the geologically ancient Canadian Shield which drains to the Hudson Bay and to the south are the younger Mississippi Lowlands draining to the Gulf of Mexico.

About four fifths of North America's rivers drain to the Atlantic or Arctic Oceans or Caribbean Sea. The River Colorado is a notable exception flowing to the Pacific, cutting its path through the Grand Canyon, one of the marvels of nature.

The plains of the interior are almost entirely drained southwards by the Mississippi, the Missouri and their tributaries. And in the far north, the Arctic plains have the Mackenzie and Nelson as their major rivers. The rivers flowing directly to the Atlantic are generally shorter but the Hudson and St. Lawrence are of great importance economically because they are linked by canals to the Great Lakes—the heart of North America's industrial and agricultural area—and are major export routes.

The Great Lakes—Superior, Huron, Erie and Ontario—lie on the border between the United States and Canada and the fifth lake—Michigan—is entirely in the United States. North America's other important lakes are Winnipeg, Great Bear, Great Slave and Athabaska, all of them in Canada.

The coldest part of the continent is the north of Canada and Alaska which is thinly inhabited, mainly by fishermen, hunters and miners.

Further south there are huge forests stretching

across the continent where pine, larch and fir trees grow. Fur trappers and lumberjacks work here where the winters are bitterly cold, but the summers are longer and warmer than in the extreme north.

In the summer months, when there is no lumbering work, many of the lumberjacks move south to the prairies where they can find work, helping with the harvesting of wheat and barley.

Between Lakes Erie and Ontario, partly in Canada and partly in the United States, are the famous Niagara Falls. They are more than 50 metres (160ft.) high and consist of the American Falls, 305 metres (1,000ft.) wide and the Canadian, or Horseshoe Falls, 762 metres (2,500ft.) wide, separated by Goat Island. The falls have been harnessed for hydro-electric power, used in factories and homes nearby. Hydro-electric power is also produced on many of the other rivers of North America.

The vast central lowlands of North America are the agricultural heart of the continent. The lowest levels flank the main channel of the south-flowing Mississippi; further west the great plains rise in a series of steps, reaching a height of over 1,375 metres (4,500ft.) where the foothills

of the Rockies begin. Within this area, the lowest areas from north to south are the centres of dairying, wheat and maize production, with much animal rearing for meat. Further west the great plains are the centre of huge cattle ranches. In much of this area as a whole, the landscape is dominated by a pattern of rectangular fields.

Some southern states of the U.S.A. are important cotton and tobacco growing areas. Originally these were produced on large plantations which were worked by negro slaves. But, the American Civil War between the northern and southern states led to the emancipation of the negroes in 1863. Today, the southern states are still important for cotton, tobacco, fruit and other farm products, but industry is now growing steadily.

Hawaii and Alaska are the latest states to be admitted to the Union, being the 49th and 50th respectively. Alaska formerly belonged to Russia but was sold to the United States in 1867. It became famous when gold was discovered there and is now being exploited for oil. There is a highway through Canada linking Alaska with the United States.

Whilst the mountain areas of the west are largely of little agricultural use, except in valleys, the areas fringing

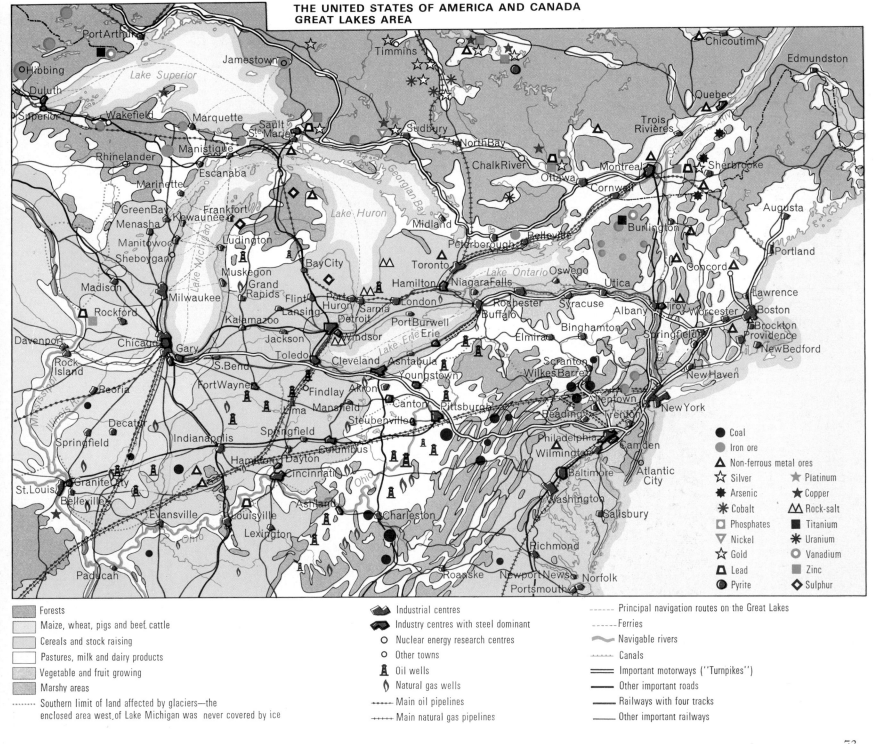

THE UNITED STATES OF AMERICA AND CANADA GREAT LAKES AREA

●	Coal
●	Iron ore
△	Non-ferrous metal ores
☆	Silver
✳	Arsenic
✳	Cobalt
▢	Phosphates
▽	Nickel
☆	Gold
△	Lead
●	Pyrite
★	Platinum
★	Copper
⋀	Rock-salt
■	Titanium
✳	Uranium
○	Vanadium
■	Zinc
◇	Sulphur

Forests
Maize, wheat, pigs and beef cattle
Cereals and stock raising
Pastures, milk and dairy products
Vegetable and fruit growing
Marshy areas

Southern limit of land affected by glaciers—the enclosed area west of Lake Michigan was never covered by ice

Industrial centres
Industry centres with steel dominant
○ Nuclear energy research centres
○ Other towns
Oil wells
Natural gas wells
Main oil pipelines
Main natural gas pipelines

Principal navigation routes on the Great Lakes
Ferries
Navigable rivers
Canals
Important motorways ("Turnpikes")
Other important roads
Railways with four tracks
Other important railways

CENTRAL AMERICA: ECONOMY

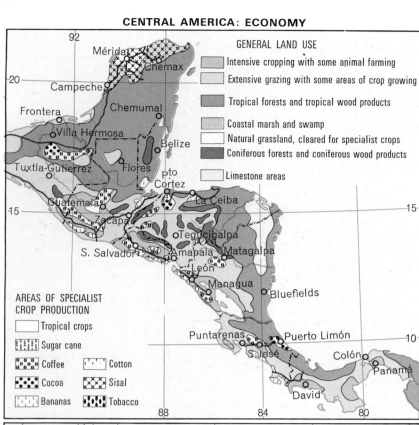

GENERAL LAND USE

Intensive cropping with some animal farming

Extensive grazing with some areas of crop growing

Tropical forests and tropical wood products

Coastal marsh and swamp

Natural grassland, cleared for specialist crops

Coniferous forests and coniferous wood products

Limestone areas

AREAS OF SPECIALIST CROP PRODUCTION

Tropical crops

Sugar cane

Coffee

Cotton

Cocoa

Sisal

Bananas

Tobacco

ECONOMIC RELATIONS BETWEEN CENTRAL AMERICA AND THE U.S.A.

Imports from the U.S.A.	Exports to the U.S.A.	
		UNITED STATES
65	67	CUBA / REP. DOMINICA
69,2	53,1	HAITI
65,2	49,3	
79,3	73,9	MEXICO
64	70	
67,6	63,7	GUATEMALA
56,9	64,4	HONDURAS
65	37,5	EL SALVADOR / NICARAGUA
59,5	53,6	COSTA RICA
59	86	PANAMA

Percentage of the total value of imports and exports

the Pacific have been turned to great use during the twentieth century. In British Columbia there are some of the finest stands of coniferous timber in the world and these are now the basis of a great timber and paper industry. Further south, fruit farming, temperate in the north and Mediterranean in California, dominate. California is also the most important industrial area on the Pacific fringe and today it is the most populous state in the U.S.A.

Further south, in Mexico, the land becomes very dry and much of it is desert. But, along the east coast, tropical fruits and sugar cane are grown.

North America's huge mineral wealth has played an important part in its development. There are great coal basins in the central states of the U.S.A. and in the Canadian provinces of Alberta and Saskatchewan which produce about one fifth of the world's supply. In addition to coal, North America also has about one fifth of the world's iron ore, one third of the copper and one fifth of the lead. There are also large deposits of sulphur, aluminium, gold and other metals. Large manufacturing industries have grown up in the north-east, originally because of the nearby deposits of coal and iron. Pittsburgh has some of the oldest steel mills of North America, and is still a very important centre; today, other locations on the Atlantic coast and the Great Lakes are growing more rapidly.

The largest city and chief port of the United States is New York. It is the leading commercial, financial and cultural centre of the United States and its port handles more than 40% of U.S. foreign trade. But Washington, in the District of Columbia, is the capital of the U.S.A. This beautiful city houses the Capitol where the U.S. Congress (parliament) sits and the White House, the official residence of the President of the U.S.A.

In Canada, Montreal is the largest city. This large port on the St. Lawrence has, in the past, handled much of Canada's Atlantic trade, during those months when the St. Lawrence River is not frozen. However, the recently completed St. Lawrence Seaway now makes it possible for large vessels to bypass the rapids on the river and sail all the way from the Atlantic into the Great Lakes.

Like the U.S.A., Canada is a Federation of States and therefore much of its government tends to be regional rather than central. Thus its capital city is not the largest one, but Ottawa, is situated in an important position between the two major interests in Canada—the French to the east and the British to the west.

North America probably has one of the most mixed populations in the world. In Alaska, most of the inhabitants are of Eskimo origin as they are too in the Yukon and most of the Northern Provinces. In Canada, the population is mostly a mixture of French and English settlers and Quebec, in particular, is pressing to be reunited with France.

PROPORTION OF RACES IN CENTRAL AMERICAN POPULATION

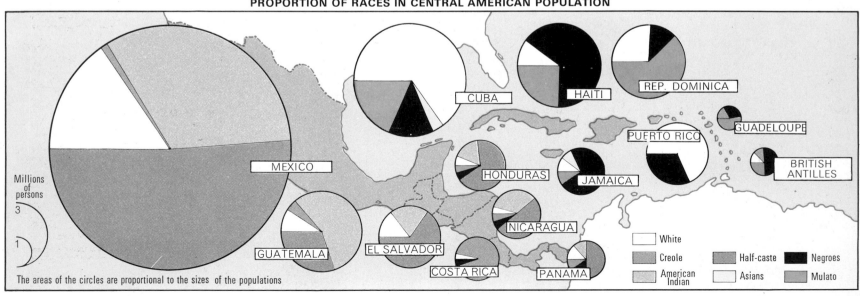

Millions of persons

The areas of the circles are proportional to the sizes of the populations

White

Creole

American Indian

Half-caste

Asians

Negroes

Mulato

The United States has traditionally been a country of immigration and between 1820 and 1956 some ten million British, seven million central Europeans, six and a half million Germans, five million Italians and one million Orientals came to settle in the country.

For many years after their emancipation, the negroes remained in the country districts where, for the most part, they continued to work on the land. Today, however, more than two-thirds of the negroes living in the United States live and work in the big cities. In addition, during the last ten years, many Puerto Ricans have left their overcrowded and relatively poor island to work in New York and other large cities.

The American Indians, the original inhabitants of the North American continent, are today one of the smallest minority groups. When Columbus landed in America, it was estimated that there were four million Indians, or Red Skins, as they were called, living there. Anthropologists believe that these tribes of people originated in Asia and that they crossed over to North America by way of the Bering Strait. Today, largely because of fighting with the settlers who were claiming their lands and through the diseases brought by these settlers, the numbers of these proud people has been seriously reduced and they are not believed to number more than half a million. Only about 15% of them live in towns; the remainder live on some 200 reservations, most of them on the west of the Mississippi. Although their standard of living tends to be low, the discovery of oil, uranium and certain other metallic ores on their reservations has brought considerable wealth.

The inhabitants of Mexico and Central America are mainly of Spanish origin and the West Indian islands are peopled by negroes, the descendants of the slaves brought there to work on the plantations.

In less than 200 years since its discovery, the continent of North America has made tremendous strides forward in commerce, industry, agriculture and culture. The United States in particular is an international, wealthy power playing a major role in world affairs.

Bermuda. **This island's pleasant climate and proximity to the United States of America makes it a popular luxury tourist centre.**

BAHAMA ISLANDS

The Bahamas are a large group of islands, reefs and cays stretching some 805 km. (500 miles) south-eastward from the coast of Florida. The islands are a British dependent territory which have internal self-government. Of the 700 islands in the group, only thirty are inhabited. Exports include vegetables, citrus fruits, cement, rum and fish. The U.S.A., Britain and Canada are leading trading partners. The sub-tropical climate attracts tourists and that industry is highly developed, catering especially for Americans. Nassau, the capital, is the leading tourist resort and is located on New Providence Island. The other most important islands are Grand Bahama, Abaco, Eleuthera and Andros. Over 80% of the population are negroes or half-castes, descendants of the slaves. *Capital: Nassau. Population: 142,000. Land area: 13,955 sq. km. (5,390 sq. miles).*

Canada. **The Algonquin Provincial Park in Ontario. Between these huge pine trees are the cabins where the lumberjacks live.**

BARBADOS

Barbados is the most easterly of the West Indian islands. It was taken by Britain and remained a colony until full internal self-government was granted in 1961. It is a member of the Commonwealth. The island is formed by coral limestones and volcanic rocks. Sugar cane is the most important crop from which sugar, rum and molasses are produced. Sugar exports amount to 155,000 tons a year. Sweet potatoes are also grown and there are coastal and deep sea fisheries. Bridgetown is an important port with a new deep water harbour with a special berth for bulk sugar handling. *Capital: Bridgetown. Population: 245,000. Land area: 430 sq. km. (166 sq. miles).*

BERMUDA

Bermuda is a British dependent territory, and a member of the Commonwealth. It consists of about 300 small coral islands, of which 20 are inhabited. The islands are 1,290 km. (800 miles) east of the U.S.A. The population, which is two thirds negro, lives largely by the tourist trade. Necessary imports are largely paid for by tourist earnings. The harbour at St. George was used as a privateer and blockade-running base in the 1812 war and the American Civil War. It was a naval base in the Second World War. The islands have been owned by Britain since 1684 but some land has been let to the U.S.A. *Capital: Hamilton. Population: 49,000. Land area: 52 sq. km. (20 sq. miles).*

CANADA

Canada is a federal union of ten provinces within the Commonwealth, occupying the north of the American continent. It is the second largest country in the world, yet has a comparatively small population. Wheat is a major crop on the prairies; fruit-growing, fishing and cattle rearing are also important. Canada has huge mineral resources; oil, copper, nickel, iron ore, zinc and asbestos are most valuable. Timber, pulp and newsprint are also highly important. Canada plays an important role in international trade, mainly in raw or semi-processed materials. Her chief customers are the U.S.A. and Great Britain. About 30% of the population are French-speaking Roman Catholics. English and French are official languages. *Capital: Ottawa. Population: 20 million. Principal river: St. Lawrence. Land area: 10.1 million sq. km. (3.9 million sq. miles).*

CAYMAN, TURKS and CAICOS ISLANDS

These two groups of islands were part of the independent West Indies Federation between 1958 and 1962; they then returned to the status of dependent territories within the Commonwealth. The Cayman Islands are some 320 km. (200 miles) north west of Jamaica. Fishing, rope making and tourism are the main occupations. *Capital: Georgetown (on the island of Grand Cayman). Population: 9,000. Land area: 259 sq. km. (100 sq. miles).* The Turks and Caicos Islands lie north of the Dominican Republic. Salt is the most important product. *Capital: Grand Turk. Population: 5,300. Land area: 430 sq. km. (166 sq. miles).*

COSTA RICA

Costa Rica (meaning Rich Coast) is an independent republic of Central America. It is a wholly agricultural area and high-quality coffee, bananas, cocoa, hemp, maize, potatoes, rice and sugar cane are all important. Cattle raising is increasing. Costa Rica was a Spanish dominion from 1530-1821 when she gained independence. Since that time she has established a tradition of peaceful, democratic government. Most Costa Ricans are Roman Catholics (of Spanish descent). Education is compulsory and the literacy rate is the highest in Latin America. *Capital: San José. Population: 1.5 million. Land area: 50,882 sq. km. (19,653 sq. miles).*

Canada. Niagara, an aerial view of the Canadian Falls which are separated from the American Falls by Goat Island.

Cuba. **These shady colonnades are a reminder that this island was influenced by Spanish styles in architecture as a result of its long association with that country.**

CUBA

Cuba is a Caribbean island republic, situated at the entrance to the Gulf of Mexico. Sugar is the major crop and accounts for 80% of her exports. Other agricultural products include bananas, rice, coffee, cocoa, maize, cotton and tobacco. Mineral resources include copper, nickel, iron ore and chromite. Cuba was discovered by Columbus in 1492 and remained a Spanish possession until 1898. An independent republic was established by 1902 and until 1959 the country was closely related economically to the U.S.A. In 1959 the constitution was suspended when Fidel Castro seized control; relations with the U.S.A. were broken off and assistance was sought from the U.S.S.R. and other communist countries. *Capital: Havana. Population: 7.9 million. Land area: 120,900 sq. km. (46,700 sq. miles).*

DOMINICAN REPUBLIC

The Dominican Republic occupies the eastern two-thirds of the island of Hispaniola. Sugar is the main crop but coffee, cocoa, bananas, tobacco, rice and livestock are also important. Mineral deposits include iron ore, bauxite and gold but production is erratic. There is some light industry, especially rum, glass, matches, paper and rope. The area was discovered by Columbus in 1492 and was under Spanish control almost continuously until it became independent in 1844. It was occupied by U.S. marines between 1916 and 1924. Again, in 1965, the U.S.A. helped to restore constitutional government after a military coup. *Capital: Santo Domingo. Population: 3.5 million. Land area: 48,700 sq. km. (18,811 sq. miles).*

EL SALVADOR

El Salvador is the smallest and most densely populated of the Central American republics. It is crossed by two volcanic ranges and, as a result of past eruptions, the soil is very fertile. Coffee, sugar, rice and tobacco are grown. Coffee accounts for half the value of the country's exports. In 1950 work started on a hydro-electric dam on the Lempa river to provide power for various light industries. The population is of mixed white and Indian descent and more than half is illiterate although educational facilities are improving. Since 1841 the republic has had a violent and turbulent history of revolutions and dictatorships. *Capital: San Salvador. Population: 3 million. Land area: 21,385 sq. km. (8,260 sq. miles).*

GUADELOUPE

Guadeloupe itself comprises two West Indian islands in the Lesser Antilles, and has five smaller dependent islands. Colonised by France in 1635, the islands have been an overseas department since 1946. The eastern island, Grand Terre, is the smallest and very flat but with a fine harbour. The western island, Guadeloupe proper or Basse Terre, is dominated by Soufriere, a volcano which last erupted in 1797 and 1836. Arable land covers about one third of the islands. The principal crop is sugar cane, which is used in the making of rum. Bananas, pineapples, coffee, cocoa, vanilla and cotton are also grown. Trade is chiefly with France. *Capital: Basse Terre. Population: 316,000. Land area: 1,700 sq. km. (657 sq. miles).*

Canada. **Snow-covered peaks in British Columbia, with a glaciated valley floor now occupied by lakes and extensive stands of coniferous forest.**

New York. **The Empire State Building, the tallest structure in the world, is one of many skyscrapers in down town Manhattan.**

GUATEMALA

Guatemala is a republic in Central America. It was under Spanish control until 1821 when it gained independence. Its chief products are coffee and bananas. 70% of its exports go to the U.S.A. The country has had a turbulent history and a long series of dictators. The population comprises 60% Indians and the remainder are mestizos and whites. *Capital: Guatemala City. Population: 4.72 million. Land area: 108,889 sq. km. (42,042 sq. miles).*

HAITI

Haiti is an island republic of the West Indies occupying the western third of the island of Hispaniola. It was once the most prosperous of the French colonies but is now densely populated and underdeveloped. Farming is largely subsistence, although there is a growing commercial side. Coffee, sugar and sisal are exported. Bauxite and copper are the leading minerals. Development plans are being prepared with overseas aid. It is the only French speaking republic in all America. *Capital: Port-au-Prince. Population: 4.5 million. Land area: 27,700 sq. km. (10,700 sq. miles).*

HONDURAS

Honduras has been an independent republic in Central America since 1838. It borders on the Caribbean Sea and the Pacific Ocean. Bananas, the chief export crop, are grown in plantations along the Caribbean coast. Other products include coffee, coconuts, rice and livestock. Gold, silver and lead are mined and exported. Most of the population is of mixed Spanish and Indian blood. Less than half the adults are literate. *Capital: Tegucigalpa. Population: 2.4 million. Land area: 111,915 sq. km. (43,227 sq. miles).*

BRITISH HONDURAS

British Honduras is a British colony in Central America, facing the Caribbean. This tropical area is very dependent on its forest products—cedar, mahogany, pine and rosewood. Citrus fruits and bananas are grown and chicle, the raw material for chewing gum, is collected. Belize, the capital, was destroyed by a hurricane in 1961; a new inland site has been selected, and building started in 1967. English is the official language but Spanish is widely used. *Capital: Belize. Population: 115,000. Land area: 22,964 sq. km. (8,870 sq. miles).*

JAMAICA

Jamaica is a Caribbean island within the Commonwealth, independent since 1962. Sugar cane and bananas are the principal crops. Cocoa, coconuts, coffee, ginger, pimentoes and tobacco are also grown. Jamaica also produces and exports large quantities of bauxite (aluminium ore). Food processing and distilling are the major industries. The island is a popular holiday resort. Kingston, the capital, has a large land-locked harbour. The English-speaking population is 95% coloured. *Capital: Kingston. Population: 1·6 million. Land area: 11,420 sq. km. (4,411 sq. miles).*

LEEWARD and WINDWARD ISLANDS

These islands are in the S.E. Caribbean; many of them are now members of the West Indies Associated States and are in the Commonwealth. Between 1958 and 1962 they were members of the independent West Indies Federation, but when Jamaica and Trinidad left that union these smaller islands returned to the status of British dependencies. These islands are largely agricultural. Sugar cane and citrus fruits are the main crops. Each island has its own capital. *Population: 415,000. Land area: 2,395 sq. km. (925 sq. miles).*

Central America. **This church is typical of the architecture of the period of Spanish colonisation.**

MARTINIQUE

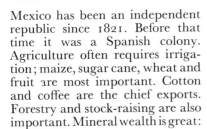

Martinique is a West Indian island; it is an overseas department of France. Less than one third of the area is arable land and used for sugar cane and bananas. Cocoa, citrus fruits and pineapples are also grown. Forests produce rosewood, mahogany and bamboo. Bananas, sugar, rum and pineapples are exported. The population consists mainly of negroes descended from the slaves brought from West Africa to work on the plantations. *Capital: Fort-de-France. Population: 320,000. Land area: 1,087 sq. km. (420 sq. miles).*

MEXICO

Mexico has been an independent republic since 1821. Before that time it was a Spanish colony. Agriculture often requires irrigation; maize, sugar cane, wheat and fruit are most important. Cotton and coffee are the chief exports. Forestry and stock-raising are also important. Mineral wealth is great: one fifth of the world's silver comes from Mexico; lead, zinc, copper and graphite are also valuable. Education is free and compulsory. Religion is Roman Catholic. *Capital: Mexico City. Population: 45.7 million. Principal river: Rio Grande. Land area: 1,971,524 sq. km. (761,500 sq. miles).*

NETHERLANDS ANTILLES

The Netherlands Antilles comprise the islands of Curacao, Aruba, Bonair and three much smaller islets in the Windward group. They are a Dutch overseas possession and have been internally autonomous since 1954. Only Curacao and Aruba are of any great economic significance; on them live over 90% of the total population. Their chief occupation is refining oil and associated activities, the oil being brought in from Venezuela, and then sent on to N. America and Europe. Each island has its own capital. *Population: 210,000. Land area: 1,010 sq. km. (390 sq. miles).*

NICARAGUA

Nicaragua is the most thinly populated of the Central American republics. It is predominantly agricultural, exporting coffee, cotton, maize, rice, sugar, bananas and beans. Gold and silver are mined and exported. Most of the people are of mixed Spanish and Indian descent and their language is Spanish. Political difficulties have hindered the country's development but progress is now more rapid under various development schemes. *Capital: Managua. Population: 1.7 million. Land area: 147,573 sq. km. (57,000 sq. miles).*

PANAMA

Panama has been an independent republic since 1903, situated between Colombia and Costa Rica. It is cut in two by the ten mile wide Canal Zone. Bananas, cereals, cocoa, coconuts, rubber and mahogany are the chief crops, many of which are exported. Rice is grown for domestic consumption. The chief source of employment is the Panama Canal. The population comprises two thirds mestizos (of mixed Spanish and Indian blood) and about 15% negroes from the West Indies. *Capital: Panama City. Population: 1.3 million. Land area: 75,622 sq. km. (29,209 sq. miles).*

PANAMA CANAL ZONE

The Panama Canal Zone is a ten-mile strip of land, bordering the Panama Canal. The land is leased in perpetuity to the U.S.A. by the Republic of Panama. The canal, which joins the Atlantic and Pacific Oceans, was built 1904-1914 and is operated for the benefit of shipping of all nations. The Canal is 51 miles long and the minimum depth is 41ft. The maximum height to which ships are raised in passage through the six locks is 85ft. Responsibility for defence lies with the U.S.A. but each country pays the same toll. *Capital: Balboa. Population: 50,000. Land area: 1,678 sq. km. (648 sq. miles).*

These are the remains of a temple probably built by the Mayans, a race who occupied parts of what is today called Guatemala and Honduras. This impressive structure probably dates back to the fourth century A.D.

PUERTO RICO

The West Indies island of Puerto Rico is a U.S.A. outlying territory. Sugar is the chief crop but tobacco, cotton, coffee and fruit are also grown. Industry is developing rapidly. San Juan, the capital, is a popular winter resort for American tourists. Columbus landed on the island in 1493 and it became an important Spanish stronghold. In 1898 it was ceded to the U.S.A. and was granted self rule in all but foreign affairs in 1952. *Capital: San Juan. Population: 2.5 million. Land area: 8,893 sq. km. (3,435 sq. miles).*

ST. PIERRE and MIQUELON ISLANDS

St. Pierre and Miquelon are a group of eight islands to the south of Newfoundland. Miquelon (216 sq. km.) is the larger of the two major islands and yet has little over 600 inhabitants—it is almost all barren rock and so there is no farming. The smaller island of St. Pierre (26 sq. km.) contains the harbour and capital, St. Pierre, which is only 24 km. (15 miles) from Newfoundland and is ice-free throughout the year. The islands lie close to the Grand Bank and fishing is thus the main occupation. There are fish canning and drying industries and a small silver fox fur industry. The islands, which are an overseas territory of France, are inhabited by about 5,000 fishermen of Norman French descent. *Capital: St. Pierre. Population: 5,000. Land area: 243 sq. km. (94 sq. miles).*

UNITED STATES OF AMERICA

The United States of America is a Federal Republic of fifty states plus the Federal District of Columbia (Washington). They occupy almost half of the land area of the North American continent. All of the states are on the mainland with the exception of Hawaii which is the smallest and most recent to join. The United States stretches across the continent from the Atlantic to the Pacific and from the Canadian border in the north to Mexico in the south.

The United States is rich in mineral resources. She ranks amongst the world's greatest producers of lead, zinc, copper, coal, iron and other less common minerals. On this basis her great industrial strength rests. Most of the manufacturing industries of this great nation are to be found in the north-eastern towns, such as Chicago, Detroit, Cleveland, Baltimore, Philadelphia, Boston and New York.

The United States is also the world's leading producer of crude oil. This mainly comes from the states bordering the Gulf of Mexico, though the states of Kansas and Oklahoma are also important. From the same locations, much natural gas is also extracted.

The range of climates found in the U.S.A. is such that a very wide variety of agricultural products are found. On the Gulf of Mexico coast, citrus fruits are grown; elsewhere in the south-east, tobacco and cotton are the leading crops, though they are now grown in carefully controlled rotations. In the Central Lowlands, maize, wheat and dairying, together with pig farming, are most important. On the Atlantic fringes, market gardening (known locally as Truck Farming) is a major activity to feed the great populations of that area.

On the Great Plains of the west, cattle farming (ranching) is most important, and on the Pacific fringes fruit is grown—both Mediterranean and temperate types. Only in the mountains of the west is farming unimportant.

Today the United States has less than 10% of the world's population yet it produces more than half the world output of manufactured goods, and its inhabitants enjoy the highest material standards of living.

Two world wars and the influx of immigrants from Europe have spurred the U.S.A.'s achievements in all fields and she leads the world in industrial mechanisation and automation and in industrial and scientific research. She holds the distinction of being the first nation to put a man on the moon.

The United States of America is a federal republic, and not a unitary country. That means that although many political decisions are made for the whole country by the federal government in Washington, such as decisions on foreign affairs, other decisions are made by each state of the union by its own state government. Thus, each citizen of the U.S.A. will pay taxes to the federal government, for such things as space research and aid to developing countries, and also taxes to his state government for such things as local roads, schools and the state police force.

The federal constitution provides for the election of a President every four years. Any President may serve for two terms in office. The President is elected through an electoral college. Members of both houses of Congress (the Senate and the House of Representatives) are elected by popular vote. Since elections of some sort are held every other year, it can happen that a President finds that he is head of a country in whose Congress his party is in a minority. *Capital: Washington. Population: over 200 million. Highest point: Mt. McKinley, 6,194 metres (20,320ft.). Land area: 9,201,000 sq.km. (3,553,890 sq.miles).*

VIRGIN ISLANDS

The Virgin Islands of the U.S.A. are a group of about 50 tiny islands in the West Indies, to the east of Puerto Rico. They are almost entirely agricultural, though tourism is of growing importance. St. Thomas, St. John, St. Croix and many smaller islets were owned by Denmark from 1671 until they were sold to the United States in 1917. They were of value since they controlled a major sea route from the Atlantic Ocean to the then recently finished Panama Canal. Today they rank as an incorporated territory of the U.S.A. *Capital: Charlotte Amalie (St. Thomas Is.). Population: 40,000. Land area: 344 sq. km. (133 sq. miles).*

N.B. The Virgin Islands which belong to the United States are the western isles of the whole Virgin group. The islands to the east are part of the British dependency of the Leeward Is.

U.S.A. **A huge oil refinery on the shores of Delaware Bay.**

SOUTH AMERICA

South America is joined to North America by the narrow isthmus of Panama. It has an area of 18.1 million sq. km. or seven million square miles and extends further south than any other continent. At its most southerly point, Cape Horn, it is separated by only 1,050 km., or 650 miles, of sea, from Graham Land in Antarctica. Yet, about three quarters of the continent lies within the tropics.

Immediately south of the Isthmus of Pamana are a continuous chain of mountains, the Andes, which run parallel with the Pacific coast to the Tierra del Fuego in the extreme south. These mountains are sometimes referred to as the backbone of South America. They contain the highest peak in the western hemisphere, Aconcagua which is 6,959 metres (22,834ft.) high, and form a barrier between the Pacific coast and the interior and the Atlantic coast. There are few low passes for roads and railways. A number of active volcanoes lie within this range, such as Cotopaxi, and there are numerous high volcanic peaks which are no longer active. These mountains are part of the great "ring of fire" which encircles the Pacific Ocean, and thus the area is liable to earth tremors as well as volcanic eruptions.

Whilst much of central and eastern South America is lowland, there are three areas of very ancient upland into which the headwaters of the rivers have cut deep valleys.

In the north there are the Guiana Highlands rising to heights of 2,810 metres (9,219ft.); in the east, the Brazilian Highlands rise quite rapidly from the Atlantic coastal plains to heights of 2,884 metres (9,460ft.); in the extreme south-east there is the lower plateau area of the Patagonian cold desert.

The extensive lowlands of eastern and central South America are drained by three river systems. In the centre, the mighty River Amazon carries more water than any other system in the world. Its source is high up in the Andes, from which it flows some 6,275 km. (3,900 miles) through dense tropical rain forest, flowing out to the Atlantic in a huge delta. The river and its tributaries drain an area almost as large as the United States—7,042,000 sq. km. (2,720,000 sq. miles).

In the south is the huge river system which ends in the Rio de la Plata. This is a 320 km. (200 miles) long inlet of the Atlantic which is the combined estuaries of the Paraguay, Parana and Uruguay rivers. On this the busy ports of Montevideo and Buenos Aires are located.

To the north, the Orinoco river system drains the eastern and northern flanks of the Andes and the Guiana Highlands. The main stream is 2,750 km. (1,700 miles) long, and the system drains an area of some 1,035,000 sq. km. (400,000 sq. miles).

Since South America extends from the Equatorial region to latitude 50°S, and it has this major physical barrier, the Andes, in the west, it is not surprising that it has a wide range of climates and natural environments. In the Amazon basin, at Manaus, the average monthly temperature is always in excess of 26°C (79°F), and the annual rainfall totals 1,775 mm. (69.8in.). This is a true equatorial climate. On the Pacific fringe of central Chile, at Valparaiso, a true Mediterranean type climate is found—the summer (January) temperature is 19°C (67°F), the winter (July) temperature is 13°C (55°F) and the annual rainfall is 500 mm. (19.7in.). In the extreme south, Puntas Arenas has a more extreme cool temperature climate; much of the Argentine enjoys the warm temperate climate of an eastern region with a marked summer maximum in its rainfall; whilst much of southern Brazil and the extreme north coast of the continent enjoys a true tropical climate.

Parallel with this great range of climates is found a similar range of natural environments. Much of the Amazon Basin is a true equatorial forest. This is often

Continued on page 86

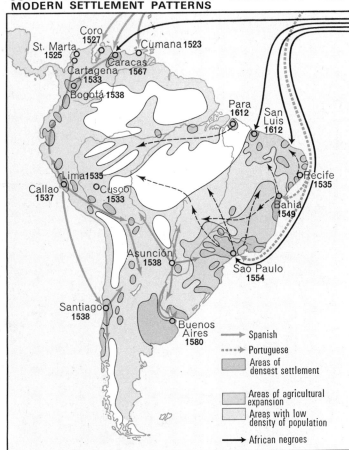

SOUTH AMERICA: POPULATION MIGRATIONS AND MODERN SETTLEMENT PATTERNS

Coro 1527
St. Marta 1525
Cumana 1523
Caracas 1567
Cartagena 1533
Bogotá 1538
Para 1612
San Luis 1612
Lima 1535
Recife 1535
Callao 1537
Cusco 1533
Bahia 1549
Asunción 1538
Sao Paulo 1554
Santiago 1538
Buenos Aires 1580

→ Spanish
┈┈→ Portuguese
▨ Areas of densest settlement
▨ Areas of agricultural expansion
▨ Areas with low density of population
→ African negroes

Brazil. **These buildings are part of the programme recently started to open up and exploit the interior of South America which is underdeveloped and very sparsely populated. The capital is being moved from Rio de Janeiro on the coast to Brasilia in the interior.**

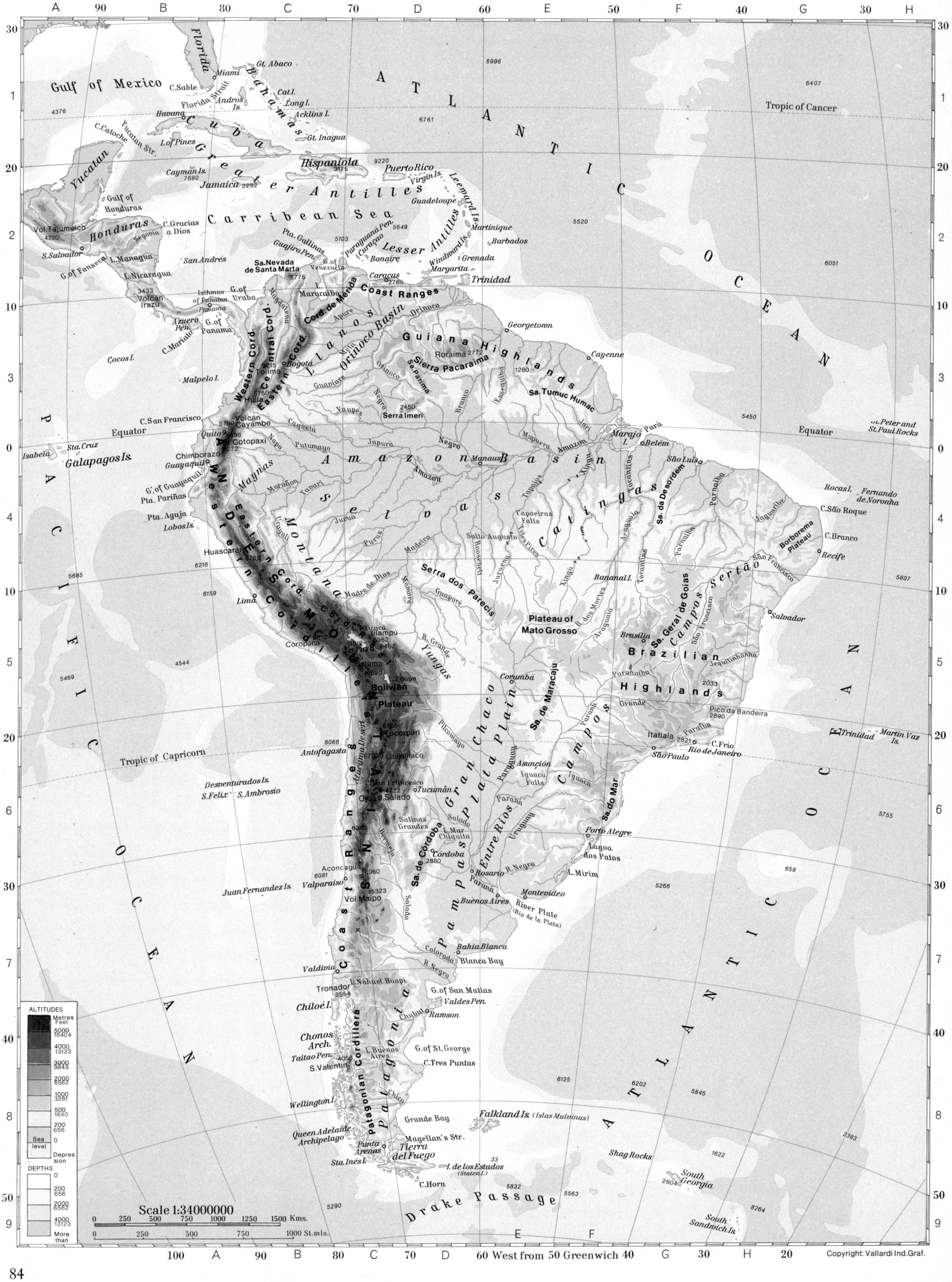

ATLANTIC OCEAN

PACIFIC OCEAN

Gulf of Mexico
Florida
Bahamas
Cuba
Greater Antilles
Hispaniola
Jamaica
Puerto Rico
Caribbean Sea
Lesser Antilles
Trinidad
Honduras
Yucatan
Gulf of Honduras

Tropic of Cancer
Equator
Tropic of Capricorn

Coast Ranges
Cord. de Mérida
Sa. Nevada de Santa Marta
Maracaibo
Llanos
Orinoco Basin
Guiana Highlands
Roraima 2772
Sierra Pacaraima
Sa. Tumuc Humac
Serra Imeri
Georgetown
Cayenne

Western Cord.
Central Cord.
Eastern Cord.
Bogotá
Tolima
Huila
Volcán Cayambe
Quito
Cotopaxi
Chimborazo
Guayaquil

Amazon Basin
Selvas
Manaus
Belém
Marajó I.
Pará

Huascarán
Lima
Montaña
Madre de Dios
Serra dos Parecis
Plateau of Mato Grosso

Catingas
São Luiz
Sertão
Campos
Brazilian Highlands
Borborema Plateau
Recife
Salvador

Western Cordillera
Eastern Cordillera
Illampú
Illimani
Yungas
Bolivian Plateau
Coropuni
Lake Titicaca

Gran Chaco
Plata Plain
Brasília
Sa. Geral de Goiás
Pico da Bandeira 2890

Antofagasta
Atacama Desert
Tucumán
Ojos del Salado
Salinas Grandes
Córdoba
Sa. de Córdoba
Aconcagua
Valparaíso
Vol. Maipo

Asunción
Iguaçu Falls
São Paulo
Rio de Janeiro
C. Frio
Porto Alegre
Lagoa dos Patos
L. Mirim
Rosario
Paraná
Uruguay
Montevideo
Buenos Aires
River Plate (Rio de la Plata)

Coastal Range
Bahía Blanca
Blanca Bay
R. Negro

Valdivia
Tronador
L. Nahuel Huapi
Chiloé I.
Chonos Arch.
Taitao Pen.
S. Valentín
Patagonian Cordillera
Patagonia
Wellington I.
Queen Adelaide Archipelago
Sta. Inés I.
Punta Arenas
Tierra del Fuego
Magellan's Str.
I. de los Estados (Staten I.)
C. Horn

Falkland Is. (Islas Malvinas)
Grande Bay
South Georgia
South Sandwich Is.
Shag Rocks
Drake Passage

Galápagos Is.
Juan Fernández Is.
Desventurados Is.
S. Félix
S. Ambrosio

ALTITUDES
Metres / Feet
5000 / 16404
4000 / 13123
3000 / 9843
2000 / 6562
1000 / 3281
500 / 1640
200 / 656
Sea level
Depression

DEPTHS
0
200 / 656
2000 / 6562
4000 / 13123
More than

Scale 1:34000000
0 250 500 750 1000 1250 1500 Kms.
0 250 500 750 1000 St.mis.

60 West from 50 Greenwich 40

Copyright: Vallardi Ind. Graf.

A 90 B 80 C 70 D 60 E 50 F 40 G 30 H

UNITED STATES

Tampa

Gulf of Mexico

Gr. Bahama I.
Gt. Abaco I.
Miami
Nassau
S. Salvador or Watling I.
Florida Str.
Bahama Is. (Br.)

ATLANTIC

Tropic of Cancer

HAVANA
Sta. Clara
CUBA
Mérida
I. of Pines
Camagüey
Guantanamo
Yucatan Str.
Santiago de C. HAITI
Guatanamo
Cayman Is. (Br.)
Port au Prince
DOMINICAN REP.
Santo Domingo
S. Juan
Virgin Is. (U.S.A.-Br.)
Puerto Rico (U.S.A.)

MEXICO
Belize
Br. Honduras
GUATEM.
HONDURAS
Tegucigalpa
EL SALVADOR
San Salvador
NICARAGUA
Managua
L. Nicaragua
Bluefields
COSTA RICA
San José
JAMAICA
Kingston
Greater Antilles

Caribbean Sea

Guadeloupe (Fr.)
Dominica (Br.)
Martinique (Fr.)
St. Lucia (Br.)
BARBADOS
Lesser Antilles

OCEAN

Panama Canal Zone
Colón
Panama
G. of Panama
PANAMA

Cocos I. (Cost.)

BARRANQUILLA
Cartagena
G. of Venezuela
Maracaibo
Maracaibo
CARACAS
Valencia
Margarita
Cumaná
Curaçao (Neth.)
Bonaire (Neth.)
Port of Spain
TRINIDAD AND TOBAGO

MEDELLIN
Bucaramanga
Manizales
BOGOTÁ
Barquisimeto
S. Cristóbal
S. Fernando de Apure
Ciudad Bolívar
VENEZUELA
Georgetown
Paramaribo
Cayenne
GUYANA
SURINAM (Neth.)
FR. GUIANA

Buenaventura
CALI
Neiva
COLOMBIA
Popayán
Pasto
S. Carlos
S. Fernando de At.
Guaviare
Roraima

Malpelo (Col.)

Quito
ECUADOR

Isabela
Sta. Cruz
Galapagos Is. (Ec.)

GUAYAQUIL
Cuenca
Piura
Chiclayo
Trujillo
Cajamarca

Mitú
Uaupés
Putumayo
Napo
Iquitos
Leticia
Japurá
Negro
Moura
Amazonas
Manaus
Amazon
Óbidos
Santarém
Marajó I.
BELEM
Mouths of the Amazon

Amapá
Macapá
Equator

St. Peter and St. Paul Rocks (Braz.)

Marañon
Maranon
PERU
Cruzeiro do Sul
Porto Velho
Humaitá
Manicoré
Itaituba
Tapajos
Pará
São Luís
Parnaíba
FORTALEZA
Rocas I.
Fernando de Noronha (Braz.)

Cerro de Pasco
Callao
La Oroya
LIMA
Huancavelica
Pisco
Ica

Rio Branco
Guajará Mirim
Riberalta
Rondonia
Guaporé
Magdalena
Trinidad
Mato Grosso
Conceição do Araguaia
Porto Nacional
Ilha do Bananal
BRAZIL
Carolina
Maranhão
Piauí
Teresina
Iguatu
Natal
Campina Grande
João Pessoa
RECIFE
Maceió
Aracajú

Arequipa
Puno
L. Poopó
La Paz
Cochabamba
Oruro
Sucre
Potosí
BOLIVIA
Santa Cruz
Puerto Suarez
Corumbá
Mato Grosso
Cuiabá
Goiânia
Brasília
Palma
Barra
S. Francisco
Bahia
SALVADOR
Ilhéus
Minas Gerais
Piraporo
Diamantina
Theofilo Otoni
Caravelas

Mollendo
Arica
Iquique
Calama
Antofagasta
Copiapó

Uyuni
Embarcación
Jujuy
Salta
Tucumán

PARAGUAY
Pto. Casado
Concepción
Campo Grande
Asunción
Villarrica
Encarnación
Paraná
Uberaba
Ribeirão Preto
Bauru
CAMPINAS
S. PAULO
Santos
Juiz de Fora
BELO HORIZONTE
Vitória
Campos
Niteroi
RIO DE JANEIRO
Trindade (Braz.)
Martin Vaz Is. (Braz.)

Desventuradas Is. (Chile)
S. Félix
S. Ambrosio

Tropic of Capricorn

La Serena
San Juan
CÓRDOBA
Valparaiso
SANTIAGO
Juan Fernández Is. (Chile)
Talca
San Rafael
Malargue
Mendoza
Mercedes
BUENOS AIRES
La Plata
Concepción
Chillan

Santiago del Estero
Catamarca
La Rioja
Santa Fe
Paraná
ARGENTINA
Rosario
Santa Rosa
Tandil
Bahía Blanca
Mar del Plata

Resistencia
Corrientes
Sta. Maria
Passo Fundo
Florianópolis
PORTO ALEGRE
Lagoa dos Patos
Pelotas
Rio Grande
Rivera
Paysandú
Mercedes
URUGUAY
MONTEVIDEO
Rocha
River Plate (Rio de la Plata)
CURITIBA
Paranagua
Blumenau

Temuco
Zapala
Neuquén
Negro
Viedma
G. of San Matías

Puerto Montt
S. Carlos de Bariloche
Esquel
Chubut
Chiloé I.
Chonos Arch.
Taitao Pen.
Pto. Aisen
Comodoro Rivadavia
Deseado
Pto. Deseado

Chico
Santa Cruz
Grande Bay
Rio Gallegos
Magellan's Str.
Punta Arenas
Tierra del Fuego
Ushuaia
I. de los Estados
C. Horn

Falkland Is. (Islas Malvinas) (Br.)
Port Stanley

Shag Rocks (Br.)
South Georgia (Br.)

South Sandwich Is. (Br.)

Drake Passage

PACIFIC OCEAN

ATLANTIC OCEAN

Scale 1:34 000 000
0 250 500 750 1000 1250 1500 Kms.
0 250 500 750 1000 St. mls.

100 A 90 B 80 C 70 D 60 West from 50 Greenwich 40 G 30 H 20

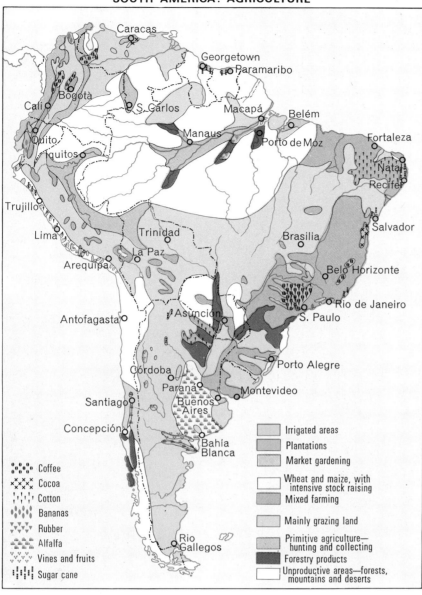

Coffee
Cocoa
Cotton
Bananas
Rubber
Alfalfa
Vines and fruits
Sugar cane

Irrigated areas
Plantations
Market gardening
Wheat and maize, with intensive stock raising
Mixed farming
Mainly grazing land
Primitive agriculture—hunting and collecting
Forestry products
Unproductive areas—forests, mountains and deserts

THE EXPANSIONS OF THE INCA CIVILISATION

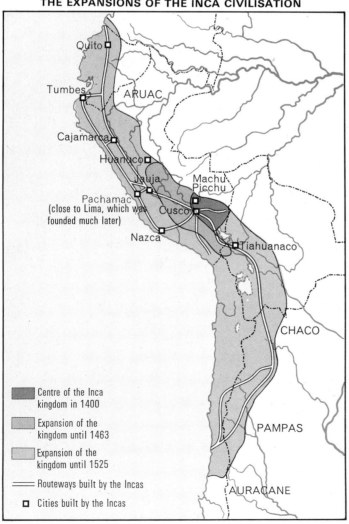

Centre of the Inca kingdom in 1400
Expansion of the kingdom until 1463
Expansion of the kingdom until 1525
Routeways built by the Incas
Cities built by the Incas

called Selvas and contains a wide variety of different trees, mainly hardwoods, which are all mixed together. The area is largely undeveloped, although rubber is one significant product of the forest.

The plateau area between the Amazon and Paraguay/Parana river systems is characterised by tropical grassland which is called the Campos; the Guiana Highlands are similarly characterised by the tropical grassland called the Llanos. Much of northern and central Argentina and the Uruguay, at a lower altitude, is the rich Pampas, a temperate grassland. And finally, the narrow coastal strip of the Pacific may be divided into four main areas from north to south: the equatorial forest lands; the deserts of coastal Peru and northern Chile; the Mediterranean region; and the southern temperate forests.

Today the continent of South America may seem to be a sleeping giant. Unlike the continent of Africa, it has been a continent of independent nations for nearly a century and a half, with one or two exceptions. Yet the resources of this large area are mainly underdeveloped and the wealth of many regions as yet unrealised.

The forest regions of northern Brazil are still the province of nomadic Indian tribesmen. The Boro tribe, for instance, live by shifting farming methods, and rely for their food on wild animals and manioc.

In contrast, the area of the Pampas has been exploited. The plains of this area are ideal for intensive cultivation; they form South America's largest cereal belt from which about 8% of the world's maize and wheat is produced each year; much of this is exported. Also on the Pampas are the great estancias, or cattle ranches, from which about one sixth of the world's beef originates. And, further south, the cooler plains are great sheep rearing country, both for fat lambs and wool.

Within tropical South America there are one or two distinctive farm products. The continent as a whole produces about half the world's coffee each year, although production varies greatly. Brazil and Columbia are the two most important countries. In addition, one sixth of the world's cocoa, one tenth of its sugar, a quarter of its linseed and 8% of its cotton come from this continent.

The mineral riches of South America are extensive and varied. However, there is comparatively little exploitation of them for local use. Production of some of them is now growing, but this is largely for export to Europe and North America. The countries who are carrying out the mining are strongly supported by money from overseas.

Venezuela, Brazil, Chile and Peru are all richly endowed with iron ore deposits. Manganese is produced in Brazil and her output ranks third in the world, behind the U.S.S.R. and South Africa. Surinam and Guyana, amongst other countries, are important for their bauxite reserves—about one fifth of the world's annual output comes from Surinam. Chile, which was once very important for its production of nitrates from the Atacama Desert, is now more distinctive for its supplies of copper, which rank second in the world, after the United States. Finally, in this survey of major minerals, the importance of Venezuela as the world's biggest producer of crude oil must not be forgotten.

Any map showing the present distribution of population in South America is very revealing. From the population map at the beginning of this atlas it is seen that with few exceptions all the major towns are within two hundred miles of the coast and that the most heavily peopled parts of the continent are the Atlantic fringes of Brazil, Uruguay and Argentina, the Mediterranean zone of Chile and parts of the extreme north-west. The heart of the continent has yet to be tamed and developed. Yet, the recent decision to move the capital of Brazil from its former location on the Atlantic coast at Rio de Janeiro to a new

The impressive waterfalls of Iguacu which are on the boundary between Brazil and Argentina.

inland site at Brasilia shows a determination on the part of Brazil to make greater use of its rich interior areas.

The present population of South America is mixed and stems from three different sources—there are the descendants of the original American Indians, who are still mainly primitive tribesmen who play very little part in the economic life of the continent. Then there are the descendants of the negro slaves who were brought to South America by various groups to work in the plantations established up to the nineteenth century. And, finally, there are the descendants of the European settlers, mainly Spanish and Portuguese, who are by far the largest group.

When European settlers first penetrated into Peru in the early sixteenth century they found that the area in the Andes extending from what is now called Ecuador, through Peru to Chile was part of an extensive and highly organised empire whose economy was in large part based on the cultivation of maize. This was the empire of the Incas (the Indian word for king or lord) who had control over a large number of tribal groups within the mountains. The administration of this empire was elaborate and efficient. There were no written languages, yet records were kept by means of a complex system of knotted cords called quipu.

The Incas did not know the use of the wheel, nor did they know about iron. However, their engineers had developed some surprising skills, constructing palaces, temples and suspension bridges which amazed the European explorers. In these they had used huge blocks of stone, up to one hundred tons in weight, and had developed incredibly fine techniques of engineering. The Incas had also developed great skill as craftsmen in precious metals. A lengthy system of roads was another of their important achievements and these communications were maintained from one end of their empire to the other.

This Inca Empire is so fascinating, since it was so highly organised and apparently successful at such an early time, and so high up in the mountains. Yet it was all overthrown by the Spanish adventurer, Pizarro, in 1531, and today we can only see the ruined remains of this great ancient civilisation.

From the sixteenth to nineteenth centuries South America was a source of attraction to Spanish and Portuguese adventurers and missionaries. The Spanish were drawn to the Pacific and the southern area where one of the greatest attractions was the chance of finding gold. On the other hand, what is now Brazil was settled by the Portuguese who began to exploit the farming possibilities of the area. Tobacco was grown at first and later sugar cane became the main source of wealth. It was only in the nineteenth century that the mineral wealth of the interior was realised.

Unlike North America, this continent did not unite into a large nation when it broke away from its European mother nations. In the early years of the nineteenth century nine Spanish-speaking countries achieved independence. And Brazil, the Portuguese-speaking eastern area, also became independent in 1822. And herein lies one major reason for the stagnation in South America during the last century and a half—there has been no unity in the continent, and no great link with the powerful nations of Europe.

Today, we are seeing the development of some of South America's potential—the great farmlands of the Argentine have been developed during the past fifty years; Brazil's tropical farming specialities are now being supported by mining and industrial ventures; Venezuelan oil and ores are exploited more and more. A lot of this development is with aid from overseas. Yet in the activities of organisations such as the Organisation of American States and the Latin American Free Trade Association, it can be seen that the "sleeping giant" is beginning at last to stir itself.

BRAZIL: THE ROADS

Asphalt roads
Dirt roads
Roads planned

BRAZIL: ACTUAL AND POTENTIAL MINERAL RESOURCES

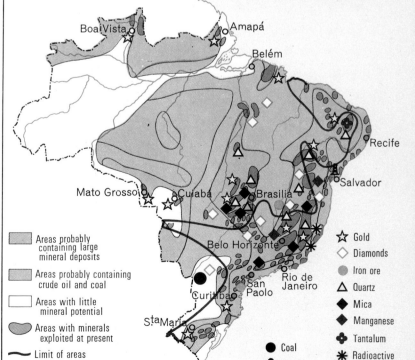

Areas probably containing large mineral deposits
Areas probably containing crude oil and coal
Areas with little mineral potential
Areas with minerals exploited at present
Limit of areas served by railways

Gold
Diamonds
Iron ore
Quartz
Mica
Manganese
Tantalum
Radioactive materials
Coal
Crude oil

ARGENTINA

Argentina is an independent republic, occupying the extreme south-eastern part of South America. It is the second largest South American country and its capital, Buenos Aires, is the largest city in the southern hemisphere. It is basically an agricultural country. The fertile Pampas is one of the greatest areas for beef and wheat production in the world. Further south, in Patagonia, large flocks of sheep are raised. In this area, too, are the huge herds of cattle. Thus Argentina is one of the world's leading exporters of canned and frozen meat, wheat and wool. Leading imports are fuel and manufactured goods. Religion is 93% Roman Catholic. The language is Spanish. *Capital: Buenos Aires. Population: 22 million. Highest point: Aconcagua, 6,959 metres (22,834ft.). Principal river: Parana. Land area: 2,775,600 sq. km. (1,072,075 sq. miles).*

BOLIVIA

Bolivia is an independent land-locked republic in the Andes. It is a mountainous country with few fertile agricultural areas. Development schemes are increasing food outputs. The most important industry is mining, tin being the principal mineral. Bolivia is the world's second most important producer. Exports of silver, lead and tungsten are also important. Petroleum has recently been discovered. Exports are carried by rail to ports on the Peruvian and Chilean coasts. The airport at La Paz is the highest civil aerodrome in the world. Two thirds of the population are Indian. Some work in the mines while others grow maize, barley and potatoes and raise wool-bearing llamas. *Capital: La Paz. Population: 3.6 million. Land area: 1,098,150 sq. km. (424,160 sq. miles).*

BRAZIL

Brazil is the largest country in South America with almost half of the continent's area and population. Brazil's economy depends largely on coffee; it produces about half of the world supply. Coffee accounts for 60% of her exports but sugar, cotton, rubber and iron ore are also important. In the interior there are valuable mineral resources, including iron ore, chromite, mica and some rarer ores. Development of these has been hampered by poor communications. Industry has grown rapidly as a result of government encouragement; iron and steel, textiles and engineering are most important. Brazil is a republic. The language is Portuguese and the religion mainly Roman Catholic. There is complete freedom of the press and free speech. There is, however, a high rate of illiteracy. *Capital: Brasilia. Population: 87.2 million. Principal river: Amazon. Land area: 8.51 million sq. km. (3.29 million sq. miles).*

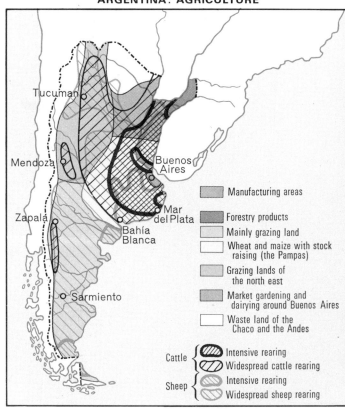

ARGENTINA: AGRICULTURE

Manufacturing areas
Forestry products
Mainly grazing land
Wheat and maize with stock raising (the Pampas)
Grazing lands of the north east
Market gardening and dairying around Buenos Aires
Waste land of the Chaco and the Andes

Cattle — Intensive rearing
Cattle — Widespread cattle rearing
Sheep — Intensive rearing
Sheep — Widespread sheep rearing

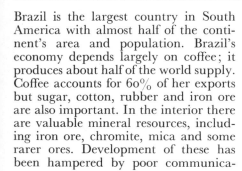

BOLIVIA: AGRICULTURE AND MINING

AGRICULTURE
Cereals and root crops
Pastures
Forests
Savanna lands
High mountain areas: some grazing animals

MINES
♨ Crude oil
☆ Silver
★ Copper
⬗ Lead
▦ Zinc
▼ Tin
▯ Antimony
✳ Uranium
☆ Gold
⋏⋏ Salt
○ Tungsten

Argentina. **Part of a huge cattle market in one of the country's important agricultural centres.**

CHILE

Chile is a republic occupying a thin strip of land on the west coast of S. America. Northern Chile is most important for mineral production—iron ore, nitrates and copper are the leading products. Iodine, potash and gold are also produced. Chile possesses nearly half of the world's copper reserves. Olives, wine grapes, citrus and other fruits and a variety of grains are grown in fertile valleys of central Chile. A number of industries—textiles, chemicals, leather and steel—have grown up in this area, particularly around Santiago. The south of Chile is densely forested and few people live there. Punta Arenas, in the far south, is the centre of a growing oil industry and a wool market. Chile was discovered in the 16th century by Spanish adventurers and remained under Spanish rule until a war of liberation established its independence in 1818. The population consists of the indigenous Indians, the Spanish descendants of the early settlers, mixed Spanish-Indians and European immigrants. Religion is Roman Catholic. *Capital: Santiago. Population: 8.75 million. Land area: 741,484 sq. km. (286,398 sq. miles), including offshore islands.*

COLOMBIA

Colombia is a republic in the north west of S. America with Atlantic and Pacific coastlines. It is the world's second largest producer of coffee which accounts for about 85% of its exports. There are also important deposits of crude oil, platinum, gold, silver, copper and coal. American companies control about 85% of the oil industry; the rest is British. Colombia was discovered by Columbus in 1502, conquered by Spain in 1536 and remained under Spanish rule until 1824. In 1830 it became the republic of New Granada and adopted the name Colombia in 1863. The language is Spanish with some Italian dialects. *Capital: Bogota. Population: 17.5 million. Highest point: Cristobal Colon, 5,775 metres (18,947ft.). Land area: 1,138,338 sq. km. (439,400 sq. miles).*

ECUADOR

Ecuador is a republic on the Pacific coast of S. America, straddling the equator. The country is still largely forested yet agricultural production and exports include bananas, cocoa, coffee, balsa wood, pyrethrum and rice. Mineral deposits such as copper, gold, lead and petroleum are rich but have not been extensively exploited. The Galapagos Islands, about 1,045 km. (650 miles) to the west, belong to Ecuador. They are well known for their rare animal life —giant tortoises, iguanas and flightless cormorants. Ecuador has more than 20 active volcanoes. Language is Spanish. *Capital: Quito. Population: 5.6 million. Highest point: Chimborazo, 6,272 metres (20,561ft.). Land area: 270,670 sq. km. (104,506 sq. miles).*

Brazil. **Rio de Janeiro, a view of the city and the bay from Mount Corcovado.**

GUIANA

Guiana is a former French colony on the north coast of South America. Since 1946 it has been governed as an overseas department of France. The country is almost wholly undeveloped. The population lives by practising subsistence agriculture. The Guiana coast was first settled by the Dutch. The lands changed hands many times between the British, French, Dutch and Portuguese and French Guiana was created in 1815 by the Vienna Congress. It was used by the French as a convict settlement (especially the notorious Devil's Island) from 1792 to 1946. *Capital: Cayenne. Population: 33,000. Land area: 88,984 sq. km. (34,370 sq. miles).*

GUYANA

Guyana became an independent country within the Commonwealth in 1966. A Dutch colony for nearly two centuries from 1620, it had been ceded to Britain in 1814. It is situated on the north-east coast of South America. The narrow coastal strip is cultivated, and rice and sugar are the most valuable crops. Further inland are huge deposits of bauxite, together with some diamonds, gold, manganese and mica. The central and southern areas are largely untouched forest lands. By value, Guyana's most important exports are sugar, bauxite, alumina, rice, diamonds and timber. Machinery, fuels, foodstuffs and textiles are the major imports. The population is of mixed origins, with East Indians making up nearly half of the total. *Capital: Georgetown. Population: 674,000. Principal river: Essequibo. Land area: 214,887 sq. km. (83,000 sq. miles).*

Peru. **Machupicchu ruins, nearly 10,000ft. up in the Andes Mountains.**

PARAGUAY

Paraguay is an independent land-locked republic of S. America, between Argentina, Brazil and Bolivia. It became a Spanish colony in 1535 and Spanish colonisation of South America radiated from Asuncion. It was here, too, that the mission establishments of the Jesuits organised the Indians into successful communities. After declaring itself independent in 1811, Paraguay was involved in war with Brazil, Argentina and Uruguay, 1865-70, after which only 22,000 males remained alive. The country is mainly agricultural and cotton, tobacco, maize, sugar cane, rice and sub-tropical fruits are grown. Principal exports include cotton, quebracho (a tanning extract), timber, maté, vanilla and meat products. Exports are sent to the Argentinian seaport of Buenos Aires by river. There are few industries and most of the population (which is largely mestizo—of mixed European and Indian blood) is poor, backward and illiterate. Spanish is the official language, but Guarani, the language of the native Indians, is spoken widely. Religion is Roman Catholic. *Capital: Asuncion. Population: 1.8 million. Principal rivers: Paraguay and Parana. Land area: 406,660 sq. km. (157,048 sq. miles).*

PERU

Peru is a republic on the Pacific coast of S. America. It is a mountainous country and agriculture is restricted to the coastal lowlands and valleys. Fishing is most important for exports. The Indians raise sheep, llamas, alpacas and vicunas in the Andes and the wool is either exported or used in local textile factories. There are many mineral resources, of which lead, copper, silver and iron ore are the most important. The way of life of the Indians has changed little since the time of the Incas. Religion is Roman Catholic. Peru was the cradle of the Inca civilisation which was destroyed in the 16th century by the Spanish Conquistador, Pizarro. It remained a Spanish colony until the S. American wars of liberation and became independent in 1821. *Capital: Lima. Population: 12 million. Land area: 1,285,215 sq. km. (496,100 sq. miles).*

Bolivia. **The desolate landscape of the Andean plateau. The Indians live close to Lake Titicaca which is on the borders of Peru and Bolivia.**

Tierra del Fuego. **This island, at the very tip of the continent, is very close to the Antarctic circle. This remote southern extremity of the Andes mountains is very sparsely populated.**

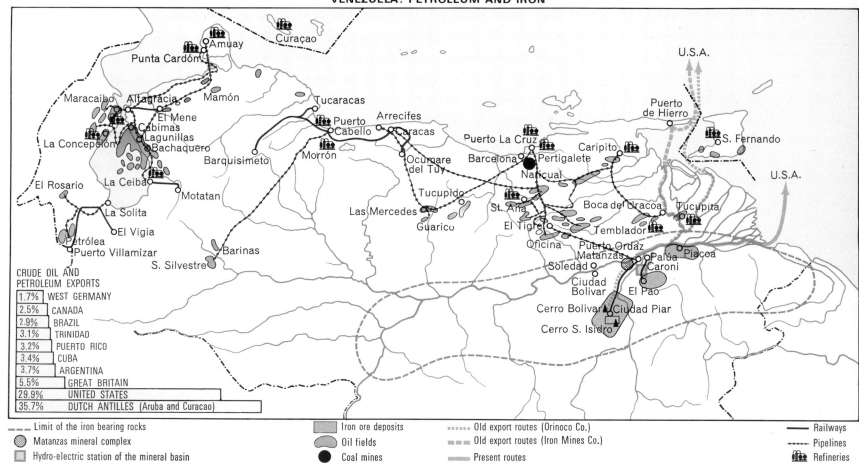

CRUDE OIL AND PETROLEUM EXPORTS

1.7%	WEST GERMANY
2.5%	CANADA
2.9%	BRAZIL
3.1%	TRINIDAD
3.2%	PUERTO RICO
3.4%	CUBA
3.7%	ARGENTINA
5.5%	GREAT BRITAIN
29.9%	UNITED STATES
35.7%	DUTCH ANTILLES (Aruba and Curacao)

- - - - Limit of the iron bearing rocks
 Matanzas mineral complex
Hydro-electric station of the mineral basin
▨ Iron ore deposits
◖ Oil fields
● Coal mines
····· Old export routes (Orinoco Co.)
- - - Old export routes (Iron Mines Co.)
▨▨▨ Present routes
—— Railways
····· Pipelines
 Refineries

SURINAM

Surinam (formerly Dutch Guiana) is an internally self-governing territory united with the European kingdom of the Netherlands. It is situated on the Atlantic coast between Guyana (formerly British Guiana, Guiana (formerly French Guiana) and Brazil. The coastal lowlands are the most significant area for farming—sugar cane,

rice and tropical fruit are the major products. Forestry is also important. Further inland, bauxite, which accounts for over 70% of the country's exports, is mined. *Capital: Paramaribo. Population: 400,000. Principal river: Surinam. Land area: 181,455 sq. km. (70,087 sq. miles).*

TRINIDAD and TOBAGO

Trinidad and Tobago are two West Indian islands which form an independent country within the Commonwealth. Trinidad (by far the larger island) is close to the north coast of Venezuela, and Tobago is 32 km. (20 miles) further north. Both islands are fertile and sugar cane, coffee, cocoa, citrus fruits and coconuts are grown. Rum is an important export. Trinidad's main source of revenue is oil which is refined on the island. Natural

asphalt is recovered from a 114-acre pitch lake and production totals about 160,000 tons per year. Trinidad was discovered by Columbus in 1498, colonised by Spain in 1532 but annexed by Britain in 1797 and formally ceded to her in 1802 by the Peace of Amiens, as was Tobago in 1814. In 1889 the two islands were amalgamated as a Crown Colony. *Capitals: Port of Spain and Scarborough. Population: 975,000. Land area: 5,128 sq. km. (1,980 sq. miles).*

Venezuela. **Caracas, Bolivar Street, one of the important commercial areas in the city.**

URUGUAY

Uruguay is the smallest South American republic, between Brazil and Argentina. Stock-raising is the principal activity. Wool is the leading export but much salted, frozen and tinned meat, leather, hides and animal fat are also sent abroad. Wheat, corn, linseed, tobacco, rice and barley are grown. Most of Uruguay's industries are concerned with food processing. The area was controlled by Portugal in the 17th century; in the early

18th century Spanish immigrants set up many ranches in what was then a province of Brazil. Independence was gained in 1828, since when Uruguay has acted as a buffer state between Brazil and Argentina. The population is mainly of Italian and Spanish origins. The official language is Spanish and Roman Catholicism the official religion. *Capital: Montevideo. Population: 2.75 million. Land area: 186,926 sq. km. (72,172 sq. miles).*

VENEZUELA

Venezuela is the most northerly S. American republic, between Colombia, Guyana and Brazil. Venezuela is the leading world exporter of crude oil which accounts for 90% of her exports. At least two thirds of this comes from an oilfield in the Maracaibo Basin, where thousands of wells can be seen along the shores and in the shallow waters of the lake. Iron ore, asbestos and diamonds are also produced. A large proportion of the population are farmers—coffee, maize and livestock are the leading products. About two thirds of the population are of mixed Spanish and Indian blood. *Capital: Caracas. Population: 8.3 million. Land area: 912,050 sq. km. (352,143 sq. miles).*

Rio de Janeiro. **This city of nearly three and a half million people on Brazil's southern Atlantic fringe is built on a narrow coastal lowland. Many of its buildings, flats, offices and hotels are fifteen and more storeys high.**

AUSTRALASIA
AND THE PACIFIC ISLANDS

Australasia is the name given to the large island of Australia, the smaller islands of New Zealand, and numerous tiny Pacific islands which are grouped to the east and north of them. The continent is spread out over an area one and a half times the size of Europe yet only about seventeen million people live there and many parts are uninhabitable. Australia is often referred to as "down under" by British people, a reminder that it is on the opposite side of the globe.

The island of Australia is the largest landmass in the continent. Although it is believed to be one of the oldest land masses in the world, it was the last to be developed by Europeans. New Holland was the name given to it by the Dutch who landed on the west coast of the York Peninsula in 1606. Later Dutch navigators reached parts of the north and western coasts but when these explorers came back with their reports of a barren land and hostile natives, Dutch interest in the continent waned.

The first Englishman to visit Australia was William Dampier in 1688. His explorations led him along the north-west coasts and his reports, like those of the Dutchmen, were unenthusiastic and did little to awaken England's interest in the continent.

It was not until 1770 that Captain James Cook first sighted the east coast of the continent. Cook had been sent to Tahiti to make astronomical observations and when he had completed his mission he sailed round New Zealand, charted the coasts of both the north and south islands and then sailed westwards. After sighting land near Cape Everard in the south-eastern corner of Australia, he sailed north and landed at Botany Bay, choosing that name because of the huge variety of botanical specimens that he found there. Then he sailed north again for 2,000 km. (nearly 1,300 miles) and, after passing through Torres Strait, landed on an island off Cape York which he called Possession Island; here he hoisted the British flag and formally took possession of the eastern parts of the continent.

The news of Cook's discovery aroused considerable interest in England but still no attempt was made at colonisation. However, with the loss of the American colonies in the American War of Independence, Britain needed an alternative overseas settlement to which she could send law breakers sentenced to deportation. Therefore, in May 1787, a fleet of ships under the command of Captain Phillip sailed to Australia with 1,030 people, 726 of them convicts, and landed at Botany Bay in the following January. About a week later, the settlement was transferred to Port Jackson which eventually grew into Australia's largest city—Sydney.

At first the colonists were dependent on food supplies from overseas but gradually the land was brought under cultivation although, for the most part, it was poor and crop yields tended to be low.

Continued on page 100

Australia. **Sydney, part of the docks, the famous harbour bridge and the new opera house.**

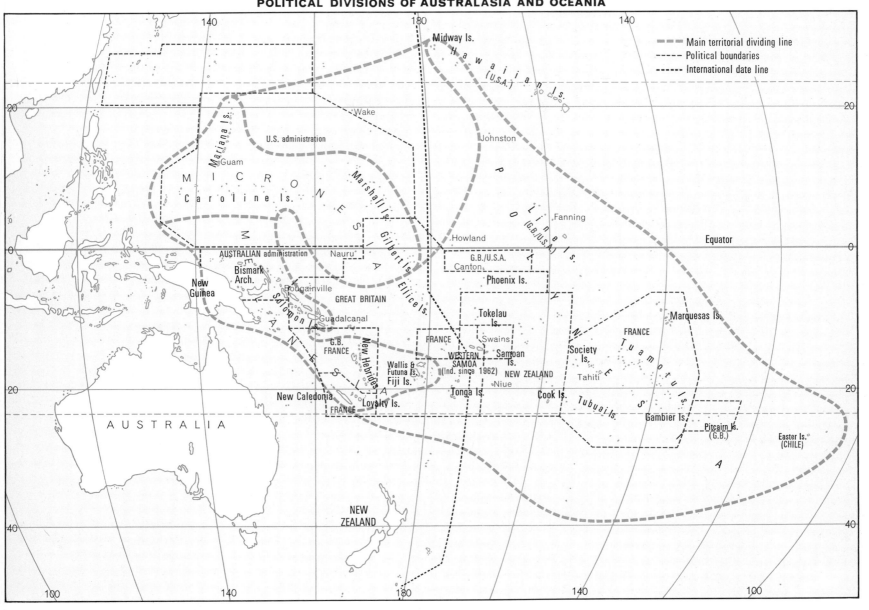

Main territorial dividing line
Political boundaries
International date line

Midway Is.

H a w a i i a n Is. (U.S.A.)

Wake

Mariana Is.

Guam

U.S. administration

M I C R O N E S I A

Caroline Is.

Marshall Is.

Gilbert Is.

Ellice Is.

Johnston

P O L Y N E S I A

Fanning

Line Is. (G.B./U.S.A.)

Equator

Howland

AUSTRALIAN administration

Nauru

G.B./U.S.A.
Canton

Phoenix Is.

New
Guinea

Bismark
Arch.

Bougainville

M E L A N E S I A

Solomon Is.

Guadalcanal

GREAT BRITAIN

Tokelau
Is.

Swains

Marquesas Is.

FRANCE

Tuamotu Is.

G.B.
FRANCE

New Hebrides

FRANCE

WESTERN
SAMOA
(Ind. since 1962)

Samoan
Is.

Society
Is.

FRANCE

Wallis &
Futuna Is.

Fiji Is.

NEW ZEALAND

Tahiti

New Caledonia

Loyalty Is.

FRANCE

Tonga Is.

Niue

Cook Is.

Tubuai Is.

Gambier Is.

Pitcairn Is.
(G.B.)

Easter Is.
(CHILE)

AUSTRALIA

A

NEW
ZEALAND

1

C h i n a

A S I A

Yangtze-Kiang

Si-kiang

East China Sea

Shikoku

Kyūshū

Nampo Shotō

Tanega

Tokara Is.

Amami Is.

Bonin Is.

Ramapo Trench
(Izu Tr.)
10554

8848

Volcano Is.

Mellis Seamount

Formosa Str.

Ryu Kyu Is.

Okinawa
7507
Miyako
Ishigaki

Daitō Is.

Minami Tori Shima
(Marcus)
877

Hong Kong

3950
Taiwan
(Formosa)

Ryukyu Trench

Hainan
1879

Batan Is.

Babuyan Is.

Philippine

Parece Vela

Farallon de Pajaros

1379

Wake I.

Paracel
Island

4224

Luzon

Basin

Asuncion
Agrihan
Pagan

Mariana Is.

P A C I

Saigon

267

Mindoro

Panay

Samar

Leyte
Philippines

10793

1859

Anatahan
Saipan
Tinian
Rota
Guam

Mariana Trench

Taongi Atoll

Palawan

Negros

10497

Balabac Str.
2867

Sulu Sea

Mindanao

2958
Apo
9580

6218

Kinabalu
4100

Brunei

Bunguran Is.

B o r n e o

Iran Ra.

Sulu Arch.

11022

Yap Is.

8527

Ulithi A.

Gaferut

Woleai A.

Eauripik A.

Pulo-Anna

Talaud Is.

Tobi

Palau Is.

C a r o l i n e

I s l a n d s

M I C R O N E S I A

Marshall Islands

Eniwetok A.

Bikini A.

Rongelap A.

Kwajalein
Atoll

Ailinglapalap A.
Jaluit A.

Ratak Chain

Ralik Chain

Maleolap A.

Arno A.

Mili A.

Makin

Tarawa Atoll

Kapuas

Schwaner Ra.

Mahakam

Celebes Sea

Molucca Sea

Morotai

Halmahera

Mapia Is.

Hall Is.

Truk Is.

Ponape

Senyavin Is.

Mortlock Is.

Kusaie

Nukuoro A.

Kapingamarangi
Atoll

6920

Nauru

Ocean I.

Kingsmill Gr.

Nonouti

G i l b e r t I s.

Billiton

Barito

Bandjarmasin

Rantemario
3440

Buru
5800

Ceram

Sula Is.

Obi Is.

Waigeo
Dampier Str.
Kwoka
2995

Biak

Japen

Sarera
B.

C.d'Urville

Ninigo Group

Sukarnapura

Admiralty
Is.

St. Matthias
Group

New Hanover I.

New Ireland

**Bismarck
Archipelago**

New
Britain

Bougainville

Nakumanu Is.

S o l o m o n   I s.

M E L A N E S I A

Nanumea

Makassar
2871

Java Sea

Semarang

Madura

Bali

Lombok

3676
Semeru

Flores Sea

Lesser Sunda Is.

Wetar

5400

Babar Is.

Tanimbar Is.

**New
Guinea**

Sukarno Peak
5030

Central Range

Kai Is.

Aru Is.

Digul

4694
Finisterre Ra.

4100

Trobriand or
Kiriwina Is.

New Georgia

Choiseul

Sta. Isabel

Malaita

Duff Is.

Ellice
Islands

Vaitupu

Semarang

Flores
2920

Timor

Arafura Sea

Kolepom I.

Fly

G. of
Papua

4073
O. Stanley Ra.

D'Entrecasteaux Is.

Guadalcanal

S. Cristobal

Rennell

Santa Cruz Is.

6061

Mitre I.

Rotuma

Java Trench
7450

6840

Sumbawa

Sumba

Roti

Timor
Sea

Melville I.

Cobourg Pen.

Torres Str.

C. York

Port
Moresby

Louisiade Arch.

Coral

4842

Louisiana Arch.

Banks Is.

Espiritu Santo Is.

Aurora

Fiji

New

Darwin

Jos.
Bonaparte
Gulf

Arnhem
Land

Groote
Eylandt

G. of
Carpentaria

Cooktown

Cape
York
Pen.

C. Melville

Sea

Mellish Reef

Malekula

Efate

Hebrides

Eromanga

Kandavu

King Sd.

Fitzroy

Kimberley

Roper

Victoria

Wellesley
Is.

Mitchell

Mt. Bartle Frere
1612

Great Barrier Reef

Chesterfield Iles

Uvea
Mt.Panie
1213

Loyalty Is.

New
Caledonia

Maré

Matthew

I. des Pins

Barrow I.

Exmouth G.

N.W. Cape

2910

De Grey

Great Sandy
Desert

L. Mackay

L. Disappointment

Macdonnell Ranges

1510

Alice Spring

Flinders

Selwyn Ra.

Barkly Tableland

Bellona Reefs

Rockhampton

Cato

Great Dividing

South Fiji

5303

Basin

Ashburton

Hamersley Ra.
1227

1106
Mt. Augustus

Gibson Desert

1515

Musgrave Range

L. Amadeus

Diamantina

Cooper Cr.

Barcoo

Brisbane
1356

C. Byron

New England
Ra.
1555

Middleton Reef

3566

Norfolk I.

T a s m a n

5548

Shark B.

Murchison

Dirk Hartog I.

425
L. Austin

L. Barlee

**Great Victoria
Desert**

L. Eyre
-12

L. Frome
90

Bourke

Darling

Liverpool Ra.
1494

Macquarie

5944

Lord Howe I.
870

4656

Sea

5655

Perth

L. Moore

L. Cowan

Nullarbor Plain

L. Torrens
1189

L. Gairdner

Pt. Augusta

Flinders Ra.

Eyre's
Pen.

Murrumbidgee

Lachlan

Murray

Canberra

Sydney

A U S T R A L I A

Geographe B.
1109

C. Leeuwin

Darling Range

Great Australian
Bight

Gawler Ra.

Kangaroo I.

Spencer G.

Encounter B.

Adelaide

1167

2228
**Australian
Alps**

Wilson Prom.

North C.

2797
Ruapehu

New

1105

I N D I A N

2498

South
Australian
Basin

5560

Melbourne

Port Phillip B.

King I.

Bass Strait

Furneaux Group

1578
Legges Tor
Hobart

South East
Cape

Tasmania

5364

T a s m a n

Basin

West C.

Mt. Cook
3764

Southern Alps

Zealand

Cook Str.

Christchurch

Canterbury Bight

South Island

Stewart I.

O C E A N

Scale 1:33 000 000

0   250   500   750   1000   1250   1500 Kms.

0   250   500   750   1000 St. mls.

NORTH AMERICA

Guadalupe I.
I. de Cedros
G. of California
Lower California
C. St. Lucas

7060

Hawaiian Islands

Midway Is.
I.
Lisianski I.
Laysan I.
Maro Reef
Gardner Pinnacles
Necker I.
Necker Ridge
Nihoa
Kauai
Niihau
Honolulu
Oahu
Lanai
Maui
4213 Manua Kea
Hawaii

Tropic of Cancer
3767

Revilla Gigedo Is.

983

833

Johnston I.

F I C   O C E A N

P A C I F I C

3092

901

Palmyra I.
Washington I.
Fanning I.

436

Christmas I.

Howland I.   7251
Baker I.

Jarvis I.

Equator

Phoenix Is.
Canton I.   7375
Phoenix I.
Gardner I.   Hull I.   Sydney I.
2204

Malden I.

Starbuck I.

Filippo Reef

Line Islands

Atafu
Fakaofo
Tokelau Is.
(Union Group)
Pukapuka Atoll
(Danger Is.)
Swains I.
ulakita
Nassau
Penrhyn A.
Vostok I.
Manihiki Atoll
Caroline I.

Eiao
Nuku Hiva   Ua Huka   Marquesas
1260   Islands
Tahuata
Fatu Hiva

Wallis Is.
eau
Savai'i   Samoa
Upolu   Tutuila
Rose
Nua

Flint I.

Suwarrow A.

Cook Islands

Tuamotu

Napuka
Pukapuka

nua Levu

Lau Group
Vava'u Gr.
Ha'apai   Tonga
Group   (Friendly Is.)
Eua I.

Tonga Trench

Rangiroa
Mataiva
Manihi
Apataki
Society Is.
Bora Bora
Maupikaa   Raiatea
Palmerston A.
Aitutaki A.
Hervey Is.
Tahiti
2241
Anaa
Makemo
Marokau
Fakarava
Rangia
Tatakoto
Pukarua
Yao   Reo
Tangatau
Archipel.

Beveridge Reef
Rarotonga
Hereherelue
Nengonengo
Pinaki

Is. Maria
Mangaia
Rurutu
Is. Duc de Gloucester
Tematangi
Tureia

10882

Rimatara
Tubuai
Raivavae
(Austral Is.)
Tubuai Is.

Mururoa
Marutea
Morane   Mangareva
Is. Gambier
Oeno I.

Tropic of Capricorn

Raoul I.
uley I.
10047
Kermadec Is.
sl.
Kermadec Trench

Haymet Rfs.

Neilson Reef   Rapa
Ilots de Bass
(Morotiri)

Pitcairn I.
Henderson I.
Ducie I.

Albatros Cordillera (East Pacific Ridge)

1088

6600

South Island

South west

Pacific

Basin

290   Chatham Is.

6010

nty Is.

ALTITUDES

Metres	Feet
4000	13123
3000	9843
2000	6562
1000	3281
500	1640
200	656
Sea Level	0
Depression	

DEPTHS

0	0
200	656
2000	6562
4000	13123
6000	19685
More than	

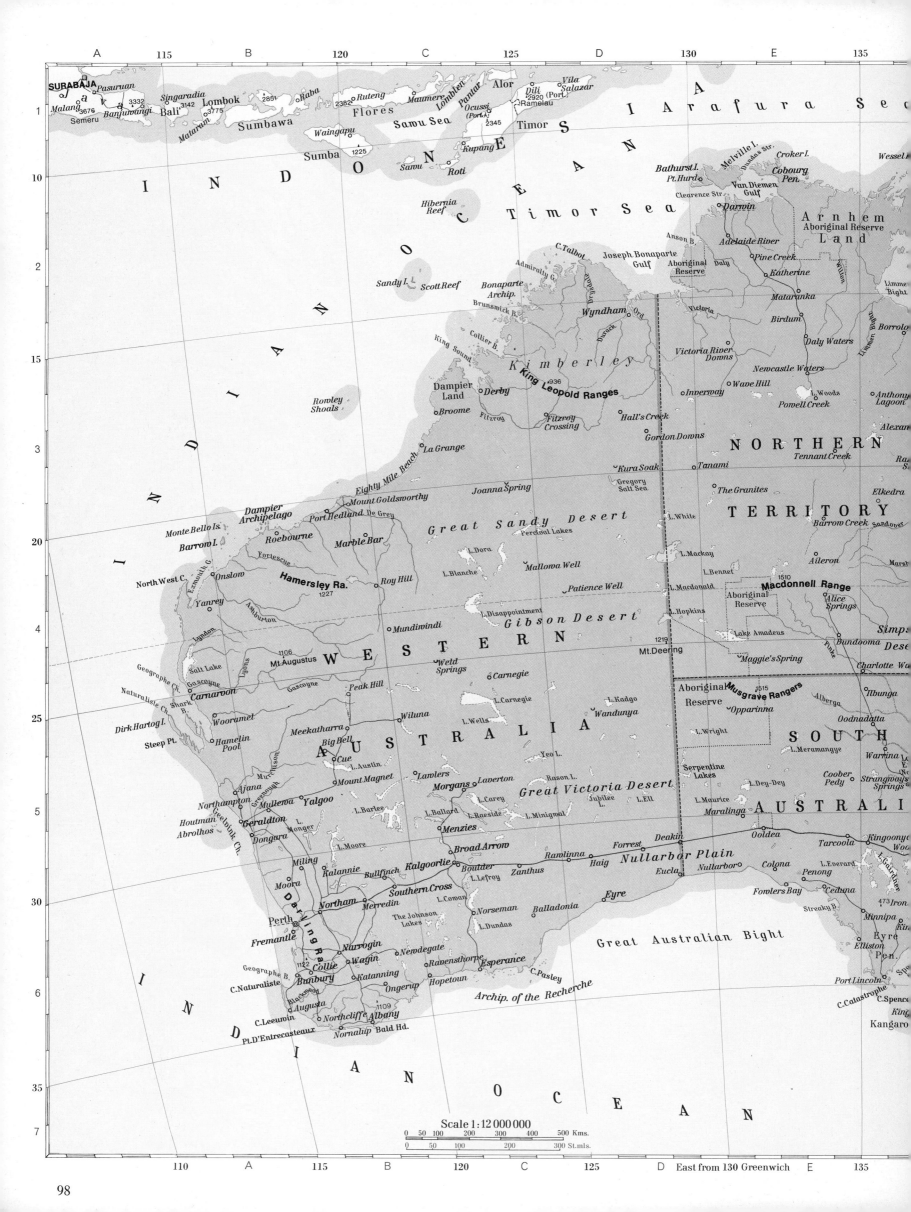

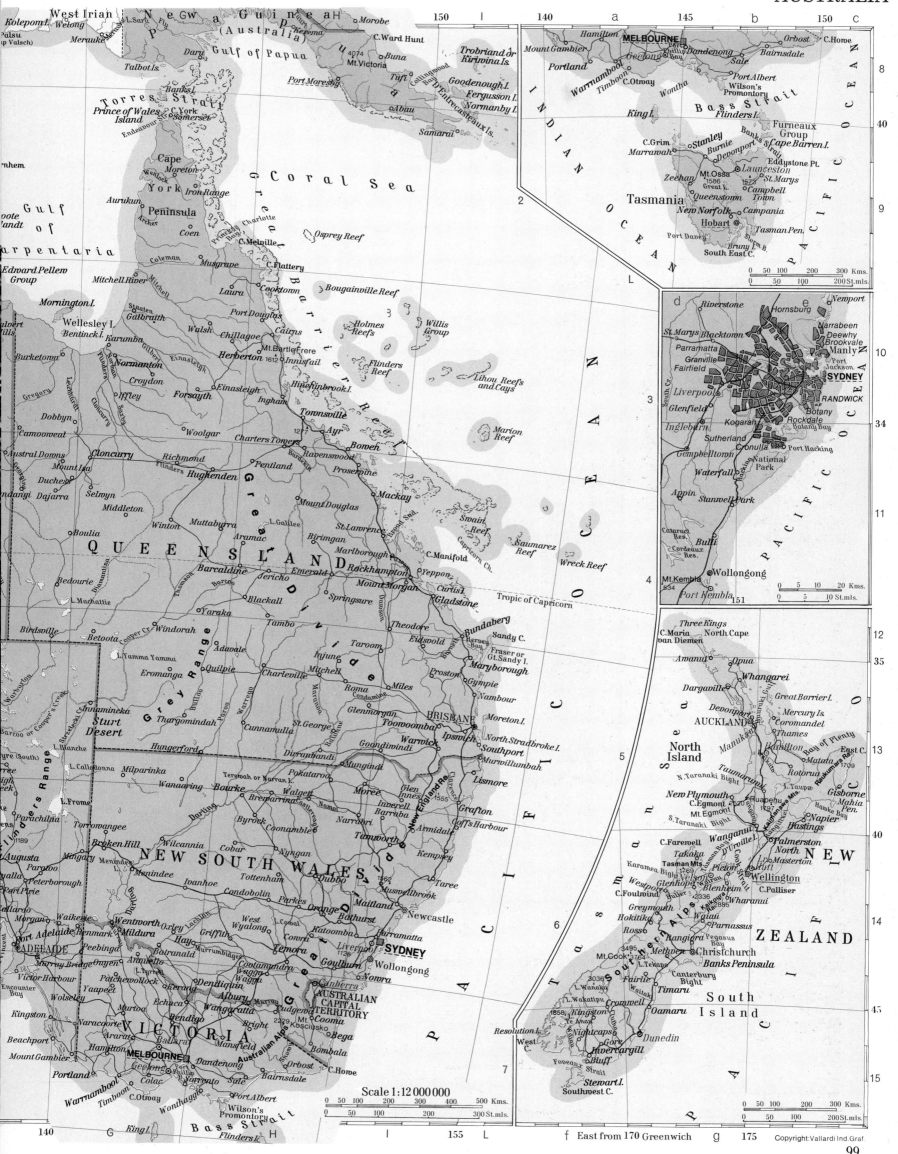

AUSTRALIA

West Irian · N e w G u i n e a H
(Australia) P a P u a
Kolepom I. Welong L.Sari Fly · Morobe
(op Valsch) Merauke Dary Kerema C.Ward Hunt
Talbot I. 4074 · Buna
Mt.Victoria Tufi Trobriand or
-nhem Gulf of Papua Collingwood Kirivina Is.
Port Moresby Bay Goodenough I.
Torres Strait D'Entrecasteaux Is. Fergusson I.
Prince of Wales C.York Abau Normanby I.
Island Somerset Samarai
Endeavour

Cape Coral Sea
-oote Moreton
-landt Wenlock York Iron Range
Gulf Aurukun Peninsula
of Archer
-arpentaria Coen C.Melville Osprey Reef
Coleman C.Flattery
Edward Pellew Musgrave Bougainville Reef
Group Mitchell River Laura
Mornington I. Mitchell Cooktown Holmes
Stanten Port Douglas Reefs Willis
-lbert Wellesley I. Galbraith Cairns Group
-lills Bentinck I. Karumba Walsh Chillagoe
Burketown Normanton Herberton Mt.Bartle Frere Flinders
Croydon Einasleigh 1612 Innisfail Reef
Iffley Forsayth Hinchinbrook I.
Dobbyn Einasleigh Ingham Lihou Reefs
Camooweal Woolgar Townsville and Cays
Austral Downs Cloncurry Richmond 1277 Ayr Marion
Mount Isa Hughenden Ravenswood Bowen Reef
-dangi Duchess Selwyn Pentland Proserpine
-ra Dajarra Middleton Mount Douglas Swain
Boulia Winton Muttaburra L.Galilee Mackay Reef
QUEENSLAND St.Lawrence Saumarez
Bedourie Aramac Marlborough Reef
Birdsville Betoota Windorah Barcaldine Emerald Rockhampton Capricorn Ch. Wreck Reef
L.Machattie Jericho Mount Morgan Yeppon Tropic of Capricorn
Blackall Springsure Curtis I.
Yaraka Tambo Theodore Gladstone

References

The state of Victoria occupies the south-eastern corner of the country and is the smallest of the mainland states. Its largest city is Melbourne, lying on the River Yarra in the south. Victoria is rich in natural resources: it has large and valuable forests; enormous reserves of brown coal; and deposits of offshore oil have recently been found. Wheat, wool, butter, beef, fruit and dried vine products are important and there are large textile, automobile, oil refining, petrochemical and aluminium industries.

Australian Capital Territory was created in 1909 when this land, lying between the cities of Sydney and Melbourne, was ceded to the Commonwealth for the establishment of a federal capital. Plans for the new city, Canberra, were drawn up in 1912, construction began in 1913 but development was hindered by world wars and the depression and its real expansion did not take place until after 1945.

Queensland is the second largest state, occupying the north-east portion of the country. It has some of Australia's finest beaches which are popular holiday resorts. It is particularly famous for the Great Barrier Reef with its wonderland of coral structures and tropical fish. Queensland is principally an agricultural state raising sheep and cattle and it is also the centre of the country's sugar industry. It has some of the richest deposits of copper, lead, zinc, bauxite and uranium in the world.

The state of South Australia occupies the centre of southern Australia. Its largest city is Adelaide and the prosperous rural economy is based on wheat, sheep and wine production. Industrially, it is important for ship-building, oil refining, automobile engineering and electrical goods manufacture. In the desert areas to the north is the Woomera Rocket Research Range.

Western Australia is the largest state but it has one of the lowest populations. In the southwest are flourishing timber forests; a little further inland is a rich wheat and sheep farming belt. Yet the major part of the state is harsh desert land in which are found some of the world's richest goldfields. In the north west there are vast reserves of iron ore.

The Northern Territory occupies the north central part of Australia, a large part of which is desert. Despite the difficulties of climate and lack of water, the area is now developing. It is rich in minerals—gold, copper, uranium and bauxite—and has extensive cattle ranching. In this state separate areas have been set aside as reserves for the Australian aborigines. There are Government settlements and mission stations on these reserves so that the administration can keep in touch with the aborigines and help them with education and social problems.

The island state of Tasmania is the only completely well-watered state in Australia. The fast-flowing rivers provide hydro-electric power for a number of industries, including copper and aluminium refining. Tasmania is the leading world exporter of apples and is also a large producer of butter, minerals and timber.

The two islands of New Zealand, to the south-east of Australia, also form part of the continent. They were discovered by Tasman in 1642 and explored by Cook in 1769 but extensive settlement did not take place until 1840 when British sovereignty was declared. The original Maori population at first resisted the gradual absorption of their land but eventually the differences were settled peacefully. The islands are much greener and more scenic than Australia and the economy is firmly based on livestock and dairy produce which is sent to markets all over the world.

To the north and east of New Zealand spread out the numerous islands of the Pacific which make up the third component of Australasia. Some of them are Australian external territories and others belong to Great Britain,

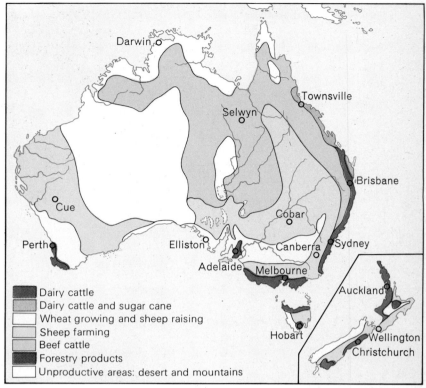

AUSTRALIA, NEW ZEALAND: AGRICULTURE

- Dairy cattle
- Dairy cattle and sugar cane
- Wheat growing and sheep raising
- Sheep farming
- Beef cattle
- Forestry products
- Unproductive areas: desert and mountains

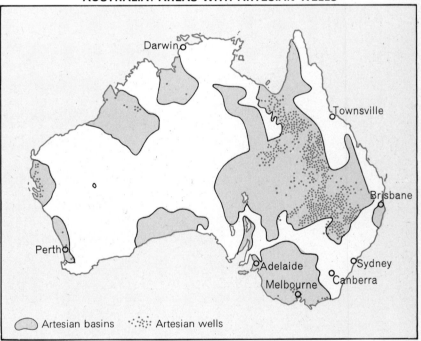

AUSTRALIA: AREAS WITH ARTESIAN WELLS

- Artesian basins
- Artesian wells

the U.S.A. and France. They stretch as far as the Hawaiian islands in the north and in the east to the mysterious Easter Island where huge stone figures reflect the ingenuity of a long-lost civilisation.

The needs of the islanders are comparatively simple. The coconut palm, which flourishes on all the islands, provides them with food, materials to build their homes, and an export product—copra. In recent years, many of these tiny specks in the ocean have been selected as re-fuelling stops on international airline routes.

The plants and animals of Australasia are very different from those found in other parts of the world. Marsupials, animals which carry their young in a pouch at the front of the female's body—such as the kangaroo and koala bear, are found almost exclusively in this continent. In addition there are strange creatures such as the duck-billed platypus, the wombat, the Tasmanian devil, the flying squirrel and the spiny anteater; brilliantly-coloured birds such as cockatoos, rainbow lorikeets, emus and black swans; and beautiful and strange trees and plants such as the acacia, eucalyptus and gum trees.

AUSTRALIA

The landmass of Australia was settled as a number of separate British colonies up to the end of the nineteenth century. Then, in 1901, these were united as the "Commonwealth of Australia" within the British Empire. Today it is one of the most senior independent states within the Commonwealth.

Australia is a federal state, like many other large nations, e.g. Canada, U.S.A., U.S.S.R. As such, each constituent state has many of its own laws and its own capital. The whole nation, however, is governed from the federal capital of Canberra, which has been built on federal territory in the last fifty years.

The individual states of Australia are listed below. Their respective capitals are: Sydney, Melbourne, Brisbane, Adelaide, Perth, Darwin, Hobart and Canberra.

State	Sq. km.	Sq. ml.	Population
New South Wales	801,122	309,433	4,300,000
Victoria	227,532	87,884	3,272,000
Queensland	1,726,863	667,000	1,689,000
S. Australia	984,001	380,070	1,107,000
W. Australia	2,526,657	975,920	864,000
Nor. Territory	1,347,005	520,280	40,000
Tasmania	68,306	26,383	376,000
Aus. Cap. Trty.	2,431	939	10,000
TOTAL	7,683,917	2,967,909	11,752,000

Australia has approximately the same area as the U.S.A. and exhibits a wide range of climates, natural environments and human activities. It extends from 11°S to 43°S, and from 113°E to 153°E. In the extreme north the summer monsoon rains and the high temperatures of tropical Australia are unattractive to European settlers. Much of the interior of the country has very little rainfall and forms the barren expanse known as "the outback". In the south west there is a small area which enjoys a climate similar to that of the extreme tip of South Africa, the "Mediterranean" type of climate. In the south east of the country the most temperate climates of all have attracted most of the settlers. Since Australia's most important mountains run parallel with the east and south-east coast, nearly all the major towns are sited along this coast.

The basis of Australia's economy is sheep raising. There are about fifteen sheep to every inhabitant in that country. However, industry has been increasing rapidly since the Second World War. Gold mining is important but coal has become increasingly important in recent years. There are also large deposits of silver, lead, iron ore, bauxite, uranium and oil. Wool and meat (chiefly mutton) account for more than half of Australia's exports. Great Britain is her most important trading partner. Most of the exports go through the ports of Sydney, Melbourne, Adelaide and Brisbane. There is a trans-continental railway from Sydney to Perth, but the aeroplane is a very important means of communication in so large a country. One distinctive use of the aircraft is the flying doctor and veterinary services of the interior. *Federal capital: Canberra. Population: 11,752,000. Highest point: Kosciusko Mountain, 2,230 metres (7,328ft.). Principal river: Murray-Darling. Land area: 7,683,917 sq. km. (2,967,909 sq. miles).*

COOK ISLANDS

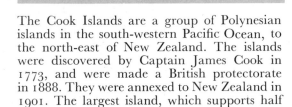

The Cook Islands are a group of Polynesian islands in the south-western Pacific Ocean, to the north-east of New Zealand. The islands were discovered by Captain James Cook in 1773, and were made a British protectorate in 1888. They were annexed to New Zealand in 1901. The largest island, which supports half the total population, is Rarotonga. Like many of the islands in the group, it is of volcanic origin. Other important islands are Aitutaki, Atiu and Mangaia. The most important export items are citrus fruits, copra and pearl shells. The group of islands obtained internal self-government in 1965. *Capital: Avarua (on the island of Rarotonga). Population: 20,000. Land area: 240 sq. km. (93 sq. miles).*

FIJI ISLANDS

Fiji is a group of over 800 islands and islets in the south-west Pacific Ocean. It is a British dependent territory but has internal self-government. Sugar and coconut products are the chief exports. There are important gold mines and saw mills. Rice is grown for home consumption. Immigrants from India were brought to Fiji in 1879 to work on the sugar plantations and by 1954 they had multiplied so rapidly that they outnumbered the native Fijians of Melanesian stock. The largest island is Viti Levu. Most of the larger islands are of volcanic origin. They have rainfalls in excess of 200in. per year on their windward slopes but only 40in. on their leeward side. *Capital: Suva. Population: 480,000. Land area: 18,265 sq. km. (7,055 sq. miles).*

FRENCH POLYNESIA

French Polynesia is the name given to The Society Islands (Leeward and Windward), the Marquesas, the Tuamotu Isles and the Tubuai Islands, all of which have been an overseas territory within the French Community since 1958. They are mainly agricultural islands producing arrowroot, breadfruit, coconuts, coffee, copra, rum, sugar and vanilla. Other important products are mother-of-pearl and pearls. Tourism is a major source of revenue. The islands were first discovered in the second half of the eighteenth century and became the "French settlements in Oceania" in 1881. The population of all the islands was drastically reduced by plague-like epidemics of European diseases. *Capital: Papeete (on Tahiti). Population: 100,000. Land area: 4,000 sq. km. (1,545 sq. miles).*

Australia. **Ayer's Rocks. Erosion has caused this unusual rock formation in the Australian interior.**

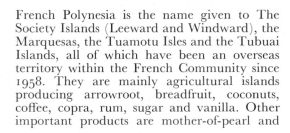

GILBERT and ELLICE ISLANDS

The Gilbert and Ellice islands are a British dependent territory. Each of five island groups (Gilbert, Ellice, Phoenix, Line and Ocean) is controlled by its own native government; the whole colony is administered by a resident commissioner. On these coral islands there is little soil. However coconut trees grow readily and provide the major export, copra. Phosphate is also exported. The majority of the people live in the Gilbert group, which is the most extensive, except for the largest of all coral atolls, Christmas Island. *Capital: Tarawa (Gilbert Is.). Population: 57,000. Land area: 932 sq. km. (360 sq. miles).*

GUAM

Guam is the largest of the Marianas Islands and the most westerly U.S. outpost in the Pacific Ocean. It was discovered by Magellan in 1521 and was taken by the United States in 1898 during the Spanish-American war. It is now an incorporated territory of the U.S.A. and has internal self-government. The island was in Japanese hands during most of the Second World War. Today it is a major naval and air base for the U.S.A. Major products are maize, bananas, citrus fruits and vegetables. The native population is mainly Malay. *Capital: Agana. Population: 74,000. Land area: 554 sq. km. (210 sq. miles).*

NAURU

Nauru is a tiny coral island in the south-western Pacific Ocean, 2,730 km. (1,700 miles) north-east of Australia. The coral reef surrounding the island is exposed. It is important for its phosphates which are exported. Much foodstuff is imported in return. Nauru is administered by Australia under a United Nations trusteeship held jointly by Great Britain, New Zealand and Australia. *Capital: Nauru. Population: 6,100. Land area: 20 sq. km. (8 sq. miles).*

NEW CALEDONIA

New Caledonia is a large volcanic island in the west Pacific. Together with a number of small dependencies, including the Loyalty, Huon and Pine Islands, it is a French overseas territory. It was discovered by Captain Cook in 1774. The principal crop is coffee, grown for export, and cattle are reared. Mineral production and exports are far more valuable; nickel is most important, chrome, iron and manganese follow. The population consists of Melanesians, Polynesians and Europeans. *Capital: Noumea. Population: 87,000. Land area: 19,094 sq. km. (7,375 sq. miles).*

NEW HEBRIDES

The New Hebrides are a group of islands in the south-western Pacific Ocean, unique in that they have been ruled jointly by Great Britain and France since 1906. They are situated to the north-east of Australia. Copra, cocoa and coffee are the main commercial crops. Subsistence crops include manioc, yams and bananas. Fishing is growing in importance. Mineral production (mainly manganese) and timber (mainly Kauri pine) is also expanding. *Capital: Vila. Population: 66,000. Land area: 14,760 sq. km. (5,700 sq. miles)*

Samoa. **One of the island's typical native villages.**

New Zealand. **Wellington, the capital, is New Zealand's second largest port. It is on North Island, at the entrance to a large bay on Cook**

NEW ZEALAND

New Zealand comprises two main islands, North and South, plus a number of smaller islands. From 1840 until 1907 it was a British colony. Since then it has been an independent state within the Commonwealth (formerly British Empire). It lies some 1,750 km. (1,100 miles) south-east of Australia and is, in both area and population, the second most important country in Australasia.

Unlike Australia, it is a predominantly mountainous country. The South Island is dominated by the Southern Alps which are still glaciated in parts. These rise to 3,764 metres (12,349ft.) in Mount Cook, and present an almost impenetrable barrier between the coastal lowlands, of which the Canterbury Plains in the east are the more important. In the North Island mountains dominate the central and eastern areas. Here there are a number of active and extinct volcanoes. In addition, there are the famous geysers, hot springs and mud pools.

The climate of New Zealand has many similarities with that of Great Britain. It is oceanic and is in large measure tempered by the rain-bearing westerly winds. However, since New Zealand is closer to the equator than Great Britain, it is generally warmer.

When New Zealand was first settled by Europeans in the mid nineteenth century, the native peoples—the Maoris of Polynesian descent—were not always friendly towards the newcomers. However, by 1871 peace was finally established and today some 200,000 Maoris enjoy equal status with the New Zealanders of white descent. Perhaps New Zealand is the most successful example of a plural society anywhere in the world.

New Zealand's economy is dominated by agriculture, especially pastoral farming. There are just over 9 million hectares (22.3 million acres) of farm land, and 90% of this is grassland. Seven and a half million cattle and sixty million sheep graze on this land and contribute greatly to the nation's exports with butter, cheese, beef, lamb and wool. In addition to this, there is a small acreage of cropland for home use and some fruit growing for both home and exports.

The mineral resources of New Zealand are limited, although in recent years new reserves of oil, natural gas and iron ore have been proved and will soon be developed. Coal is found in both islands whilst gold is mined on the west coast of the South Island. Hydroelectric power is a major source of energy. The Waikato River in the North Island and many lakes in South Island have been harnessed. This power is used domestically and for the growing range of manufacturing industries.

New Zealand is essentially an exporter of farm produce and an importer of manufactured goods. In order of value, wool, butter, lamb, beef and cheese are her main exports. Machinery of various kinds, iron and steel and chemicals/plastics are her main imports. The United Kingdom, Australia, U.S.A. and Japan are her leading trading partners. *Capital: Wellington. Population: 2.9 million. Land area: 268,572 sq. km. (103,736 sq. miles).*

PACIFIC ISLANDS

In 1946 the U.S.A. was appointed trustee to the former Japanese islands between 1°N and 20°N and 130°E and 172°E, often called Micronesia ('land of small islands'). Only 96 of the 2,100 islands are inhabited. *Capital: Saipan (Mariana Island). Population: 92,000. Land area: 1,812 sq. km. (700 sq. miles).* Then, in the 1952 Japanese peace treaty, the U.S.A. assumed control of the Ryukyu and some other small islands south of Japan. Okinawa is by far the most important. *Capital: Naha City (Okinawa). Population: 950,000. Land area: 2,330 sq. km. (900 sq. miles).*

Pacific Islands of the U.S.A. **This plug of volcanic lava is all that remains of an old volcano.**

PAPUA and NEW GUINEA

The eastern part of the island of New Guinea and many smaller islands nearby is an Australian trust territory. It is one of the world's least explored inhabited regions. The native population is very primitive. Yet coffee, cocoa, copra and tropical fruits are produced commercially. Pastoral farming, fishing and forestry are developing slowly. Copra, coffee, timber and gold are the main exports. *Capital: Port Moresby. Population: 2,183,000. Land area: 461,541 sq. km. (178,270 sq. miles).*

PITCAIRN ISLANDS

Pitcairn Island itself is a very small volcanic island in the Pacific Ocean, about halfway between New Zealand and South America. It is a British colony which is controlled by the governor of Fiji, a much larger British dependency away to the west. In 1790 the mutineers from the "Bounty" settled on this island, and eighteen natives from Tahiti joined them. In 1856 the then population of 194 were taken to Norfolk Island. A few years later 43 of them returned. The modern population is approximately 100. In 1902 the larger neighbouring islands of Henderson, Ducie and Oeno were added to the Pitcairn colony, but so far they have never been settled. Today much foodstuff is imported and fruit and trinkets are sold to ships which call at the islands. With so small a population there is no "Capital city" in the normal sense. *Population: 100. Land area: 47 sq. km. (18 sq. miles).*

Fiji. **A village on the banks of the river Rewa, not far from Viti-Levu, the capital.**

SAMOA

The Samoan islands are a chain in the South Pacific Ocean, about halfway between Hawaii and Eastern Australia. They were discovered in 1722 and are today inhabited by the native Polynesians and the American naval personnel at the Pago Pago base. Sometimes referred to as American Samoa, to distinguish it from Western Samoa, it comprises the islands of Tutuila and six smaller ones. They are a United States unincorporated territory. Polynesian native laws are respected. By one of these laws there is no public land and only persons with at least one half Samoan blood may own land. Copra, yams and tropical fruit are the most important products. Principal exports include copra, tuna fish and traditional native handicrafts. *Capital: Fagatoga. Population: 26,000. Land area: 199 sq. km. (77 sq. miles).*

SOLOMON ISLANDS

The Solomon Islands are a group of mountainous islands in the south-western Pacific Ocean, east of New Guinea. They were discovered in 1568 and taken under British control in the late nineteenth century. Copra is the only important crop and some is exported. Gold was recently discovered on Guadalcanal. All of the islands, except two, are a British protectorate. These exceptions are Bougainville and Buka which are part of the Australian trust territory of Papua and New Guinea. The population are mainly of Melanesian stock. Their way of life is somewhat primitive and malaria is a prevalent disease amongst them. *Capital: Honiara. Population: 146,000. Land area: 29,773 sq. km. (11,500 sq. miles).*

This koala bear is a native of eastern Australia. It lives in eucalyptus trees and feeds on their leaves. It is a marsupial, the female carrying her young in a pouch at the front of her body.

TONGA

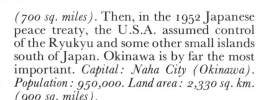

The Tonga or Friendly Islands consist of about one hundred and fifty coral and volcanic islands in the South Pacific Ocean. Most of the population are engaged in farming or fishing. Farming is nearly all copra and banana growing, for local use and export. The islands were visited by Captain James Cook in 1773 and he became very friendly with the natives—hence the name, Friendly Islands. The islands are a monarchy with their own royal family. They have been a British protectorate since 1900. *Capital: Nuku'alofa. Population: 77,500. Land area: 699 sq. km. (270 sq. miles).*

French Polynesia. **A view of the western coast of Tahiti, one of the Society Islands.**

New Zealand. **Sheep, reared both for wool and meat, are a major part of New Zealand's most important economic resource, agriculture. They number, at present, about 58 million and graze over about two-fifths of New Zealand's farmed area.**

WALLIS and FUTUNA

The Wallis Islands, together with the islands of Futuna and Alofi, lie some 600 km. (370 miles) northeast of Fiji. For more than a century, from 1842 until 1961, they were a French protectorate in which a local commissioner was immediately responsible to the French High Commissioner in Noumea (capital of New Caledonia). Then, in 1959, as all of France's overseas possessions were deciding upon their future status, these islands voted to become an overseas territory within the French Community. Farming is the main local occupation. Coffee, copra and vegetables are the main products. There are also some cattle and sheep. *Capital: Mata-Utu. Population: 8,500. Land area: 430 sq. km. (166 sq. miles).*

WESTERN SAMOA

Western Samoa is an independent Pacific state, within the Commonwealth, comprising Savaii, Upolu and a number of other small islands. It belonged to Germany before the First World War. From 1920 until 1962 it was administered by New Zealand as a trust territory. These islands are of volcanic origin and are surrounded by coral reefs. They are mountainous, peaks rising to 1,857 metres (6,094ft.) on Savaii. On the lower coastal areas copra, bananas and cocoa are important crops for export. For all that Savaii is the largest island, much of it is wasteland. Thus, the smaller island of Upolu is far more heavily peopled. *Capital: Apia (on Upolu). Population: 132,000. Land area: 2,848 sq. km. (1,100 sq. miles).*

Reefs and small islands built up out of coral are quite common in Australasia. The Australian Great Barrier Reef has been built up at some distance from the shore and is separated from it by a deep lagoon.

POLAR REGIONS

When we talk about the Polar Regions, we are referring to those areas of the world around the North and South Poles. The regions stretching from the North Pole to $66\frac{1}{2}°$N and from the South Pole to $66\frac{1}{2}°$S are said to be within the Arctic and Antarctic Circles respectively.

At both poles the sun is out of sight for six months in each year. In the Arctic Circle, because of the inclination of the earth's axis, the daily period of sunlight varies from twenty-four hours at the summer solstice (21st June) to complete darkness at the winter solstice (22nd December). The reverse happens in the Antarctic.

Some of the more unusual sights seen in the sky are visible from the polar regions. For instance, the Aurora Borealis is seen in the Arctic Circle and the Aurora Australis in the Antarctic Circle. These auroras, or Northern and Southern Lights as they are often called, are streams of coloured lights, usually seen in the night sky. They are the result of magnetically charged particles from the sun being attracted to the earth's magnetic field and when they hit the upper atmosphere some of the gases make them glow.

Although $66\frac{1}{2}°$N is strictly the limit of the Arctic, a boundary of much greater significance is the northern limit of forest land. On the polar side of this boundary the annual average temperature is $0°$C ($32°$F) and continental land areas have permanently frozen sub-soil. These include parts of North America, Europe and Asia, northern Canada and the whole of Greenland.

Monthly average temperatures in the Arctic range from $0°$C ($32°$F) to $-36°$C ($-33°$F) over the pack ice and from $15°$C ($60°$F) to $-40°$C ($-40°$F) in continental areas.

Literal desert conditions prevail in much of the Arctic where precipitation is less than 10in. per year. Snow seldom exceeds a depth of more than a few inches although drifts do sometimes build up in strong winds. Fogs occur quite regularly, especially along the coasts, because of the difference in heat between land and sea.

A huge ice cap, believed to be as thick as 3,000 metres (10,000ft.) covers the whole of Greenland. The weight of the ice tends to depress the central part of the land and the ice flows outwards in the form of glaciers. These moving "rivers of ice" reach the coast in many places and quite often masses of ice break off the end of these glaciers, or from ice sheets, and drift out to sea as icebergs. Only about one ninth of the volume of an iceberg is visible above the water. Because the size and extent of their undersea area cannot be seen, they are a great danger to shipping. This danger is particularly great off Greenland where icebergs are carried south by the Labrador Current towards the Grand Banks of Newfoundland. In this area they are in the lanes of North Atlantic shipping. Since the loss of the Titanic in 1912, when 1,517 people died when that ship struck an iceberg, a warning service has been in operation.

Smaller ice caps occur on some Canadian islands, and in Iceland, Spitsbergen and Franz Josef Land. All other land areas in the Arctic have a tundra type of vegetation with stunted grasses, mosses, lichens and a few dwarf trees. Even in the most northerly areas, numerous brightly-coloured flowers bloom briefly in the spring.

The Arctic is very rich in animal life. There are seals, walruses, whales, foxes, hares, wolves, polar and grizzly bears, reindeer, and musk oxen, as well as a wide variety of fish and bird life.

It is estimated that this vast animal population provides support for some 70,000 hunters and trappers of which about 40,000 are Eskimos who live in northern Canada and Greenland.

The Eskimos, who are of Mongoloid origin from Siberia, still pursue a traditional way of life. The mammals that they hunt—seals, walruses, polar bears—and the fish, provide them with skins for their clothing and tents, oil for heat, light and cooking, and of course, food. Their tools and weapons are also made out of the bones of some of these animals.

The Eskimos build igloos only in Greenland. They are constructed either of sticks covered with snow or entirely of blocks of snow, arranged as a dome, in which the temperature must be kept just below freezing point. These igloos are often large and elaborate, containing many rooms linked by passages.

Eskimos use dog sledges for long-distance travel and they fish from kayaks which are a type of canoe made from animal skins. They tend to live communal lives, sharing nearly all their possessions, but during the past one hundred years governments and missionaries have supplied them with food, clothing and permanent dwellings and brought to these people much of the paraphernalia of more advanced societies.

Other primitive people living in the Arctic regions include the Lapps of northern Scandinavia, the Samoyeds, Chukchees and other Siberian tribes, all of whom herd reindeer as well as being hunters and fishermen.

The rest of the inhabitants of the Arctic regions comprise Danes, Russians, Canadians and Americans. They have come to the area quite recently to exploit the Arctic's great mineral wealth and to trade and operate transport routes. Russia has established permanent mining, agricultural and trading centres and has succeeded in growing cereals and vegetables. As strains of wheat and other crops able to withstand colder temperatures and to ripen more quickly are developed, so more northerly lands can be farmed.

The Arctic provides the shortest air routes between many centres of population in the northern hemisphere. Already several airlines are operating between Europe on the one hand and America and the Pacific on the other and this has brought a new importance to Greenland, Northern Canada and Alaska which have been used as refuelling points. The new use of icebreakers in the Arctic Seas is opening up the area for shipping; it is likely to be of importance for oil tankers serving north west Canada and Alaska.

The Arctic is very rich in natural resources. There are

Continued on page 112

The penguin is one of the few inhabitants of the desolate Antarctic regions.

ARCTIC REGIONS

ALTITUDES
Metres / Feet
3000 / 9843
1500 / 4921
500 / 1640
200 / 656
0

DEPTHS
0
200 / 656
1000 / 3281
2000 / 6562
3000 / 9843
More than

PACIFIC OCEAN

Aleutian Islands
Andreanof Is.   Rat Is.   Near Is.
Komandorskije Is.
C. Lopatka   Kuril Islands
Urup I.   Iturup I.
Paramushir I.   La Pérouse Str.
Petropavlonsk-Kamchatski
Hokkaido
Sea of Japan

Bering Sea
Únimak I.
Pribilof Is.
Mt. 4850 Klyuchevsk
Kamchatka Pen.
Shelekhov Gulf
Sea of Okhotsk
Sakhalin
Amur
Nikolayevsk

Kodiak I.
Nunivak I.
St. Matthew I.
C. Navarin
Koryak Ra.
Magadan
Okhotsk
Shantar Is.
Dzhugdzhur Ra.
Stanovoy Ra.

G. of Alaska
Seward
Nome
Norton Sound
Gulf of Anadyr
Anadyr
Gydan Ra. (Kolyma)
Chersky Ra.
Verkhoyansk Ra.

Queen Charlotte Islands
Alexander Archipelago
Juneau
Mt. McKinley 6196
6050
Kotzebue
Bering Strait
Chukchee Pen.
Chukot Ra.
Nizhne Kolymsk
Indigirka
Yakutsk

Coast Range
Rocky Mountains
Alaska Ra.
Fairbanks
Alaska (U.S.A.)
Yukon
Kolyma
Verkhoyansk
Aldan
Vilyuisk

Mackenzie Mts.
Brooks Ra.
Dawson
Barrow
2816
C. Barrow
De Long Str.
Wrangel I.
Bear Is.
Kazache
New Siberia
Lena

Fort Liard
Peace
Ft. McPherson
Beaufort Sea
De Long Is.
New Siberian Islands
Lyakhov Is.
Tiksi
Olekma
Vitim

Great Slave Lake
Great Bear Lake
L. Athabasca
Mackenzie
Amundsen Gulf
Banks I.
Koteiny I.
Laptev Sea
Nordvik
Tunguska

Dubawnt L.
Victoria I.
M'Clure Str.
Melville
Parry Is.
Pr. Patrick I.
Borden I.
C. Chelyuskin
Bolshevik I.
Severnaya Zemlya
October Revolution I.
L. Taimyr
Taimyr Pen.
Dudinka

Churchill
King William
Prince of Wales I.
Queen Elizabeth Islands
Sverdrup Is.
A. Heiberg I.
ARCTIC OCEAN
Komsomolets I.
Gyda Pen.
Yenisey
Surgut

Hudson
Boothia Pen.
Somerset I.
G. of Boothia
Brodeur Pen.
Devon I.
Ellesmere I.
North Pole
Franz Josef Land
Graham Bell I.
Wilczek Ld.
Gyda Pen.
Salekhard
Tobolsk

Southampton I.
Melville Pen.
Foxe Basin
Foxe Pen.
Nettilling L.
Bylot I.
Smith Sc.
Thule
Peary Ld.
North East Land
George Land
Alexandra Ld.
Novaja Zemlya
Kara Sea
Bely I.
Gulf of Ob
Narodnaya 1894
Ob

Labrador
Hudson Strait
Ungava Bay
C. Chidley
Baffin Island
Cumberland Peninsula
Cumberland Str.
Disko I.
Baffin Bay
Shannon
Ely Christian X Ld.
West Spitsbergen
80
Barents Sea
Bear I.
Ob
Kanin Pen.
Kolguyev I.
Pechora
Murmansk
North C.
Kola Pen.
Arkhangelsk
Kama
Yaman Tau 1638

Davis Strait
2941
Greenland (Den.)
King Christian IX Ld.
Mt. Forel 3360
King Frederik VI Ld.
Frederikshaab
Angmagssalik
Denmark Strait
C. Farewell
Scoresby Sd.
Jan Mayen
Greenland Sea
Norwegian Sea
Lofoten Is.
Narvik
Lapland
Inari
White Sea
N. Dvina
Onega
L. Onega
Kazan
Gorki
Volga
Kuybyshev

Reykjavik
Oraefajökull 2119
ICELAND
Arctic Circle
Trondheim
Umeå
Luleå
Oulu
G. of Bothnia
Helsinki
L. Ladoga
L. Onega

Faeroe Is.
Shetland Is.
2481
Bergen
60
Oslo
Stockholm
Åland
Åbo
Gotland
Riga
Estonia
Latvia
Lithuania
Kaliningrad

Rockall
British Isles
Scotland
Glasgow
North Sea
Denmark
Copenhagen
G. of Finland
NORWAY
SWEDEN
FINLAND
Vänern
Vättern
Skagerrak
Kattegat

Dublin
IRELAND
England
London
Bristol Ch.
St. George's Ch.
English Channel
GREAT BRITAIN
Friesian Is.
Hamburg
Elbe
Berlin
GERMANY
Bonn
POLAND
Warsaw
Vienna
CZECHOSLOVAKIA
Prague
AUSTRIA HUNGARY

Le Havre
BELGIUM
LUX.
FRANCE
The Hague
Danube

South Limit of Drift Ice

Scale 1:30000000
0 250 500 1000 1250 1500 Kms.
0 250 500 750 1000 St. mls.

Itineraries of the main Arctic expeditions
Peary - 1908-1909
Amundsen-Nobile (Norwegian) - 1926
Byrd - 1926
Nobile - 1928
Limit of the inhabited areas

SPITZBERGEN
Scale 1:10000000
Sjuöyane
North C.   C. Platen   C. Smith   White I.
Danskøya
Moffen
Haakon VII Land
Ny Ålesund
Prins Karls Forland
West Spitsbergen
North-East Land
Storøya
C. Mohn
King Karls Land
Abelöya
Barents
Kongsöya
Svensköya
Edge
Storfjorden
Negerpynten
C. South

0 50 100 150 200 Kms.

INDEX

INDEX TO COUNTRIES OF THE WORLD

The first column of figures indicates page number and the second the map reference.

Countries marked with an asterisk appear on the world map on pages 12/13 and are referred to by their lines of latitude and longitude.

GENERAL INDEX

Hadramaut, S. Yemen 36 GH8
Hague, The, Netherlands 22 G5
Haig, Australia 98 D6
Hail, Saudi Arabia 38 G7
Hailar, China 39 P5
Hainan, China 39 P8
Haiphong, N. Vietnam 39 O7
Hair, Muscat & Oman 36 H7
Hakodate, Japan 39 S5
Haleb, Syria 38 F6
Halifax, Canada 71 O5
Hall Is., Pacific Ocean 96 F4
Halle, Germany 22 I5
Hallett, Antarctica 111 A2
Halley Base, Antarctica 111 M2
Halmahera I., Indonesia 39 Q9
Hallingdal R., Norway 20 H3
Hall's Creek, Australia 98 D3
Hamar, Norway 22 I3
Hamadan, Iran 38 G6
Hamburg, Germany 22 H5
Hamelin Pool, Australia 98 A5
Hamersley Range, Australia 98 B4
Hamilton, Australia 99 G7
Hamilton, New Zealand 99 h13
Hamilton Inlet, Canada 70 OP4
Hamilton R., Canada 70 O4
Hammada, Libya 52 E3
Hangay Mts., Mongolia 36 N5
Hang Chow, China 39 PQ6
Hanoi, N. Vietnam 39 O7
Hanover, Germany 22 H5
Hao I., Pacific Ocean 97 N6
Harbin, China 39 Q5
Hargeisa, Somali 53 H5
Hari R., Afghanistan 36 I6
Harz Mts., Germany 22 I5
Hastings, New Zealand 99 h13
Hatteras, Cape, U.S.A. 71 N6
Haugesund, Norway 22 H4
Hauriki G., New Zealand 99 h13
Havana, Cuba 71 M7
Hawaii, Pacific Ocean 97 M3
Hawaiian I., Pacific Ocean 97 ILM2
Hawke Bay, New Zealand 99 h13
Hay, Australia 99 G6
Hay R., Australia 99 F4
Haymet Rfs., Pacific Ocean 97 L7
Hebrides U.K. 22 E4
Hebron, Canada 71 O4
Hejaz, Saudi Arabia 38 F7
Heligoland, N. Europe 20 H5
Helmand R., Afghanistan 38 I67
Helsinki, Finland 23 N3
Henderson I., Pacific Ocean 97 P7
Hengyang, China 39 P7
Herat, Afghanistan 38 I6
Herberton, Australia 99 H3
Hercegovina, Yugoslavia 20 L7
Hereherelue I., Pacific Ocean 97 N6
Hermosillo, Mexico 71 H7
Hervey Bay, Australia 99 I5
Hervey Is., Pacific Ocean 97 M6
Hibernia Reef, Australia 98 C2
High Atlas Mts., Morocco 52 C2
High Veld, S. Africa 52 F8
Himalyas, S. Asia 36 LMN 67
Hindu Kush Range, W. Pakistan 36 IL6
Hinehinbrook, Australia 99 H3
Hiroshima, Japan 39 R6
Hispaniola, C. America 70 N7
Hitra, Norway 20 H3
Hobart, Australia 99 b9
Hobbs Coast, Antarctica 111 rS2
Hodeida, Yemen 38 G8
Hoggar Mts., Algeria 52 D3
Hoihow, China 39 P8
Hokitika, New Zealand 99 g14
Hokkaido, Japan 39 S5
Holmes Reefs, Australia 99 H3
Hollick Kenyon Plateau, Antarctica 111 Q1
Homs, Syria 38 F6
Honduras, Gulf of, C. America 70 M8
Hong Kong, Asia 39 P7
Honolulu I., Pacific Ocean 97 M2
Honshu, Japan 39 RS56
Hope Bay, Antarctica 111 n3
Hopetoun, Australia 98 C6
Hopkins L., Australia 98 D4
Horlick Mts., Antarctica 111 R1
Hormuz Str. of, Persian Gulf 36 H7
Horn Cape, Iceland 22 B2
Horn C., S. America 85 D9
Hountman Abrolhos Is., Australia 98 A5
Howe C., Australia 99 H7
Howland I., Pacific Ocean 97 I4
Howrah, India 38 M7
Huancavelica, Peru 85 C5
Huascarari, Peru 84 C4
Hubli, India 38 L8
Hudson Bay, Canada 71 M34
Hudson Bay Lowland, Canada 70 LMN 4
Hudson C., Antarctica 111 B3
Hudson Mts., Antarctica 111 p2
Hudson Str., Canada 71 NO3
Hue, S. Vietnam 39 O8
Huelva, Spain 20 E8
Hughenden, Australia 99 G4
Huhenot, China 39 P5
Huila, Colombia 84 C3
Hull, U.K. 22 F5
Humaita, Brazil 85 D4
Humber, U.K. 20 G5
Huna Bay, Iceland 22 B2
Hungerford, Australia 99 G5
Hunsruck Mts., Germany 20 H6
Huon Gulf, New Guinea 37 o14
Hurd Point, Australia 98 E2
Huron L., N. America 71 M5
Hwang Ho R., China 39 P6
Hyderabad, India 38 L8
Hyderabad, Pakistan 38 I7

I
Iasi, Rumania 23 N6
Ibadan, Nigeria 53 D5
Iberian Mts., Spain 20 G7
Iberian Pen., Europe 20 EF78
Ibiza, Balearic Is. 22 G8
Ica, Peru 85 C5
Idaho State, U.S.A. 71 H5
I. de los Estados, Argentina 85 D9
Idhra, Greece 21 M8
Idjil, Mauritania 53 B3
Iffley, Australia 99 G3
Iguacu Falls, Argentina/Brazil 84 E6
Iguaeu R., Brazil 84 E6
Iguatu, Brazil 85 G4
Ilbunga, Australia 98 F5
Ilebo, Congo 53 F6
Ile d'Oleron, France 22 F6
Ilek R., U.S.S.R. 23 T5
Ilheus, Brazil 85 G5
Ili R., Asia 36 LM5
Illampu Mt., Bolivia 84 D5
Illots de Brass, Pacific Ocean 97 N7
Ilmen L., U.S.S.R. 21 O4
Iloilo, Philippines 39 Q8
Imandra L., U.S.S.R. 21 O2
Imphal, India 36 N7
Inari L., Finland 21 N2
Inchon, S. Korea 38 Q6
Indals R., Sweden 20 L3
Indianapolis, U.S.A. 71 M6
Indigirka R., U.S.S.R. 39 S23
Indore, India 38 L7
Indus Plain, Pakistan 36 IL67
Indus R., India 36 IL67
Indus R., Pakistan 38 IL67
Ingham, Australia 99 H3
Ingrid Christensen Land, Antarctica 111 Fe23
Inhambane, Mozambique 53 G8
Injune, Australia 99 H5
Inn R., Austria 20 I6
Innamincka, Australia 99 G5
Inner Mongolia, Asia 38/39 OPQ5
Innisfail, Australia 99 H3
Innsbruck, Austria 22 I6
Interior Lowlands, U.S.A. 70 LM5
Invercargill, New Zealand 99 f15
Inverell, Australia 99 I5
Inverness, U.K. 22 F4
Inverway, Australia 98 D3
Ioannina, Greece 23 M8
Ionian Is., S. Europe 20 L8
Ionian Sea, S. Europe 22 L8
Iowa State, U.S.A. 71 L5
Ipin, China 39 O7
Ipoh, Malaysia 38 O9
Ipswich, Australia 99 I5
Ipswich, U.K. 22 G5
Iquique, Chile 85 C5
Iquitos, Peru 85 C4
Iraklion, Crete 23 N8
Iran, Plateau of, Iran 36 H67
Iran Range, Malaysia 35 P9
Irish Sea, British Isles 22 EF5
Irkutsk, U.S.S.R. 38 O4
Iron Gate, Rumania/Yugoslavia 23 M7
Iron Knob, Australia 98 F6
Iron Range, Australia 99 G2
Irrawaddy R., Burma 38 N78
Irtysh, U.S.S.R. 38 L4
Isabela I., Ecuador 85 A4
Ishigaki I., Asia 39 Q7
Ishim R., U.S.S.R. 38 I4
Islamabad, Pakistan 38 L6
Islay I., U.K. 20 E4
Isle of Man, U.K. 22 F5
Isle of Wight, U.K. 22 F5
Issyk-Kul L., U.S.S.R. 34 L5
Istanbul, Turkey 38 E5
Isthmus of Panama, Panama 70 N9
Isthmus of Tehuantepec, Mexico 70 L8
Itaituba, Brazil 85 E4
Itatiaia, Brazil 84 F6
Iturup, U.S.S.R. 39 S5
Ivanhoe, Australia 99 G6
Ivanovo, U.S.S.R. 23 Q4
Izhevsk, U.S.S.R. 23 S4
Izmir, Turkey 38 E6

J
Jabalpur, India 38 M7
Jackson, U.S.A. 71 L6
Jacksonville, U.S.A. 71 M6
Jaffna, Ceylon 38 M9
Jaguaribe R., Brazil 84 G4
Jaladi, Ethiopia 53 H5
Jaluit At., Pacific Ocean 96 G4
Jamdena, New Guinea 37 n14
James Bay, Canada 70 M4
Jammu, India 38 L6
Jamnagar, India 38 L7
Jan Mayen Is., Arctic Ocean 71 U2
Japan, Sea of, Asia 39 R56
Japen, New Guinea 37 n14
Japura R., Brazil 85 D4
Jaipur, India 38 L7
Jari R., Brazil 84 E34
Jarvis I., Pacific Ocean 97 L5
Java, Indonesia 39 OP10
Java Sea, Indonesia 39 P10
Jequilinhonha R., Brazil 84 FG5
Jericho, Australia 99 H4
Jerusalem, Jordan/Israel 38 F6
Jesselton, Malaysia 39 P9
Jidda, Saudi Arabia 38 F7
Jima, Ethiopia 53 G5
Joanna Spring, Australia 98 C4
Joao Pessoa, Brazil 85 G4
Jodhpur, India 38 L7
Joerg Plateau, Antarctica 111 O2
Johannesburg, S. Africa 53 F8
Johnson Lakes, Australia 98 C6
Johnston I., Pacific Ocean 97 L3
Joinville I., Antarctica 111 n3
Jones Sound, Canada 70 M2
Jonkoping, Sweden 22 I4
Joseph Bonaparte Gulf, Australia 98 D2
Juan Fernandez Is., Chile 85 BC7
Juazeiro, Brazil 85 F4
Juba R., Somali 53 H5
Jubilee Lake, Australia 98 D5
Jucar R., Spain 20 F8
Juiz de Fora, Brazil 85 F6
Jujuy, Argentina 85 D6
Julianehaab, Greenland 71 Q3
Julian Alps, Jugoslavia/Italy 20 I6
Juneau, Alaska 71 F4
Jura Mts., Europe 20 H6
Jurua R., Brazil 84 D4
Juruena R., Brazil 85 E45
Jutland, Denmark 20 H4

K
Kabalo, Congo 53 F6
Kabul, Afghanistan 38 I6
Kadgo Lake, Australia 98 D5
Kaduna, Nigeria 53 D4
Kafue R., Zambia 52 F7
Kagoshima Japan 39 R6
Kai Is., Indonesia 37 R10
Kaikoura Range, New Zealand 99 g14
Kaimanawa Mts., New Zealand 99 h13
Kain Nos Cape, U.S.S.R. 21 Q2
Kalahari Desert, Botswana 53 F8
Kalamai, Greece 23 M8
Kalannie, Australia 98 B6
Kalgan, China 39 P5
Kalgoorlie, Australia 98 C6
Kalima, Congo 53 F6
Kalinin, U.S.S.R. 23 P4
Kaliningrad, U.S.S.R. 22 M5
Kalmar, Sweden 22 L4
Kama R., U.S.S.R. 21 S3
Kama Reservoir, U.S.S.R. 21 T4
Kamchatka Pen., U.S.S.R. 37 TU4
Kamina, Congo 53 F6
Kampala, Uganda 53 G5
Kamrau Bay, Indonesia 37 n14
Kananga, Congo 53 F6
Kanazawa, Japan 39 R6
Kandahar, Afghanistan 38 I6
Kandalaksha, U.S.S.R. 23 O2
Kandalaksha Bay, U.S.S.R. 21 OP2
Kandavu I., Pacific Ocean 96 H6
Kandi, Dahomey 53 D4
Kandy, Ceylon 38 M9
Kane Basin, Canada 70 NO2
Kangaroo I., Australia 98 F7
Kanin Pen., U.S.S.R. 23 QR2
Kankan, Guinea 53 C4
Kansas City, U.S.A. 71 L6
Kansas State, U.S.A. 71 IL6
Kano, Nigeria 53 D4
Kanpur, India 38 M7
Kantse, China 38 O6
Kaolack, Senegal 53 B4
Kapingamarangi At., Pacific Ocean 96 F4
Kapuas R., Indonesia 39 OP10
Kara Sea, U.S.S.R. 38 I2
Karachi, Pakistan 38 I7
Karaganda, U.S.S.R. 38 L5
Karaginski I., U.S.S.R. 39 U4
Karakoram Range, India 36 L6
Kara Kum, U.S.S.R. 36 H6
Karamai, China 38 M5
Karamea Bight, New Zealand 99 g14
Karelia, U.S.S.R. 23 O23
Karema, Tanzania 53 G6
Kariba L., Zambia/Rhodesia 53 F7
Karisimbi Mt., Congo 52 F6
Karlskrona, Sweden 22 L4
Karonga, Malawi 53 G6
Karumba, Australia 99 G3
Kasai R., Congo 53 E6
Kasanga, Tanzania 53 G6
Kashgar, China 38 L6
Kashmir, Pakistan/India 38 L6
Kassala, Sudan 53 G4
Katanga, Congo 53 F67
Katanning, Australia 98 B6
Katharine, Australia 98 E2
Katmandu, Nepal 38 M7
Katoomba, Australia 99 H6
Katowice, Poland 22 L5
Kattegat, Denmark 22 I4
Kauai I., Pacific Ocean 97 M2
Kaunas, U.S.S.R. 23 M4
Kavalla, Greece 23 M7
Kayes, Mali 53 B4
Kay I., Antarctica 111 a2
Kayseri, Turkey 38 F6
Kazakh Uplands, U.S.S.R. 36 L5
Kazakhstan, U.S.S.R. 38 HIL5
Kazan, U.S.S.R. 23 R4
Kazbek Mt., U.S.S.R. 21 QR7
Kebnekajse Mts., Norway 20 L2
Kefallinia, Greece 22 M8
Kem, U.S.S.R. 23 O3
Kemerovo, U.S.S.R. 38 M4
Kemi R., Finland 23 N2
Kemp Coast, Antarctica 111 G3
Kempsey, Australia 99 I6
Kenai Pen., Alaska 70 DE3
Kennedy, Cape, U.S.A. 70 M7
Kentucky State, U.S.A. 71 M6
Kenya Mt., Kenya 52 G5
Kerang, Australia 99 G7
Kerch, U.S.S.R. 21 P6
Kerch Str., U.S.S.R. 23 P67
Kerkira, Greece 22 L8
Kermadec Is., Pacific Ocean 97 I8
Kermadec Trench, Pacific Ocean 97 I78
Kerman, Iran 38 H6
Kermansha, Iran 38 G6
Kerulen R., Mongolia 37 P5
Key West, U.S.A. 71 M7
Khabarovsk, U.S.S.R. 37 R5
Khalkis, Greece 23 M8
Khanka L., U.S.S.R. 37 R5
Kharkov, U.S.S.R. 23 P6
Kharpatos, Greece 23 N8
Khartoum, Sudan 53 G4
Khatanga, U.S.S.R. 38 O2
Kherson, U.S.S.R. 21 O6
Khios, Greece 23 N8
Khiuma, U.S.S.R. 23 M4
Khiva, U.S.S.R. 38 I5
Khoper R., U.S.S.R. 23 Q5
Khotan, China 38 L6
Khyber Pass, India 36 L6
Kichiga, U.S.S.R. 39 U3
Kiel, Germany 22 I5
Kiev, U.S.S.R. 23 O5
Kiffa, Mauritania 53 B4
Kigali, Rwanda 53 F6
Kigoma, Tanzania 53 G6
Kilimanjaro Mt., Tanzania 52 G6
Kimba, Australia 98 F6
Kimberley, Australia 98 D3
Kimberley, S. Africa 53 F8
Kinabalu, Indonesia 35 P9
Kindu Port Empain, Congo 53 F6
King Christian IX Land, Greenland 71 RS3
King Christian X Land, Greenland 71 RS2
King Frederik VI Coast, Greenland 71 Q3
King Frederik VIII Land, Greenland 71 S2
King George I., S. Shetland Is. 111 n3
King I., Australia 99 G7
King Leopold Ranges, Australia 98 D3
Kingoonya, Australia 98 F6
King Oscars Fjord, Greenland 70 ST2
Kingscote, Australia 98 F7
Kingsmill Is., Pacific Ocean 96 H5
King Sound, Australia 98 C3
Kingston, Australia 99 F7
Kingston, Jamaica 71 N8
Kingston, New Zealand 99 f15
King William I., Canada 70 L3
Kinshasa, Congo 53 E6
Kirensk, U.S.S.R. 38 O4
Kirgizia, U.S.S.R. 38 L5
Kirgiz Steppes, U.S.S.R. 21 STUV 6
Kirin, China 39 Q5
Kiriwina Is., Pacific Ocean 96 F5
Kirkuk, Iraq 38 G6
Kirovabad, U.S.S.R. 23 R7
Kirov, U.S.S.R. 23 R4
Kirthar Range, W. Pakistan 36 I7
Kisangani, Congo 53 F5
Kishinev, U.S.S.R. 23 N6
Kismayu, Somali 53 H6
Kisumu, Kenya 53 G5
Kitakyushu, Japan 39 R6
Kita, Mali 53 C4
Kiuchuan, China 38 N6
Kivu R., Congo 52 E6
Kivu L., Congo 53 F6
Klaipeda, U.S.S.R. 23 M4
Klar R., Sweden 20 I3
Klazma R., U.S.S.R. 21 PQ4
Klyuchevsk Vol., U.S.S.R. 37 U4
Knox Coast, Antarctica 111 d3
Knud Rasmussen Land, Greenland 71 OP2
Kobe, Japan 39 R6
Kodiak I., Alaska 71 D4
Kodok, Sudan 53 G5
Kordofan, Sudan 53 F4
Koko Nor, China 36 NO6
Kola Pen., U.S.S.R. 23 P2
Kolepom I., New Guinea 35 n14
Kolguyev I., U.S.S.R. 23 R2
Kolyma, U.S.S.R. 35 TU3
Kolyma Pl., U.S.S.R. 37 T23
Kolyma R., U.S.S.R. 39 T3
Komandorskiye Is., U.S.S.R. 39 U4
Kompasberg, S. Africa 52 F9
Komsomolets Bay, Caspian Sea 21 S6
Komsomolets I., U.S.S.R. 38 N1
Komsomolsk, U.S.S.R. 37 R4
Konosha, U.S.S.R. 23 Q3
Konotop, U.S.S.R. 23 O5
Konya, Turkey 38 F6
Konzhakovskiy Kam., U.S.S.R. 21 T4
Korab Mt., Yugoslavia 21 M7
Korea Bay, N. Korea 37 Q5
Korea Str., S. Korea 37 Q6
Korce, Greece 23 M7
Koryak Range, U.S.S.R. 37 UV3
Kosciusko Mt., Australia 99 H7
Kosice, Czechoslovakia 23 M6
Kota Bharu, Malaysia 39 O9
Kotelny I., U.S.S.R. 38 R2
Kotlas, U.S.S.R. 23 R3
Kotto R., C. Africa 52 F5
Kotuy R., U.S.S.R. 36 O23
Kotzebue, Alaska 71 C3
Kozhikode, India 38 L8
Kozhva, U.S.S.R. 23 T3
Kra, Isthmus of, Malaysia 34 N89
Krakow, Poland 22 L5
Krasnodar, U.S.S.R. 23 P6
Krasnovodsk, U.S.S.R. 38 H6
Krasnoyarsk, U.S.S.R. 38 N4
Krios Cape, Crete 21 M8
Krishna R., India 38 L8
Kristiansund, Norway 22 H3
Krivoy Rog, U.S.S.R. 23 O6
Kroonstad, S. Africa 53 F8
Kuala Lumpur, Malaysia 39 O9
Kuban R., U.S.S.R. 23 P67
Kuban Steppe, U.S.S.R. 23 PQ6
Kuching, Malaysia 39 P9
Kufra Oasis, Libya 53 F3
Kuibyshev Reservoir U.S.S.R. 23 R5
Kulaly I., U.S.S.R. 23 R7
Kuldja, China 36 M5
Kuma R., U.S.S.R. 23 R7
Kumasi, Ghana 53 C5
Kunlun Shan, China 36 MN6
Kunming, China 38 O7
Kuopio, Finland 23 N3
Kupang, Indonesia 37 Q10
Kura R., U.S.S.R. 23 R7
Kura Soak, Australia 98 D3
Kurdistan, Asia Minor 36 FG6
Kure I., Pacific Ocean 97 I2
Kuria Muria Is., Muscat & Oman 38 H8
Kuril Is., U.S.S.R. 39 ST5
Kursk, U.S.S.R. 23 P5
Kusaie I., Pacific Ocean 96 G4
Kushiro, Japan 39 S5
Kustany, U.S.S.R. 38 I4
Kutaisi, U.S.S.R. 23 Q7
Kutaradja, Indonesia 38 N9
Kuwait, Kuwait 38 G6
Kuybyshev, U.S.S.R. 23 S5
Kwajalein At., Pacific Ocean 96 G4
Kweiyang, China 39 O7
Kwoka, New Guinea 37 n14
Kyoto, Japan 39 R6
Kyoya L., Uganda 53 G5

Kyushu, Japan 39 R6
Kyzyl, U.S.S.R. 38 N4
Kyzyl Kum, U.S.S.R. 36 I5
Kzyl Orda, U.S.S.R. 38 I5

L

Labrador, Canada 71 OP4
Laccadive Is., Indian Ocean 38 L89
Lachlan R., Australia 99 G6
Ladoga L., U.S.S.R. 23 O3
Lagoa dos Patos, Brazil 85 E7
Lagos, Nigeria 53 D5
La Grande, Canada 70 N4
La Grange, Australia 98 C3
Lahore, Pakistan 38 L6
Lambarene, Gabon 53 E6
Lampedusa I., Italy 20 I8
Lanai I., Pacific Ocean 97 M2
Lancaster Sound, Canada 71 LM2
Lanchow, China 38 O6
Land's End, U.K. 22 E5
Languedoc, France 20 G7
Laoag, Philippines 39 Q8
La Paz, Bolivia 85 D5
La Paz, Mexico 71 H7
La Perouse Str., Japan 37 S5
Lapland, N. Europe 23 MN2
La Plata, Argentina 85 E7
Laptev Seas, U.S.S.R. 36 QR2
L'Aquila, Italy 22 I7
Laredo, U.S.A. 71 L7
La Rioja, Argentina 85 D6
Larisa, Greece 23 M8
La Rochelle, France 22 F6
Larsen Ice Shelf, Antarctica 111 O3
La Sagra Mt., Spain 20 F8
La Serena, Chile 85 C6
Lashio, Burma 38 N7
Las Palmas, Canary Islands 53 B3
La Spezia, Italy 22 H7
Las Tablas, Panama 71 M9
Las Vegas, U.S.A. 71 H6
Latvia, U.S.S.R. 23 MN4
Lau Group, Pacific Ocean 97 I6
Launceston, Australia 99 b9
Laura, Australia 99 G3
Laurentian Plateau, Canada 70 NO45
Laurie I., S. Orkney I. 111 N3
Laverton, Australia 98 C5
Lawlers, Australia 98 C5
Laysan I., Pacific Ocean 97 I2
Lebanon Mts., Lebanon 36 F6
Leeds, U.K. 22 F5
Leeuwin Cape, Australia 98 B6
Lefroy L., Australia 98 C6
Legaspi, Philippines 39 Q8
Leghorn, Italy 22 I7
Le Havre, France 22 G6
Leichhardt R., Australia 99 F3
Leigh Creek, Australia 99 F6
Leipzig, Germany 22 I5
Le Mans, France 22 G6
Lena R., U.S.S.R. 38 Q34
Leninakan, U.S.S.R. 23 Q7
Leningrad, U.S.S.R. 23 O4
Lenkoron, U.S.S.R. 23 R8
Leon, Mexico 71 I7
Leon, Spain 22 E7
Leopold and Astrid Coast, Antarctica 111 e3
Leopold Coast, Antarctica 111 mM2
Leopold II L., Congo 53 E6
Lerida, Spain 22 G7
Lesser Caucasus, U.S.S.R. 21 QR7
Lesser Sunda Is., Indonesia 39 PQ10
Lesvos, Greece 23 N8
Lethbridge, Canada 71 H4
Leticia, Colombia 85 C4
Levick Mt., Antarctica 111 a2
Lewis, I. of, U.K. 22 E4
Leyte, Philippines 37 Q8
Lhasa, Tibet 38 N7
Liard R., Canada 70 G3
Libenge, Congo 53 E5
Libreville, Gabon 53 D5
Libyan Desert, Libya 52 F3
Liechtenstein, Europe 22 H6
Liege, Belgium 22 H5
Ligurian Sea, S. Europe 20 H7
Lihou Reefs and Cays, Australia 99 I3
Likasi, Congo 53 F7
Lille, France 22 G5
Lima, Peru 85 C5
Limerick, S. Ireland 22 E5
Limmen Bight, Australia 98 F2
Limoges, France 22 G6
Limpopo R., Africa 53 G8
Linares, Spain 22 F8
Line Is., Pacific Ocean 97 LM45
Lindesnes Cape, Norway 20 H4
Lingga Arch., Indonesia 37 O10
Linosa, Italy 20 I8
Linz, Austria 22 I6
Lions, G. of, France 22 G7
Lipaja, U.S.S.R. 23 M4
Lipari Is., Italy 20 I8
Lisala, Congo 53 F5
Lisburne Cape, Alaska 70 C3
Lisbon, Portugal 22 E8
Lisianski I., Pacific Ocean 97 I2
Lismore, Australia 99 I5
Lithuania, U.S.S.R. 23 MN4
Little America, Antarctica 111 T2
Little Khingan Mts., China 37 Q45
Little Rock, U.S.A. 71 L6
Little Uzen R., U.S.S.R. 21 R56
Liuchow, China 39 O7
Liullaillaco Vol., Argentina 84 D6
Liverpool, Australia 99 I6
Liverpool, U.K. 22 F5
Livingstone Falls, Congo 52 E6
Livingston I., S. Shetland Is. 111 O3
Livingstone, Zambia 53 F7
Ljubliana, Yugoslavia 22 I6
Ljungan R., Sweden 20 L3
Ljusnan R., Sweden 20 I3
Llano Estacado, U.S.A. 70 I6
Llanos, S. America 84 CD3
Lobito, Angola 53 E7
Lobos Is., Peru 84 B4
Lodz, Poland 22 L5
Lofoten Is., Norway 22 I2
Logane R., Chad 52 E45
Logan Mt., Canada 71 F3
Loire R., France 20 G6
Lolland, Denmark 22 I5
Loma Mts., Guinea 52 C5
Lomami R., Congo 52 F6
Lombok, Indonesia 39 P10
Lome, Togo 53 D5
Londonderry, N. Ireland 22 E4
London, U.K. 22 F5
Long Beach, U.S.A. 71 H6
Long Is., Bahamas 71 N7
Long Island, U.S.A. 70 N5
Long Xuyen, S. Vietnam 39 O8
Lopatka Cape, U.S.S.R. 39 T4
Lopez C., Gabon 53 D6
Lop Nor, China 38 N5
Lord Howe I., Pacific Ocean 96 F8
Lorient, France 22 F6
Lorraine, France 20 H6
Los Angeles, U.S.A. 71 H6
Louisana State, U.S.A. 71 L6
Louisiade Arch., Pacific Ocean 96 F6
Lourdes, France 22 FG7
Lourenco Marques, Mozambique 53 G8
Lower California, Mexico 71 H67
Lower Hutt, New Zealand 99 g14
Lower Tunguska R., U.S.S.R. 38 N3
Loyalty I., Pacific Ocean 96 G67
Lualaba R., Congo 53 F6
Luanda, Angola 53 E6
Luang Prabang, Laos 38 O8
Luangwa R., Zambia 52 G7
Luanshya, Zambia 53 F7
Lubeck, Germany 22 I5
Lubeck Bay, Germany 20 I5
Lublin, Poland 23 M5
Lubumbashi, Congo 53 F7
Lucknow, India 38 M7
Luderitz, S.W. Africa 53 E8
Lugenda R., Mozambique 52 G7
LughFerrandi, Somali 53 H5
Lulua R., Congo 52 F6
Lulea, Sweden 23 M2
Lule R., Sweden 22 M3
Lunda Plateau, W. Africa 52 EF6
Lungwebungu R., Angola 52 F7
Lurio R., Mozambique 52 G7
Lusaka, Zambia 53 F7
Lusambo, Congo 53 F6
Lu-Ta, China 39 Q6
Lutzowholm Bay, Antarctica 111 H3
Luxembourg, Luxembourg 22 H6
Luzon, Philippines 39 Q8
Lvov, U.S.S.R. 23 M6
Lyndon R., Australia 98 A4
Lyons, France 22 G6
Lyons R., Australia 98 B4
Maan Selka, N. Europe 23 O2
Macao, China 39 P7
Macapa, Brazil 85 E3
Macauley I., Pacific Ocean 97 I7
MacDonald L., Australia 98 D4
Macdonnell Range, Australia 98 E4
Macedonia, Yugoslavia 23 M7
Maceio, Brazil 85 G4
Machattie L., Australia 99 F4
Mackay, Australia 99 H4
Mackay L., Australia 98 D4
MacKenzie Bay, Canada 70 F2
MacKenzie Bay, Antarctica 111 F3
MacKenzie Lowlands, Canada 70 GH3
MacKenzie Mts., Canada 70 FG3
MacKenzie R., Canada 71 FG3
Mac Robertson Land, Antarctica 111 f3
McClintock Mt., Antarctica 111 B2
M'Clure Str., Canada 70 GH2
McCluer Str., Indonesia 37 n14
McKinley Mt., Alaska 71 DE5
McMurdo Scott, Antarctica 111 a2
McMurdo Sound, Antarctica 111 a2
Madeira I., Atlantic Ocean 53 B2
Madeira R., Brazil 85 D4
Madras, India 38 M8
Madre de Dios R., Bolivia 84 D5
Madrid, Spain 22 F7
Madura, Indonesia 39 P10
Madurai, India 38 L9
Mafeking, S. Africa 53 F8
Mafia I., Tanzania 53 G6
Magadan, U.S.S.R. 39 T4
Magdalena, Bolivia 85 D5
Magdalena R., Argentina 84 C3
Magdeburg, Germany 22 I5
Magellan's Str., Chile 85 CD9
Maggie's Springs, Australia 98 E5
Magnitogorsk, U.S.S.R. 23 T5
Mahakam R., Indonesia 37 P10
Mahanadi R., India 36 M7
Mahenge, Tanzania 53 G6
Mahia Pen., New Zealand 99 h13
Maiduguri, Nigeria 53 E4
Maimanda, Afghanistan 38 I6
Main R., Germany 22 HI56
Maine, U.S.A. 71 O5
Mainland, Orkney Is. 22 F4
Mainland, Shetland Is. 22 F3
Maintirano, Malagasy 53 H7
Maipo Vol., Argentina 84 C7
Maitland, Australia 99 I6
Majorca, Balearic Is. 22 G8
Majunga, Malagasy 53 H7
Makarikari Salt Pan, Botswana 53 F8
Makassar, Indonesia 39 P10
Makassar, Str. of, Indonesia 39 P9/10
Makemo I., Pacific Ocean 97 N6
Makhachkala, U.S.S.R. 23 R7
Makindu, Kenya 53 G6
Makin I., Pacific Ocean 96 H4
Makokou, Gabon 53 E5
Makran, Iran 36 HI7
Makurdi, Nigeria 53 D5
Malabar Coast, India 36 L8
Malacca, Malaysia 39 O9
Malacca Str., Indonesia 36 NO9
Maladetta Mt., Spain 22 G7
Malaga, Spain 22 F8
Malaita I., Pacific Ocean 96 G5
Malange, Angola 53 E6
Malaren, Sweden 22 L4
Malargue, Argentina 85 D7
Malawi L., Malawi 53 G7
Malay Pen., Asia 38/39 OP9
Malden I., Pacific Ocean 97 M5
Maldive Is., Indian Ocean 38 L9
Male, Maldive Is. 38 L9
Malea Cape, Greece 23 M8
Maleolap At., Pacific Ocean 96 H4
Malindi, Kenya 53 G6
Mallowa Well, Australia 98 C4
Malmo, Sweden 22 I4
Malpelo I., Colombia 85 B3
Malta I., Europe 22 I8
Mamberamo R., Indonesia 37 n14
Mamore R., Bolivia 84 D5
Managua, Nicaragua 71 M8
Manakara, Malagasy 53 H8
Manaus, Brazil 85 D4
Manchester, U.K. 22 F5
Manchuria, China 39 QR45
Manchurian Plain, China 37 Q5
Manda, Tanzania 53 G7
Mandalay, Burma 38 N7
Mangaia I., Pacific Ocean 97 M7
Mangalore, India 38 L8
Mangareva I., Pacific Ocean 97 O7
Mangyshlak Pen., U.S.S.R. 21 S7
Manicore, Brazil 85 D4
Manifold C., Australia 99 I4
Manihiki At., Pacific Ocean 97 L6
Manila, Philippines 39 Q8
Manini I., Pacific Ocean 97 N6
Manitoba, Canada 71 L4
Manitoba L., Canada 70 L4
Manizales, Colombia 85 C3
Mannar, Gulf of, Indian Ocean 36 L9
Mannheim, Germany 22 H6
Manokwari, Indonesia 37 n14
Manono, Congo 53 F6
Mansfield, Australia 99 H7
Manua Kea, Pacific Ocean 96 M3
Manukau, New Zealand 99 g13
Manycg Gudilo L., U.S.S.R. 23 Q6
Manych, U.S.S.R. 23 Q6
Manzanillo, Mexico 71 I8
Mao, Chad 53 E4
Mapuera R., Brazil 84 E4
J. Marra Mt., Sudan 52 F4
Marabo, Brazil 85 F4
Maracaibo, Venezuela 85 C2
Maracaibo L., Venezuela 85 C3
Marajo I., Brazil 85 F4
Maralinga, Australia 98 E5
Maranhao, Brazil 85 F4
Maranoa R., Australia 99 H5
Maranon R., Peru 85 C4
Marble Bar, Australia 98 B4
Mar Chiquita L., Argentina 84 D7
Mar del Plata, Argentina 85 E7
Mare I., Pacific Ocean 96 G7
Margarita I., Venezuela 85 D2
Marguerite Bay, Antarctica 111 O3
Maria Is., Pacific Ocean 97 M7
Mariana Is., Pacific Ocean 96 E3
Mariana Trench, Pacific Ocean 96 E3
Mariato Punta, Panama 70 M9
Maria Van Diemen C., New Zealand 99 g12
Marie Byrd Land, Antarctica 111 R2
Marion Is., Antarctica 111 H5
Marion Reef, Australia 99 I3
Maritime Atlas Mts., Algeria 52 D2
Maritsa R., Bulgaria 21 N7
Markham Mt., Antarctica 111 B1
Marlborough, Australia 99 H4
Marne R., France 20 G6
Maroantsetra, Malagasy 53 H7
Marokau I., Pacific Ocean 97 N6
Maro Reef, Pacific Ocean 97 I2
Maroua, Cameroun 53 E4
Marquesas Is., Pacific Ocean 97 O5
Marrakesh, Morocco 53 C2
Marrawah, Australia 99 a9
Marree, Australia 99 F5
Marsabit, Kenya 53 G5
Marsala, Sicily 22 I8
Marseilles, France 22 H7
Marshall Is., Pacific Ocean 96 GH3
Marshall R., Australia 98 F4
Martin Pen., Antarctica 111 q2
Martin Vaz Is., S. America 85 GH6
Marutea I., Pacific Ocean 97 O7
Maryborough, Australia 99 I5
Masbate, Philippines 39 Q8
Maseru, Lesotho 53 F8
Mashhad, Iran 38 H6
Masson, Antarctica 111 E3
Masterton, New Zealand 99 h14
Masurian Lakes Plateau, Poland 21 M5
Matadi, Congo 53 E6
Matapan C., Greece 23 M8
Mataranka, Australia 98 E2
Matata, New Zealand 99 h13
Matavia I., Pacific Ocean 97 N6
Mato Grosso Plateau, Brazil 85 E5
Matthew I., Pacific Ocean 96 H7
Maui I., Pacific Ocean 97 M2
Mauikao I., Pacific Ocean 97 M6
Maun, Botswana 53 F8
Maurice L., Australia 98 E5
Mawsil, Iraq 38 G6
Mawson, Antarctica 111 f3
Maykop, U.S.S.R. 23 Q7
Maynas, S. America 84 C4
Mazar-i-Sharif, Afghanistan 38 I6
Mazatlan, Mexico 71 I7
Mbabane R., S. Africa 53 F8
Mbandaka, Congo 53 E5
Mecca, Saudi Arabia 38 G7
Medan, Indonesia 38 N9
Medellin, Colombia 85 C3
Medford, U.S.A. 71 G5
Medicine Hat, Canada 71 H4
Medina, Saudi Arabia 38 G7
Meekatharra, Australia 98 B5
Mekong R., S. Asia 39 O8
Melanesia, Pacific Ocean 96 CDEFG 456
Melbourne, Australia 99 G7
Melilla, Morocco 53 C2
Mellis Seamont, Pacific Ocean 96 H1
Mellish Reef, Pacific Ocean 96 F6
Melville Bay, Greenland 71 O2
Melville C., Australia 99 G2
Melville I., Australia 98 E2
Melville I., Canada 71 HI2
Melville Pen., Canada 71 M3
Menado, Indonesia 39 Q9
Menam R., Thailand 36 NO8
Mendocino Cape, U.S.A. 71 GH5
Mendoza, Argentina 85 D7
Mengtsz, China 39 O7
Menindee L., Australia 99 G6
Mentawai Is., Indonesia 38 NO10
Meramangye L., Australia 98 E5
Mercedes, Argentina 85 D7
Mercedes, Uruguay 85 E7
Mercury Is., New Zealand 99 h13
Mergui Arch., Burma 38 N8
Merida, Mexico 71 M7
Merka, Somali 53 H5
Merredin, Australia 98 B6
Merrick Mt., U.K. 20 F4
Mesewa, Ethiopia 53 G4
Mesopotamia, Asia Minor 36 FG6
Messina, S. Africa 53 F8
Messina, Sicily 22 L8
Messina, Str. of, Sicily 22 L8
Meta R., Colombia 84 D3
Methuen, New Zealand 99 g14
Metz, France 22 H6
Meuse R., Europe 22 H5
Mexicali, Mexico 71 H6
Mexican Plateau, Mexico 70 IL8
Mexico City, Mexico 71 L8
Mexico, Gulf of, North America 71 LM7
Mezen, U.S.S.R. 23 Q2
Mezen Bay, U.S.S.R. 21 Q2
Mezen R., U.S.S.R. 21 R2
Miami, U.S.A. 71 M7
Michigan L., N. America 71 M5
Michigan State, U.S.A. 71 M5
Micronesia, Pacific Ocean 96 EFG4
Middleton, Australia 99 G4
Midway I., Pacific Ocean 97 I2
Mila At., Pacific Ocean 96 H4
Milan, Italy 22 H6
Mildura, Australia 99 G6
Miles, Australia 99 I5
Miling, Australia 98 B6
Mill I., Antarctica 111 d3
Millerovo, U.S.S.R. 23 Q6
Milparinka, Australia 99 G5
Milwaukee, U.S.A. 71 M5
Minami Tori Shima, Pacific Ocean 96 F2
Minas Gerais, Brazil 85 F5
Mindanao, Philippines 39 Q9
Mindoro, Philippines 39 Q8
Minho R., Spain 20 E7
Minigwal L., Australia 98 C5
Minneapolis, U.S.A. 71 L5
Minnesota State, U.S.A. 71 L5
Minnipa, Australia 98 F6
Minorca, Balearic Is. 22 G8
Minsk, U.S.S.R. 23 N5
Minto L., Canada 70 L4
Minya Konka Mt., China 36 O7
Miquelon I., N. America 71 P5
Mirim L., Brazil/Uruguay 85 E7
Mirnyy, Antarctica 111 E3
Miskolc, Hungary 23 M6
Mississippi, U.S.A. 71 L6
Mississippi Delta, U.S.A. 70 LM7
Mississippi R., U.S.A. 71 L6
Misool, Indonesia 37 n14
Missouri R., U.S.A. 71 L5
Missouri State, U.S.A. 71 L6
Mitchell, Australia 99 H5
Mitchell Mt., U.S.A. 70 M6
Mitchell River, Australia 99 G3
Mitre I., Pacific Ocean 96 H6
Mitteland Canal, Europe 20 HI5
Mitu, Colombia 85 C3
Mitumba Mts., Congo 52 F6
Mjosa, Norway 22 I3
Mlanje Mt., Mozambique 52 G7
Mocuba, Mozambique 53 G7
Mogadishu, Somali 53 H5
Mokpo, S. Korea 39 Q6
Moksha R., U.S.S.R. 21 Q5
Moldavia, U.S.S.R. 23 N6

Mollendo, Peru 85 C5
Molucca Sea, Indonesia 37 Q9
Moluccas Is., Indonesia 39 Q10
Mombasa, Kenya 53 G6
Monaco, Europe 22 H7
Mona Passage, Puerto Rica 70 O8
Moncayo Mt., Spain 20 F7
Mongalla, Sudan 53 G5
Monger Lake, Australia 98 B5
Mongolia, Plateau of, Mongolia 36 O5
Mongu, Zambia 53 F7
Monrovia, Liberia 53 B5
Montagu Is., S. Sandwich Is. 111 M4
Montana State, U.S.A. 71 HI5
Monte Bello, I., Australia 98 B4
Monterrey, Mexico 71 I7
Montevideo, Uruguay 85 E7
Montgomery, U.S.A. 71 M6
Montpelier, France 22 G7
Montreal, Canada 71 N5
Moora, Australia 98 B6
Moore Embaym, Antarctica 111 a2
Moore Lake, Australia 98 B5
Moosonee, Canada 71 M4
Mopti, Mali 53 C4
Morane I., Pacific Ocean 97 O7
Morava R., Czechoslovakia 22 L6
Moravia, Czechoslovakia 20 L6
Moray Firth, U.K. 22 F4
Morea, Greece 21 M8
Moree, Australia 99 H5
Moreton, Australia 99 G2
Moreton I., Australia 99 I5
Morgan, Australia 99 F6
Morgans, Australia 98 C5
Mornington I., Australia 99 F3
Morondava, Malagasy 53 H8
Moroni I., Comoro Arch. 53 H7
Morris Jessup, Greenland 70 R1
Mortlock Is., Pacific Ocean 96 F4
Moscow, U.S.S.R. 23 P4
Mosquitos, Gulf of, Panama 70 M89
Mossamedes, Angola 53 E7
Mosul, Iraq 38 G6
Motopo R., South Africa 52 F8
Mouila, Gabon 53 E6
Moulmein, Burma 38 N8
Mount Douglas, Australia 99 H4
Mount Gambier, Australia 99 G7
Mount Isa, Australia 99 F4
Mount Magnet, Australia 98 B5
Mount Morgan, Australia 99 I4
Mt. Panie I., Pacific Ocean 96 G7
Moura, Brazil 85 D4
Moyata, Ethiopia 53 G5
Mozambique, Mozambique 53 H7
Mozambique Channel 53 GH78
Mozambique Coastal Plain, Mozambique 52 G7
Mtwara, Tanzania 53 H7
Muang Ubon, Thailand 39 O8
Muchinga Mts., Zambia 52 G7
Mui Varella, S. Vietnam 37 O8
Mukalla, South Yemen 38 G8
Mukden, China 39 Q5
Mulhouse, France 22 H6
Mull I., U.K. 22 E4
Mullewa, Australia 98 B5
Mulobezi, Zambia 53 F7
Multan, Pakistan 38 L6
Mundi Windi, Australia 98 C4
Mungbere, Congo 53 F5
Mungindi, Australia 99 H5
Munich, Germany 22 I6
Munster, Germany 22 H5
Muonio R., Finland 23 MN2
Mura R., Austria 20 L6
Murchison Falls, Uganda 52 G5
Murchison R., Australia 98 B5
Murcia, Spain 22 F8
Mures R., Rumania 21 M6
Murmansk, U.S.S.R. 23 O2
Murray Bridge, Australia 99 F7
Murray R., Australia 99 H7
Murrumbidgee R., Australia 99 H6
Murtoa, Australia 99 G7
Maruroa I., Pacific Ocean 97 O7
Murwillumbah, Australia 99 I5
Murzug, Libya 52 E3
Musala, Bulgaria 21 M7
Muscat, Muscat & Oman 38 H7
Musgrave, Australia 99 G2
Musgrave Rangers, Australia 98 E5
Muswellbrook, Australia 99 I6
Mutankiang, China 39 Q5
Muttaburra, Australia 99 G4
Muyum Kum, U.S.S.R. 36 I5
Mwanza, Tanzania 53 G6
Mweru L., Zambia 53 F6
Myitkyina, Burma 38 N7
Mysore, India 38 L8

N

Nafud, Saudi Arabia 38 FG7
Nafud Desert, Saudi Arabia 36 FG7
Nagelle, Ethiopia 53 G5
Nagasaki, Japan 39 Q6
Nagoya, Japan 39 R6
Nagpur, India 38 L7
Naha I., Asia 39 Q7
Nairobi, Kenya 53 G6
Nakhichevan, U.S.S.R. 23 R8
Nakumanu Is., Pacific Ocean 96 F5
Nambour, Australia 99 I5
Namib Desert, S.W. Africa 52 E78
Namoi R., Australia 99 H6
Nampula, Mozambique 53 G7
Nam Sham, China 36 LO6
Namsos, Norway 22 I3
Nam Tse R., China 36 N6
Nanchang, China 39 P7
Nancy, France 22 H6
Nanking, China 39 P6
Nanpo Shato, Pacific Ocean 96 D1
Nanning, China 39 O7
Nansen Mt., Antarctica 111 t1
Nan Shan, China 37 P7
Nantes, France 22 F6
Nanumea I., Pacific Ocean 96 H5
Nao C., Spain 20 G8
Napier, New Zealand 99 h13
Naples, Italy 22 I7
Napo R., Peru 85 C4
Napuka I., Pacific Ocean 97 N6
Naracoorte, Australia 99 G7
Narbonne, France 22 G7
Narodnaya, U.S.S.R. 21 T3
Narrabri, Australia 99 H6
Narran L., Australia 99 H5
Narrogin, Australia 98 B6
Narvik, Norway 22 L2
Naryan-Mar, U.S.S.R. 23 S2
Nashville, U.S.A. 71 M6
Nassau, Bahamas 71 N7
Nassau I., Pacific Ocean 97 L6
Nasser L., U.A.R. 53 G3
Nassob R., South Africa 52 EF8
Natal, Brazil 85 G4
Natal, S. Africa 53 G8
Naturaliste Cape, Australia 98 AB6
Naturaliste Channel, Australia 98 A5
Naury I., Pacific Ocean 96 G5
Navarin C., U.S.S.R. 37 V3
Ndola, Congo 53 F7
Neagh L., N. Ireland 20 E5
Nebraska State, U.S.A. 71 IL5
Necker I., Pacific Ocean 97 L2
Necker Ridge, Pacific Ocean 97 L2
Negoiu Mt., Rumania 21 MN6
Negro R., Argentina 85 D78
Negro R., Brazil 85 D4
Negros, Philippines 39 Q9
Neilsson I., Pacific Ocean 97 N7
Neisse R., N. Europe 20 I5
Neiva, Colombia 85 C3
Nejd, Saudi Arabia 38 G7
Nelson R., Canada 71 L4
Nelson, New Zealand 99 g14
Nengonengo I., Pacific Ocean 97 N6
Neman R., U.S.S.R. 21 M4
Nermada R., India 36 L7
Nettilling L., Canada 70 N3
Neuquen, Argentina 85 D7
Nevada State, U.S.A. 71 H56
Nevers, France 22 G6
New Britain, New Guinea 96 F5
New Brunswick, Canada 71 O5
New Caledonia, Pacific Ocean 96 G7
New Castile, Spain 20 F78
Newcastle, Australia 99 I6
Newcastle, U.K. 22 F4
Newcastle Waters, Australia 98 E3
Newdegate, Australia 98 B6
New England, U.S.A. 70 NO5
New England Range, Australia 99 I56
Newfoundland, Canada 71 OP4
New Georgia I., Pacific Ocean 96 F5
New Hanover I., New Guinea 96 F5
New Haven, U.S.A. 71 N5
New Hebrides, Pacific Ocean 96 GH6
New Hebrides Trench, Pacific Ocean 96 G6
New Ireland, New Guinea 96 F5
New Mexico State, U.S.A. 71 I6
New Norfolk, Australia 99 b9
New Orleans, U.S.A. 71 M6
New Plymouth, New Zealand 99 g13
New Schwabenland, Antarctica 111 LiI2
New Siberia, U.S.S.R. 38 ST2
New Siberian Is., U.S.S.R. 38 RS2
New South Wales, Australia 99 GH6
New York State, U.S.A. 71 N5
New York, U.S.A. 71 N5
Ngami L., Botswana 53 F8
N'Guigmi, Niger 53 E4
Nguru, Nigeria 53 E4
Niagara Falls, N. America 70 N5
Niamey, Niger 53 D4
Nias, Indonesia 38 N9
Nicaragua L., Nicaragua 71 M8
Nice, France 22 H7
Nicobar Is., Indonesia 38 N9
Nicosia, Cyprus 38 F6
Nigata, Japan 39 R6
Niger R., W. Africa 53 CD45
Nightcaps, New Zealand 99 f15
Nihoa I., Pacific Ocean 97 L2
Niihau I., Pacific Ocean 97 L2
Nikolayev, U.S.S.R. 23 O6
Nikolayevsk, U.S.S.R. 39 R4
Nile River, Africa 53 G345
Nimba Mts., Guinea 52 C5
Nimes, France 22 G7
Ninnis Glacial Tongue, Antarctica 111 b3
Nipigon L., Canada 71 M5
Nis, Yugoslavia 23 M7
Niteroi, Brazil 85 F6
Niulakita, Pacific Ocean 97 H6
Nizhne Kolymsk, U.S.S.R. 39 U3
Nome, Alaska 71 C3
Nonouti I., Pacific Ocean 96 H5
Nordvik, U.S.S.R. 38 P2
Norfolk I., Pacific Ocean 96 G7
Norman R., Australia 99 G3
Normandy, France 20 FG6
Norman Wells, Canada 71 G3
Noumanton, Australia 99 G3
Nornalup, Australia 98 B6
Norrkoping, Sweden 22 L4
Norseman, Australia 98 C6
Northam, Australia 98 B6
Northampton, Australia 98 A5
North Bay, Canada 71 N5
North Cape, Antarctica 111 a2
North Cape, Norway 23 N1
North Carolina State, U.S.A. 71 MN6
North Channel, U.K. 20 E4
North Cliffe, Australia 98 B6
North Dakota State, U.S.A. 71 IL5
North Dvina R., U.S.S.R. 23 Q3
Northeast Cape, Greenland 70 T1
Northern Territory, Australia 98 EF34
North European Plain 23 MNOP345
North Island, New Zealand 99 g13
North Minch, U.K. 20 E4
North Saskatchewan R., Canada 70 HI4
North Sea, Europe 22 G4
North Sporades Is., Greece 21 M8
North Tranaki Bight, New Zealand 99 g13
North Stradbroke I., Australia 99 I5
North West Cape, Australia 98 A4
North West Highlands, U.K. 20 EF4
Northwest Territories, Canada 71 GHILMN3
Norwegian Sea, N. Europe 22 DEFG3
Norwich, U.K. 22 G5
Notec R., Poland 22 L5
Nouakchott, Mauritania 53 B4
Nova Lisboa, Angola 53 E7
Nova Scotia, Canada 71 O5
Novgorod, U.S.S.R. 23 O4
Novi Sad, Yugoslavia 22 L6
Novokuznetsk, U.S.S.R. 38 M4
Novosibirsk, U.S.S.R. 38 M4
Nowra, Australia 99 I6
Nua I., Pacific Ocean 97 I6
Nubian Desert, Sudan 52 G3
Nuevo Laredo, Mexico 71 L7
Nuhuel Huapi L., Argentina 84 C8
Nui I., Pacific Ocean 96 H5
Nukhd, U.S.S.R. 23 R7
Nuku Hiva I., Pacific Ocean 97 N5
Nukuoro At., Pacific Ocean 96 F4
Nullarbor, Australia 98 E6
Nullarbor Plain, Australia 98 DE6
Nunivak I., Alaska 71 C34
Nunkiang, China 39 Q5
Nuoro, Sardinia 22 H7
Nura kita, Pacific Ocean 97 H6
Nuremberg, Germany 22 I6
Nuweveldberge, South Africa 52 EF9
Nyala, Sudan 53 F4
Nyngan, Australia 99 H6

O

Oahu I., Pacific Ocean 97 M2
Oakland, U.S.A. 71 G6
Oamaru, New Zealand 99 g15
Oates Coast, Antarctica 111 aB2
Oaxaca, Mexico 71 L8
Ob, Gulf of, U.S.S.R. 38 L23
Ob R., U.S.S.R. 38 I3
Obbia, Somali 53 H5
Obidos, Brazil 85 E4
Obshchiy Syrt, U.S.S.R. 21 RS5
Ocean I., Pacific Ocean 96 G5
October Revolution I., U.S.S.R. 38 N2
Odense, Denmark 22 H4
Oder R., Germany 20 I5
Odessa, U.S.S.R. 23 O6
Odienne, Ivory Coast 53 C5
Oekma R., U.S.S.R. 37 Q4
Oena, U.A.R. 53 G3
Oeno I., Pacific Ocean 97 O7
Ogbomosho, Nigeria 53 D5
Ogden, U.S.A. 71 H5
Ogoue, Gabon 53 DE6
Ohio, U.S.A. 71 M5
Ohio R., U.S.A. 70 M6
Oimyakon, U.S.S.R. 39 S3
Ojos d. Salado, Chile 84 D6
Oka R., U.S.S.R. 21 Q45
Okango Swamps, Botswana 52 F7
Okhotsk, U.S.S.R. 39 S4
Okhotsk, Sea of, U.S.S.R. 39 ST4
Okinawa I., Asia 39 Q7
Oklahoma City, U.S.A. 71 L6
Oklahoma State, U.S.A. 71 L6
Oland, Sweden 22 L4
Olbia, Sardinia 22 H7
Old Castile, Spain 20 EF7
Olekminsk, U.S.S.R. 39 Q3
Olenek, U.S.S.R. 38 P3
Olenek R., U.S.S.R. 36 Q2
Oleron, I. de, France 22 F5
Olsztyn, Poland 23 M5
Olympus Mt., Greece 21 M7
Omaha, U.S.A. 71 L5
Oman, Gulf of, Asia 36 H7
Omdurman, Sudan 53 G4
Omo Bottego R., Ethiopia 52 G5
Omolon R., U.S.S.R. 37 T3
Omsk, U.S.S.R. 38 L4
Onega, U.S.S.R. 23 P3
Onega, G. of, U.S.S.R. 21 P3
Onega L., U.S.S.R. 23 OP3
Onega R., U.S.S.R. 21 P3
Ongerup, Australia 98 B6
Onslow, Australia 98 A4
Ontario, Canada 71 MN45
Ontario, L., N. America 71 N5
Oodnadatta, Australia 98 F5
Ooldea, Australia 98 E6
Oporto, Portugal 22 E7
Opparinna, Australia 98 E5
Opua, New Zealand 99 g13
Oradea, Rumania 23 M6
Oraefaj Mt., Iceland 20 C3
Oran, Algeria 53 C2
Orange, Australia 99 H6
Orange Free State, S. Africa 53 F8
Orange R., S. Africa 53 EF89
Orbost, Australia 99 H7
Orcadas, S. Orkney Is. 111 N3
Ord R., Australia 98 D3
Ordos Plateau, China 37 OP6
Ordzhonikidze, U.S.S.R. 23 Q7
Orebro, Sweden 22 L4
Oregon State, U.S.A. 71 G5
Orel, U.S.S.R. 23 P5
Orenburg, U.S.S.R. 23 T5
Orense, Spain 22 E7
Orinoco R., Venezuela 85 D3
Orkney Is., U.K. 22 F4
Orleans, France 22 G6
Oroya, Peru 85 C5
Orsk, U.S.S.R. 23 T5
Oruro, Bolivia 85 D5
Osaka, Japan 39 R6
Oslo, Norway 22 I4
Osprey Reef, Australia 99 H2
Ossa Mt., Australia 99 b9
Ostend, Belgium 22 G5
Ostersund, Sweden 22 I3
Ostrava, Czechoslovakia 22 L6
Otranto, Italy 22 L7
Otranto Str. of, Italy 20 L78
Ottawa, Canada 71 N5
Ottawa R., Canada 70 N5
Otway C., Australia 99 G7
Ouadai, Chad 52 EF4
Ouagadougou, Volta 53 C4
Ouanda Djale, Cen. Africa 53 F5
Oubangui R., Congo 53 E5
Ouesso, Congo 53 E5
Oulu, Finland 23 N3
Oulu L., Finland 21 N3
Ouse, R., U.K. 20 G5
Outjo, S.W. Africa 53 E7
Ouvea I., Pacific Ocean 96 G67
Ouyen, Australia 99 G7
Ovamboland, S.W. Africa 52 E7
Oviedo, Spain 22 E7
Owen Stanley Range, New Guinea 37 o14
Oxley, Australia 99 G6
Ozark Plateau, U.S.A. 70 L6

P

Padang, Indonesia 38 O10
Padua, Italy 22 I6
Pagan I., Pacific Ocean 96 E3
Palau Is., Caroline Is. 39 R9
Palawan, Philippines 39 P89
Palembang, Indonesia 39 O10
Palermo, Sicily 22 I8
Palk Str., India/Ceylon 36 LM9
Palliser C., New Zealand 99 h14
Palma, Majorca 22 G8
Palmas Cape, Liberia 52 C5
Palmer Arch., Antarctica 111 O3
Palmer Land, Antarctica 111 n2
Palmerston At., Pacific Ocean 97 L6
Palmerston North, New Zealand 99 h14
Palmyra I., Pacific Ocean 97 L4
Pamirs, Asia 36 L6
Pampas, Argentina 84 D7
Pamplona, Spain 22 F7
Panama City, Panama 71 N9
Panama, Gulf of, Panama 70 N9
Panay, Philippines 39 Q8
Panjim, India 38 L8
Panonian Basin, Hungary 20 LM6
Pantelleria Is., Italy 22 I8
Paotow, China 39 P5
Papua, Gulf of, Papua 37 o14
Para, Brazil 85 E4
Para R., Brazil 85 F4
Parachilna, Australia 99 F6
Paraguana, Brazil 85 F6
Paraguana Pen., Venezuela 84 D2
Paraguay R., Paraguay 85 E6
Paraiba R., Brazil 84 F6
Paramaribo, Surinam 85 E3
Paramushir I., U.S.S.R. 37 T4
Parana, Argentina 85 D7
Parana, Brazil 85 F5
Parana R., S. America 85 E6
Paranaiba R., Brazil 85 F5
Paranger Fjord, Norway 21 N1
Paratoo, Australia 99 F6
Parecis, Serra dos, Brazil 84 DE5
Parinar, Punta, Peru 84 B4
Paris, France 22 G6
Paris Basin, France 20 G6
Parkes, Australia 99 H6
Parma, Italy 22 I7
Parnaiba, Brazil 85 F4
Parnassos, Greece 21 M8
Parnassus, New Zealand 99 g14
Paroo R., Australia 99 H5
Parramatta, Australia 99 I6
Parry Is., Canada 71 HI2
Pasley Cape, Australia 98 C6
Passero Cape, Sicily 20 L8
Passo Fundo, Brazil 85 E6
Pasto, Colombia 85 C3
Patagonian Cordillera, S. America 84 C89
Patchewollock, Australia 99 G7
Patience Well, Australia 98 D4
Patna, India 38 M7
Patria, Greece 23 M8
Paulding Bay, Antarctica 111 c3
Pavlodar, U.S.S.R. 38 L4
Paysandu, Uruguay 85 E7
Peace R., Canada 71 H4
Peak Hill, Australia 98 B5
Peary Land, Greenland 71 RS1
Pechenga, U.S.S.R. 23 O2
Pechora Bay, U.S.S.R. 21 ST2
Pechora R., U.S.S.R. 23 S2
Pecos R., U.S.A. 70 I6
Pecs, Hungary 22 L6
Pegasus Bay, New Zealand 99 g14
Peking, China 39 P6
Pelotas, Brazil 85 E7
Pemba I., Tanzania 53 G6
Penck C., Antarctica 111 e3
Pennines, U.K. 20 F5
Penong, Australia 98 E6
Penrhyn At., Pacific Ocean 97 M5
Pensacola Mts., Antarctica 111 m1